Childhood, Philosophy, and Dialogical Education

SUNY series, Horizons in the Philosophy of Education

David J. Blacker, editor

Childhood, Philosophy, and Dialogical Education

(R)evolutionary Essays

DAVID KENNEDY

Published by State University of New York Press, Albany

© 2024 State University of New York

All rights reserved

Printed in the United States of America

No part of this book may be used or reproduced in any manner whatsoever without written permission. No part of this book may be stored in a retrieval system or transmitted in any form or by any means including electronic, electrostatic, magnetic tape, mechanical, photocopying, recording, or otherwise without the prior permission in writing of the publisher.

Links to third-party websites are provided as a convenience and for informational purposes only. They do not constitute an endorsement or an approval of any of the products, services, or opinions of the organization, companies, or individuals. SUNY Press bears no responsibility for the accuracy, legality, or content of a URL, the external website, or for that of subsequent websites.

For information, contact State University of New York Press, Albany, NY
www.sunypress.edu

Library of Congress Cataloging-in-Publication Data

Name: Kennedy, David, author.
Title: Childhood, Philosophy, and Dialogical Education : (R)evolutionary Essays / David Kennedy.
Description: Albany : State University of New York Press, [2024] | Includes bibliographical references and index.
Identifiers: ISBN 9781438499437 (hardcover : alk. paper) | ISBN 9781438499451 (ebook) | ISBN 9781438499444 (pbk. : alk. paper)
Further information is available at the Library of Congress.

For those who will come after

Contents

Acknowledgments ix

Foreword xi
    Walter Omar Kohan

Introduction 1

1. The Politics of Subjectivity, Philosophy of Childhood, and Dialogical Education 7

2. Neoteny, Dialogical Education, and an Emergent Psychoculture 21

3. Young Children and Ultimate Questions: Romancing at Day Care 41

4. Becoming Child: Wild Being and the Post-Human 53

5. Paths in Utopia: School as Holding Environment for the Dialogical Self 65

6. Practicing Philosophy of Childhood: Teaching in the (R)evolutionary Mode 85

7. Intermezzo One: *My Name Is Myshkin* 97

8. Anarchism and Education: In Search of a New Reality Principle 113

9. Community of Philosophical Inquiry and the Play of
   the World   127

10. Intermezzo Two: *Dreamers*   145

11. Rhizomatic Curriculum Development in Community of
    Philosophical Inquiry   153

12. Dialogue and Dialectic in the Politics of the Self   163

Bibliography   183

Index   195

Acknowledgments

The following articles have been adapted and/or excerpted for use in this publication and are included by permission.

"The Politics of Subjectivity, the Philosophy of Childhood, and Dialogical Education." *Critical and Creative Thinking* 7, no. 2 (Spring 1999).
"Neoteny, Dialogical Education, and an Emergent Psychoculture." *Journal of Philosophy of Education* 48, no. 1 (February 2014).
"Young Children and Ultimate Questions: Romancing at Day Care." *Analytic Teaching* 12, no. 1 (November 1991).
"Becoming Child: Wild Being and the Post-Human." In *Thinking, Childhood, and Time: Contemporary Perspectives on the Politics of Education*, edited by Barbara Weber and Walter Kohan. Lanham MD: Lexington Books, 2020.
"Paths in Utopia: School as Holding Environment for the Dialogical Self." *Journal of Constructivist Psychology* (December 2020). DOI:10.1080/10720537.2020.1848668.
"Practicing Philosophy of Childhood: Teaching in the (R)evolutionary Mode." *Journal of Philosophy in Schools* 2, no. 1 (2015).
My Name Is Myshkin: A Philosophical Novel for Children. Munster: Lit Verlag, 2006.
"Anarchism and Education: In Search of a New Reality Principle." [Published as "Introduction: In Search of a New Reality Principle."] *Civitas Educationis: Education, Politics, and Culture* 8, no. 2 (December 2019). Published by Mimesis edizioni.
"Community of Philosophical Inquiry and the Play of the World." *Teaching Philosophy* 41, no. 3 (September 2018).

"Rhizomatic Curriculum Development in Community of Philosophical Inquiry." In *Educating for Complex Thinking through Philosophical Inquiry. Models, Advances, and Proposals for the New Millennium*, edited by Marina Santi and Stefano Oliverio, 210–30. Napoli: Liguori, 2012.

Foreword

David Kennedy's *Childhood, Philosophy and Dialogical Education: (R)evolutionary Essays* is a utopian, childlike, and philosophical book, as well as a mature synthesis of decades of studying and practicing in communities of philosophical inquiry. These three descriptors may seem contradictory, especially when they include the term *childlike*. As such, it might be appropriate to unpack some of their meanings and senses.

A "utopian, childlike, and philosophical" approach to education has characterized not only this book but also Kennedy's extended work over decades. His practical engagement in the educational movement known as philosophy for children with its emphasis on dialogical pedagogy referred to as "community of philosophical inquiry" is consistently enriched in his scholarly work by insights from multiple traditions, including phenomenology, hermeneutics, psychohistory, psychoanalysis, evolutionary biology, human development studies, history of education, and play theory. As a result, this book is a mature expression of the richly polyvocal oeuvre of a committed and playful scholar.

Utopian is a term that Kennedy employs in the sense of Herbert Marcuse's meaning as "that which is blocked from coming about by the power of the established societies." In this sense, his writing is an attempt to liberate childhood, philosophy, and education from what blocks them in contemporary and historical institutions. A utopian understanding of the possibilities inherent in childhood and education—the latter specifically understood as school, or what he reconstructs in evocation of the ancient Greek term *skholé*, meaning "free time"—is based on an understanding of the condition of childhood as, not just a stage of life but a form of subjectivity, a way of being in the world and as such a form of temporality or lived time. Childhood is here understood as a utopian form of a non-age-related subjectivity, as opposed to the standardized vision of childhood as a chronologically defined stage of life whose destiny is to disappear into a socially legitimized form of adulthood, to be made into the "not-child."

Childlike is a word we might both smile while pronouncing, echoing Heraclitus's (2003) iconic Fragment 52 with its reference to the Greek word *aion*—or, roughly translated, "timeless time" as the time of the child, as opposed to *kronos*, the time of the clock. *Skholé* is, in Kennedy's formulation, the institutional space where this childlike time might emerge, where the adult-child relationship might find its most fruitful, nourishing, and epiphanic context. And aion is the time, the space, and the interactive milieu in which that form of dialogical pedagogy known as a community of philosophical inquiry is given space to function in its deepest and most educational dimension. And finally, *philosophy* is the name of a practice and a form of life, a way of relating to ideas, knowledge, being, and beings that Kennedy reconnects with its Socratic roots, returning it to that historical moment when Plato's master took it to the polis, the public, and reinvented it as a form of dialogical examination, not just of concepts, but of our shared ways of living. In other words, philosophy is a dimension of education, inseparable from it and, in the form of what he calls community of philosophical inquiry, it is a necessary feature of the educational formation of childhood.

The book is organized in twelve chapters, two of which are composed of short selections from Kennedy's two novels, and function as what he calls intermezzos. *My Name Is Myshkin* and *Dreamers* are philosophical novels for middle school children and up, written in the format inaugurated by Matthew Lipman, originator of the Philosophy for Children program, and designed as narrative stimuli for triggering conceptual dialogue in the community of philosophical inquiry—that field of shared meaning in the context of which what he calls, after Marcuse, a "new sensibility" may be nourished The novels are a concrete and singular testimony to the presence of Lipman's heritage in Kennedy's educational and philosophical approach, not only theoretically but also methodologically.

The movement and structure of chapters in this book form a kind of spiral, each advance building on the path opened by the previous one, while developing one of its most crucial aspects or dimensions, and at the same time introducing new interlocutors. Throughout the book, Kennedy follows, in his distinctively evolutionary manner, the transformation of Western subjectivity from a hierarchical to a dialogical model by identifying the role that the adult construction of childhood has played in this process. Aristotle's and Plato's formulations are first statements of a perennial symbolization of the child as both deficit and danger that has raised among adults the uneasy relationship between desire and reason. The enlightenment task of reason was to dominate desire, and of civilization to colonize nature. The dialogical model embodied in the pedagogy of community of philosophical inquiry represents, for him, the possibility of a shift in human subjectivity, and education based on adult-child dialogue constitutes a primary site for the reconstruction of belief.

This transformation of Western subjectivity is a fundamental theme throughout the book, calibrated on the idea of the emergence of a new sensibility and form of reason. Again, education is the cultural energy field in which this emergence can take place, and the school its institutionalized locale. Kennedy assumes the mutual modifiability of adult and child when put together in dialogical relation and identifies *skholé* as the form of schooling through which this relation is operationalized. Childhood appears as a model of what adults need in order to reverse the actual process of planetary dystopia. The work explores the conditions under which *aion* as the living time of a childlike education might emerge not only in schooling but also in human subjectivity in the form of *infantia*, another word for the distinctive form of childish becoming and embodiment, with implications for the singular self-actualization process of education for which Kennedy is constantly searching.

In identifying "child" as "prophet of futurity" and "experimental being" he also implicitly identifies the new sensibility as a form of subjectivity that cultivates what John Dewey (1916) called "social democracy" as a path towards authentic political democracy. Kennedy identifies Dewey's political agenda as made possible through a dialectical deconstruction of three forms of self-understanding: Plato's hierarchical tripartite soul; Descartes's isolated dualistic subject, and Freud's inversion of Plato's hierarchy with the introduction of the unconscious and the ego "that is not master in its own house." Moving beyond these three models, the birth of a dialogical self is one condition for the birth of a democratic society. As the book spirals thematically upward, Kennedy's political agenda appears more explicitly and clearly: the Deweyan ideal of social democracy is identified, in keeping with the new sensibility and the dialogical self, as a "clear evolutionary bio-social potential in the human brain for a certain organization of the relations between the prefrontal cortex and the limbic system—reason and feeling and desire—that is promised in every human infant [. . .] is only interrupted by toxic culture and bad education" (52). This evolutionary movement unfolds through an argument that calls on both hermeneutical and sociohistorical approaches to childhood to justify the arrival of what Kennedy identifies as the "empathic child-rearing mode," identified as a necessary condition for the onset of adult-child dialogue and the emergence of *skholé* as an institutional form. And journeying forward, he offers further characterizations of *skholé* as grounded in anarchist principles; as, that is, a social assemblage where the three key concepts of order, authority, and agency are practiced, questioned, and continually under reconstruction in an intensively social context. For Kennedy, *skholé* is the utopian name for a school that is democratized on principles of philosophical anarchism.

Kennedy also identifies a form of professional development that embodies the empathic mode in the practice of community of philosophical inquiry among teachers devoted specifically to exploring the concept of *child*. In his view, teachers should be engaged with other adults in the continual exercise of recognizing, deconstructing, and reconstructing their beliefs about childhood in general and children in particular. In this context, he also offers an example of what he considers a complementary formative practice to communal inquiry in the descriptive review process, a form of assessment developed by the philosopher-educator Patricia Carini, based on phenomenological observation and thick description of children in classroom and home settings.

This practical proposal is followed by a chapter devoted to the ontological and epistemological rudiments of play, particularly as it manifests in the community of philosophical inquiry. Can the community of philosophical inquiry be understood as a game with rules? What kind of play is philosophical play? What kind of power is exercised in the game of philosophical communal inquiry? And the implications of his excursus on play and community of philosophical inquiry are extended epistemically in a chapter on the rhizome—a horticultural concept extended to cognitive and social psychology, which expresses epistemologically what anarchy expresses politically: a nonhierarchical, flexible, and intercommunicative order where ideas, individuals, relationships, and social organizations can freely interact through philosophical dialogue. And finally, Kennedy's last chapter focuses on the form of human subjectivity that education as an ongoing dialectical and dialogical process of transformative reconstruction fosters, albeit, as he assures us, it has always been there, if only as a latent possibility. The book's finale is a kind of dialectical synthesis of previous chapters, which reaffirms democracy both as a communicative sociocultural practice and as a model for new forms of life emerging out of the adult-child relationship practiced in *skholé*.

Kennedy's book offers a rare and richly interdisciplinary and evolutionary approach to childhood, full of historical, cultural, and philosophical references woven together in a deeply connected narrative. A variety of educational and philosophical concepts are problematized, deconstructed, and reconstructed, in dialogue with a remarkable reading of different traditions in philosophy and the human sciences. Anyone interested in the educational dimension of philosophy or in the child/adult relationship would feel thankful after reading this scholarly and thoughtful book. Thanks to David Kennedy for a stellar example of utopian, childlike, and philosophical thinking and writing.

Walter Omar Kohan
State University of Rio de Janeiro
August 2023

Introduction

This volume is about three things: childhood, philosophy, and education—or, more particularly, schooling—and consists of an exploration of their relationships both actual and potential. It appears in times that are riven by fundamental conflicts on a global scale, driven by everything from massive economic inequalities and political greed and corruption to a change in the biosphere that threatens the ultimate survival of human life as we know it. In light of this planetary crisis, these essays, although they trade in concepts that have a long history in the annals of education, may appear utopian—a descriptor that I accept as long as the term is understood in the social philosopher Herbert Marcuse's sense as "that which is blocked from coming about by the power of the established societies" (1969, 4); here utopia is understood etymologically, not as a "no space" (ou topos) but as a "good" (eu topos) one.

These essays may best be described as messages from a virtual future system state—a strange attractor that directs and guides the development of the system in the present—a field of meaning and value that is a "not yet," a novum, deeply connected with Ernst Bloch's (1995) and Paulo Freire's ontology of the "unfinished," which Freire (2005) identified as our "ontological vocation" as a species. And yet this "not yet" is already here to the extent it is already exemplified in the sensibilities of so many humans. Using Freire's terms again, the biophilic sensibility far outweighs the necrophilic in the human community; it's just that the necrophiliacs carry guns. The fact that eutopia is already, albeit virtually, here, both renders our current planetary ordeal doubly painful and allows us to hope for (r)evolution, a term by which I mean to suggest the ambiguous and fruitful relation between the meanings of these two words—revolution and evolution—one representing a historical event and the other an ever-present teleological impulse.

The practical theme upon which all of these essays converge is a form of schooling. Early on, the theme of *skholé* is introduced, a term taken from the ancient Greek, meaning "leisure" or "free time," and from which we get the term *school*. Here *skholé* stands for an originary form of gathering and adult-child encounter, an archetypal model of an intentional learning community that is based on dialogical pedagogy, interdisciplinary study, philosophical inquiry, and direct democratic self-governance. In its association with the "invention" of democracy in fifth-century-BC Athens, *skholé* is as much a useful myth as a strictly historical phenomenon. However, it represents the first (that we know of) educational impulse directly associated with political democracy. As such, it has informed educational thought and practice for the last two centuries—when democracy became a Western project—in the form of what we know as "progressive" education.

For fifth-century-BC Athenians, *skholé* in its primary sense of leisure seems to have been a necessary condition for practicing philosophy, and, in Socrates's conversational, dialogical form at that—but not with children, whom traditional philosophy has considered uniquely unsuited for the activity. And today's "school" hardly understands itself as a place for open-ended philosophical inquiry; on the contrary, it purports to be a place of preparation for the "real world" of "production," suffused by a form of temporality hounded by a doubtful future. It's where you get ready to survive: to win (for a while) in the savage planetary game of global capitalism, which means, among other things, learning not to ask unsettling questions. In its present institutional form, school function as an ideological corporate-state worker-consumer preparation apparatus, for which philosophy represents an unwelcome interruption. In fact, philosophy is what must be guarded against in conventional schooling, because it inevitably leads to questioning power and the status quo, and the typical status quo is characterized by some pretty dramatic offenses against both humanity and the natural world. So there are two contradictory forces operating here: (1) school as *skholé*: a kind of intellectual sanctuary or (Gk.) *temenos* dedicated to free inquiry and study (Lat. *studium*: passion, enthusiasm) that is undergirded by the most fundamental form of inquiry, philosophy; and (2) school as a primary zone of ideological indoctrination and mental stultification. As such, philosophy is the elephant in the room of school constructed as an ideological state apparatus.

Even apart from school as *skholé*, childhood and philosophy have always been associated through the phenomenon of wonder—Gk. *thaumazein*—and its primary cognitive and linguistic expression, the question. Like a hand sweeping across a chess board mid-match, the philosophical question not only interrupts the particular discursive game we are playing, but also returns us to the beginning, the invisible point that Hannah Arendt (1958) called "natality," which is the primary characteristic of childhood. We may say that the child—both the child before us and the child within us—is always in the process of giving birth to an adult, and it could always be a new kind of adult: hence *natality*. This is what the philosopher of childhood Walter Kohan has called the "power" of childhood. It is a progenitive power, as Kohan (2014) points out, and its source is in a kind of lived time: an experience of temporality, aion, which we underrepresent by translating as "eternity." The best we can do is to identify it as not-*kronos*: not an infinite linear movement of protensions and retentions, but a being there all at once. This experience does not disappear with childhood, but rather is pushed impatiently and often despairingly out of the adult lifeworld by our finitude and what Heidegger (2010) called our "care" (*Sorge*).

Childhood is, then, the locus of the question prompted by wonder, the most direct and evocative of which is the philosophical question, and *skholé* is the cultural space that creates a place for this questioning. Philosophical questioning, when allowed its own direction and momentum, is transformative, progenitive, playful: it has the potential to break out of discursive molds, to reconstruct and invent and reinvent concepts, to rearrange the pieces on the checkerboard of life's meanings. In school as *skholé*, childhood and philosophy belong together. Children's play is itself a kind of bodily philosophical activity: a way of holding things at arm's length, of imagining different worlds, different selves, of taking different perspectives, of building and tearing down, of recombining, of thinking feelingly and feeling thoughtfully.

But what role do adults play in this? As a cultural sanctuary—a secular *hieron*—dedicated to inquiry as deep play, school as *skholé* is where children and adults meet in dialogue and not in unequal confrontation. There are multiple ways to formulate the dimensions of adult-child dialogue: impulse and habit; history and the present; libido and superego; youth and age; and so on. In *skholé*, the primary discursive ground of this dialogue is the philosophy circle. In the form of yet another central practice that combines *skholé* with Socratic dialogue in the public space or agora—what is known as "community of philosophical inquiry" (CPI)—adults are found engaging children in philosophical dialogue. Teachers are not instructing, transmitting, explicating, or inculcating, but practicing with, their students:

not talking about philosophy and its heroes, not delivering the central ideas of the canon, but doing it, directly. On this pedagogical model, the teacher as convener, coach, and model facilitates the group's ongoing reconstruction of the concepts that we—child and adult—live by, or that live in or through us, or that are becoming in us, through an emergent process of questioning, hypothesizing, exemplifying, and reformulating. And as befits *skholé*, we are doing it as a community: collectively, collaboratively, deliberatively, reflectively. Philosophy as here understood is not to be found in its traditions, schools, vocabularies, and methodologies: those are simply its artifacts, or even traces. Philosophy is there when we are doing it, and when we are doing it, we bring it out in each other.

Philosophy in schools, practiced with children, carries certain utopian implications. When philosophy is in the room, *skholé* emerges, and *skholé* is an evolutionary play space, virtual and transitional, an epistemological studio/laboratory where natality has its first big chance, where the new can emerge: new kinds of thinking and valuing, and sensibilities that emerge from thresholds, border crossings, and becomings triggered by the dynamics of the adult-child relationship as they are engaged in the ongoing reconstruction of concepts. The most mundane but perhaps most significant potential element of this space for transformation is its political dimension: it is where what Benjamin Barber (2004) calls "strong" democracy can emerge, again through its actual practice. Here the connection between philosophical investigation and ethics, right action, justice—*dikaiosune* (righteousness)—is actualized in a democratic speech community, a miniature polis, interrogating real issues and making real decisions. As such, *skholé* is the site for the cultural reinvention of democratic structures and processes. So, Dewey (1959) spoke of school as an "embryonic society," a "genuine form of active community life"(49) a special sort of ecological niche with generative and transformative potential for the political environment of the larger society. The democratization of philosophy is intimately linked with democracy tout court; they share similar affects and intensities. A functional democratic school is a necessary condition for a functional democratic society where, as Dewey (1916) pointed out, the communicative habits of social democracy—without which genuine political democracy is impossible—can emerge. The community of philosophical inquiry is at the heart of the democratic speech community. It is the site where *parrhesia*—frank and open speech—allows for practical ethical discourse and is connected to ethical action.

A second, related utopian implication that suggests itself in the theory and practice of philosophical dialogue with children in *skholé* is associated with the reconstruction of philosophy not just as a communal cognitive and metacognitive activity but also as an embodied practice. It means, first, the border-crossings of philosophical discourse into other expressive modalities: drawing, writing, film and photography, dance, and psychodrama. It returns philosophy to the body and breaks the spell of the exclusionary cogito. As a holistic practice, it also acts to subvert the binaries that hold the current epistemological paradigm in place, through interrogating their founding assumptions, thinking against their grain, and finding their "between" through playfully moving the pieces about, as Heraclitus's aionic child—"Eternity [*Aion*] is a child playing at draughts" (2003)—does, thus clearing space for reconstruction. And closely related to this, because of its re-inclusion of the body, it has the potential to return philosophy to the position of a contemplative practice, a particular form of the search for wisdom. This tradition is, as Pierre Hadot (1995) has shown us, an ancient one in philosophy; it is based on that movement of desire that seeks an actual alteration of perception—a form of attention that reveals the world differently, and as such is coextensive with the emergence of new modes of perception and action and new modes of exchange—in short, of a new sensibility.

And indeed it is this concept—developed by Marcuse amid the social and cultural turbulence of the 1960s—that is most likely to trigger skepticism in the reader of this book, but it is also the most central to its argument. A new or emergent sensibility is implicit in the notion of natality as an ever-present new beginning, which is embodied in the fact and the value and the possibilities of the long human childhood, known among evolutionary biologists as neoteny. It holds the promise of the emergence of "new" brains that connect higher cortical functions with lower reactive and emotional ones. This leads, in his words, to "an emergent organization of the relation between reason and desire, an emergent form of subjectivity" as "express[ing] the ascent of the life instincts over aggressiveness and guilt," dedicated to "the collective practice of creating an environment . . . in which the nonaggressive, erotic, receptive faculties of man [sic], in harmony with the consciousness of freedom, strive for the pacification of man and nature." It represents the actual felt "liberation of the mind, and of the body from aggressive and repressive needs" (1969, 29, 31).

Although Marcuse doesn't address the issue directly, the assumption in these essays is that the new sensibility—or as the anarchist philosopher Murray Bookchin (2005) called it, "second nature"—given that being is relational, is an emergent form of social character, and therefore as much a cultural as an individual or biological phenomenon. The ongoing evolutionary transformation of social character is fundamental to the notion of education understood as individual and social reconstruction as opposed to reproduction, which is at the heart of progressive educational ideals. It is also inextricably connected with the theory and practice of democracy as a form of life: the latter may be said to require a new sensibility in order to reach its potential, and, conversely, democracy acts as a social and political framework for the emergence of the new sensibility. Above all, it is already present in the species among members of a psychoclass composed of individuals who, for reasons that typically combine genetic, environmental, and cultural factors are, to quote Marcuse on a path of "liberation from aggressive and repressive needs." It is also implicit in the notion, offered by Gilles Deleuze and Felix Guattari (1987), of "becoming-child" as a human ontological vocation, by which they mean "an affective capacity or capacity to be affected . . . to grow and connect in new ways, which can be activated at any stage of life" (261). It is in this sense that this volume is witness to the power of childhood that we, as adults, must recognize and make a space for before it can become effective in culture and society. When combined with the redefinition of philosophy as a popular and democratic process, understanding children as originators is to take a different view of the species: to open that view to an ontological optimism, which recognizes in childhood a promissory note for new forms of individual and collective subjectivity, and understands the school as a potential evolutionary outpost, an experimental zone, a place where new cultural meanings and values can emerge.

A note on sources: The majority of the chapters in this volume originated as journal articles, all of them focusing on the same narrative thematics, and as such, lending themselves to their collation in one blended volume. Each has been altered more or less extensively in the interest of cross-reference and continuity. My hope is that this reconstructive synthesis results in the emergence of new meanings and new understandings.

Chapter One

The Politics of Subjectivity, Philosophy of Childhood, and Dialogical Education

The Western onto-theological tradition has long been preoccupied with two symbolizations of childhood: as original unity of being and knowing, exemplar of completed identity; and as deficit and danger, exemplar of the untamed appetite and the uncontrolled will. In the economy of Plato's and Aristotle's tripartite self, the child is ontogenetically out of balance. She is incapable of bringing the three parts of the self—reason, passion (spiritedness), and instinct—into a proper hierarchical relation based on the domination of reason. On this model, attaining adulthood means eradicating the child. Freud's reformulation of the Platonic community of self as horizontal rather than vertical creates an opening for shifting power relations between the elements of the self: for intrigue, transgression, and the possibility of dialogue. He opens the way towards what Julia Kristeva calls the "subject-in-process" (in Marchak 1990)—a pluralism of relationships rather than an organization constituted by exclusions and hierarchies—which in turn opens a way toward what is now known as "dialogical self theory," which will play an important role in the thematic organization of this book.

After Freud, the child comes to stand for the inexpugnable demands of desire, the marginalized "other" within. It is through dialogue with this child that the postmodern adult undergoes the dismantling of a notion of subjectivity based on domination, and the continuous reconstruction of the subject-in-process. In the realm of education, the new model of subjectivity leads to curriculum and pedagogy based on dialogue, and a new respect for the child's voice.

School-based education is a form of life that on its most basic level has to do with relations between adults and children. The traditional structure of schooling—which even today either characterizes or haunts the contemporary classroom—is a clear indication of the extent to which those relations have been founded on adult domination, based on a model of selfhood that denies children reason, and construes children's subjectivity as chaotic, unbalanced, and in need of correction. The deconstruction of this adultist model of selfhood has a number of consequences, both personal and cultural. It implies a new definition of reason, for when the functions of self are understood as in dialogue rather than in relations of domination, the function of reason—which Plato, in his original formulation of the plural self, called logos, *tò logistikón*, or *hò logismós*—is transformed. It recognizes its debt to the other two elements of the tripartite model, and loses its rationalistic, hierarchical, and separative character. In this process, the whole self becomes more "reasonable" as opposed to just "rational." One outcome of a decentered, interactive model of subjectivity—which we will encounter further along in dialogical self theory—is that adults recognize that reasonableness develops through dialogue between reason and the irrational, and to that extent, they learn to see that process as an aspect of childhood as well as adulthood. The net result for the adult-child relation, upon which education is based, is that adults begin to recognize children's capacity to reason, which opens the way for an educational model based on dialogue rather than domination.

Because it is children and their relations with adults that is the fundamental issue here, I want to begin by tracing in broad outlines the transformation of Western subjectivity from a hierarchical to a dialogical model by identifying the role that the adult construction of childhood has played in this process. Adults have long used the child iconically—as a symbol and often as a "proof text"—for human nature, and for understanding the direction of and the potential for psychological and cultural development. As adults' interpretations of childhood—of both the child before them and the child within—change, so changes not just education, but also the lived world we share in common. When looked at over time, adult representations of childhood can be seen to have both perennial and historical characteristics.

The Child and the Second Harmony

The child first appears in the known ancient texts, not as a beginning, but as an end. She represents the idea of the fulfillment of spiritual growth as a reversal of the life cycle. In the sixth century BC Lao Tzu says, "He who is in harmony with the Tao is like a newborn child. Its bones are soft, its muscles are weak, but its grip is powerful. . . . The Master's power is like this. He lets all things come and go effortlessly, without desire" (Lao Tzu 2006). Jesus speaks of the attainment of spiritual maturity as "becoming like little children" (Mark 10:13 KJV). Plotinus contrasts children with adults "whose faculty and mental activity are busied upon a multitude of subjects passed quickly overall, lingering on none." Among children, on the other hand, objects "achieve presence," because the child's attention is not "scattered," dispersed in the world of multiplicity (Bales 1990, 142).

In this grand perennial Western mythos, the child represents an original ontological unity of being and knowing, thought and experience—identity realized, the "single eye." The child is premoral, the realized adult post-moral. The story of the journey from one to the other begins with a Fall into division. It is a necessary fall, because it inaugurates a psychological and spiritual journey that, if you don't die in the desert of adulthood, promises self-reintegration on a higher level. G. W. F. Hegel's logic of history replicates this universal myth of the individual life cycle: "The harmoniousness of childhood is a gift of the hand of nature: the second harmony must spring from the labor and culture of the spirit" (Abrams 1971, 380).

Not just in Hegel, but also in his Romantic contemporaries, the mythos of the arduous psychological journey of regained unity leaves its religious otherworldly moorings and enters time. Friedrich Schiller articulated the Romantic ideal in 1796 in reference to children: "They are what we were; they are what we should once again become. We were nature just as they, and our culture, by means of reason and freedom, should lead us back to nature. They are, therefore, not only the representation of our lost childhood, . . . but they are also representations of our highest fulfillment in the ideal" (Schiller 1966, 85). Original unity, self and nature given as one, the concrete universal. Romanticism rediscovers the archetypal "divine" child of mythology right here on earth as a prophet (Jung and Kerenyi 1969), a mute seer, an enigmatic sign of life without division. The language of the child as prophet is play. Heraclitus says, "Time is a child moving counters in a game. The royal power is a child's" (2003, Fragment 52). Augustine in crisis, pacing in frantic agony in the garden, hears the "singsong voice of a child in a nearby house," chanting "take it and read, take it and read." He opens the Bible in his hand to the passage that changes his understanding of his life forever (Augustine 1961, 177). In 1933, Henri Cartier-Bresson photographs a band of twelve school-aged children playing in the ruins of a house in Naples. Framed by a gaping hole in a plaster wall, their ecstatic revel has the appearance both of a celebratory dance and a war skirmish, as they grab, flee, scream, and giggle. In Leonardo's *Virgin and Child with Saint Anne* (c. 1508, Louvre), the naked Christ Child frolics with the lamb that represents his sacrificial murder. In Stefan Lochner's *Madonna of the Rose Bower* (c. 1450, Cologne), the tiny naked Child holds in his hand a golden ball, proffered to him by an angel.

Play, says Melanie Klein, is "the child's most important medium of expression." In that his "conscious is as yet in close contact with its unconscious," the language of play is the same language "that we are familiar with in dreams" (Klein 1980, 7–9). For the Romantic imagination, play expresses an ontological principle. In it, the universal and the particular converge, as well as the possible and the given, the random and the determined, accident and purpose, is and ought. The world of nature plays, and human play represents this meta-play and becomes it, thereby overcoming our separation from the world of nature. In play the tyranny of means and ends is broken, and causality gives way to synchronicity. Play implies a different subject-object, self-world, inner-outer relationship. "The players," philosopher Hans-Georg Gadamer says, "are not the subjects of play: instead play merely reaches presentation through the players" (Gadamer 1975, 92). Play is located in what D. W. Winnicott, describing young children, called "transitional space," which is also the space of art, fantasy, and profound emotion, in which ego-boundaries become permeable, and the wall that we have built between reality and imagination is temporarily overcome. Because play is neither "inside" nor "outside," it is experienced as the (play-) marriage of the pleasure principle and the reality principle (Winnicott 1989, 41). N. O. Brown calls this the "psychoanalytic meaning of history." He says, "Our indestructible unconscious desire for a return to childhood, our deep childhood-fixation, is a desire for a return to the pleasure-principle, for a recovery of the body from which culture alienates us, and for play instead of work" (Brown 1959, 38). Play is pure presence, access to a life without the play of difference. Schiller puts it bluntly: "The play impulse would aim at the extinction of time in time and the reconciliation of becoming with absolute being, of variation with identity" (Schiller 2004, 74). And finally, Jungian psychologist Erich Neumann (1973b) characterizes the experience of infancy as "oceanic feeling," and "paradisiacal" in "the unity of the I and thou, self and world . . . which set its imprint on all future development, and is of particular importance for the psychology of creative individuals. . . . The child lives in a total participation mystique . . . a psychic mother-fluid . . . from which the opposites, ego and Self, subject and object, individual and world have yet to be crystalized" (14, 15).

The Child and the Divided Self

Plato's theory of the tripartite self places the child as original unity and symbol of the second harmony under erasure. In his child, and Aristotle's as well, the balance between the three dimensions of self is ontogenetically out of off. The child lacks reason, and as such is exemplar of the untamed appetite and the uncontrolled will. Children are liable—along with women, slaves, and the "inferior multitude"—to the "great mass of multifarious appetites and pleasures and pains" of the naturally immoderate (Plato 1941, 125, IV:31c). "They are full of passionate feelings from their very birth" (Plato 1941, 138, IV:440b). The "boy," just because "he more than any other has a fount of intelligence in him which has not yet 'run clear,' . . . is the craftiest, most mischievous, and unruliest of brutes. So, the creature must be held in check . . ." (Plato 1961, 1379, VII: 807d). Children's only virtue appears to be that they are "easily molded," and as such they are capable of being made into adults. This calls for a certain form of education as a personal and social necessity, and as such the Republic is the first Western educational tract.

Aristotle develops Plato's argument by showing just how the community of self is skewed in children. The preponderance of their appetitive nature either leads to or is a result of the lack of the capacity for choice, or "moral agency," (i.e., the ability to deliberately engage in an action toward a final end) (Aristotle 1987, 197b:7–10, 104 and 1224a:27–29, 492–93). For this reason, the child cannot be called "happy," because happiness is a result of "activity in accordance with virtue," which is a state in which the executive function of reason controls instinct and will: "Happiness requires full grownup goodness and a complete life." Children do not fulfill the requirements of a "complete life." If we do call a child happy, "we do so by reason of the hopes we have for his future" (Aristotle 1962, 1099b:25–1100a:5, 22–23). And, although we can love her, we cannot call a child "friend": "It would be absurd for a man to be the friend of a child" (Aristotle 1987, 1239a:1–6).

Aristotle's and Plato's formulations are first statements of a perennial symbolization of the child as both deficit and danger. Aristotle's might even be read as an implicit theory of monsters, in the sense that children are "like" humans—"human" understood as adult, male, free-born, and governed by reason—but are not. They combine the same elements in a different and deficient mixture. It is true that the child, if not born a slave or a female, has the chance of becoming an adult (i.e., developing reason in right relation to will and appetite) whereas the woman and the slave never will. But the transition becomes problematic. Indeed, says Plato, some children never become "adults" in the sense of a harmony of the tripartite self: "Some, I should say, never become rational, and most of them only late in life" (Plato 1941, 138, IV:441b). A technology becomes necessary in order to accomplish adulthood, namely education, which Aristotle, following Plato, defines as being "brought up from childhood to feel pleasure and pain at the proper things; for this is correct education" (Aristotle 1962, 1104b, 37). Education-as-training then presents itself as a ritual of force and an absolute cultural necessity.

The tripartite self is not so much a plural self as a structural community of separate functions, in which the attainment of adulthood represents the parts coming into a normative balance, of bringing the "elements into tune with one another by adjusting the tension of each to the right pitch" (Plato 1941, 102, III:411e). The metaphor travels down through the Western philosophy of self into Sigmund Freud's late nineteenth-early twentieth-century formulation. The child of Western patriarchal rationalism represents the ambiguity of what's given as the human at the beginning of the life cycle, and the possibility of the construction of an ideal self in which "each part of his nature is exercising its proper function, of ruling or of being ruled" (Plato 1941, 141, IV: 443b). This construction is carried on into adult life in what Michel Foucault has called "the technologies of the self" (Martin, Gutman, and Hutton 1988). Unity of self is accomplished only through the eternal vigilance of reason over appetite and will, a product of constant self-examination and readjustment through self-discipline. This system of internal domination is replicated macrocosmically, not just in Plato's Republic, but also in the Indo-European social political system as a whole, where kings (reason) control warriors (spirited will) who in turn rule over the agricultural classes (appetite) (Dumezil 1970).

The Child and the Politics of Subjectivity

It is not coincidental that the philosophy of childhood should share location with the philosophy of self and of the construction of subjectivity. The child has always found symbolic use as a proof text for views of human "nature," whether in the original depravity of the Puritan's child, the primary wholeness of the child of the Romantics, or the stage-bound developmentalism of biologistic psychology's version of childhood. But each "child" also represents a corresponding "adult." Given the inseparability of the two concepts, to say what a child is, is in the same breath to say what an adult is, if only through saying what it is not. To say what a child is is also to say how one becomes an adult; and to say what an adult is is to say what relationship one has with one's childhood.

The narrative that has informed the relationships between this contrastive pair at least since Aristotle and Plato is the story of the uneasy relationship among adults between desire and reason. The child is ambivalent in the adult imagination because she represents a limit condition of the human. Like the mad, the divine, the animal—or, in patriarchy, woman—all of which are representations of desire in some "pure" form, the liminality of the child both excludes and privileges her; so, it was a child who went before the worshipers in the secret Eleusinian mysteries to meet the god (Golden 1990, 44).

In our time, Freud took up this familiar narrative and described it as the relation between instinct and repression. He continued the Platonic construal of development as the struggle to integrate a subjectivity divided by a fundamental quarrel. His importance to the philosophy of childhood lies in his combination of the two symbolizations of childhood—the original ontological unity and the dangerous deficit—showing their interrelationship.

The original unity that the child represents for Freud is described in what he calls "infantile narcissism," the paradise of desire in which the boundaries of the self are the boundaries of the world. In infancy, thought and act are one, self and (m)other are one. The snake in this garden is the twofold contradictory nature of desire: Eros and Thanatos, love and death. Eros cannot complete its drive for unity in time and multiplicity. It is only Death and its agent, Aggression, which can achieve the final homeostasis that is Love's goal.

In Freud's mythic story, the child's Fall into division is inscribed on the body. First, the dismemberment of pleasure in the ontogenetic separation of the erogenous zones. The Oedipal crisis cements the fixation of pleasure in the genitals and establishes the prohibition of desire as a principle of property. The child falls slowly but surely out of the grace-state of polymorphic sexuality, out of existence as spontaneous erotic play, out of the magic symbiosis of subject and object, self and world, inside and outside.

For Plato, Aristotle, and Freud, childhood disappears when reason or ego assumes its executive function. However, for Freud, ego is not completely reason; it is part conscious and part unconscious. Nor is it dominant, but a mediator, a fourth function that arises as a result of the interplay between the id, the superego, and the reality principle, and attempts to integrate them. Furthermore, to the extent that neurosis (i.e., chronic non-integration of the functions of self) is the human condition, the experience of infantile narcissism remains as an existential surd. Jean-François Lyotard speaks of this surd as infantia, or "that which resists, after all." He says, "But something will never be defeated, at least as long as humans will be born infants, infantes. Infantia is the guarantee that there remains an enigma in us, a not easily communicable opacity—that something is left that remains, and that we must bear witness to it" (Lyotard and Larochelle 1992, 416). The "miserable and admirable indetermination" of infancy is for Lyotard all that can resist the Enlightenment ideal of "emancipation," the "inhuman" of systematization and complexification disguised as "development." The goal of emancipation is to "secure full possession of knowledge, will and feeling; so as to give oneself the authority of knowledge, the law of the will, and control over one's affections" (Lyotard 1992, 421; Lyotard 1991; Lindsay 1992, 389–401).

The "emancipated" adult of Enlightenment is inaugurated in the West by Plato and Aristotle. He (sic) dominates appetite through reason, which uses will as the Indo-European rulers use the military to control the masses. To achieve control, the child and the "native," both of whom represent instinctual life, appetite, pleasure, the body (i.e., the transgressive) must be excluded and subjugated. Ashis Nandy analyzes the relationship between what he calls "the ideology of adulthood" and colonialism:

> To the extent adulthood itself is valued as a symbol of completeness and as an end-product of growth or development, childhood is seen as an imperfect transitional state on the way to adulthood, normality, full socialization and humanness. This is the theory of progress as applied to the individual life-cycle. The result is the frequent use of childhood as a design of cul-

> tural and political immaturity or, it comes to the same thing, inferiority. Much of the pull of the ideology of colonialism and much of the power of the idea of modernity can be traced to the evolutionary implications of the concept of the child in the Western world view. (Nandy 1987, 57)

Freud presages but does not accomplish a break in this picture of internal and external colonization. In his formulation, the politics of the Platonic self shift, and the child and the instinctual life she represents get repositioned. The child is no longer dominated, expunged, under erasure in the adult personality, but comes to represent the ever-present voice of the demands of the id. These demands are experienced both on the inside and the outside: as the haunting memory of the experience of the hallucinatory omnipotence of primary process in one's own infancy; and as the adult's relationship with the real child—"reason" in conflict and dialogue with the desire-self in parenting and education. The politics of subjectivity are also the politics of child-rearing and the politics of difference.

The picture is complicated by a deep-seated ambivalence. For the "civilized" Freud, the child is the voice of neurosis. The neurotic is unwilling to give up the demands of childhood, the possibility of a world undivided. The adult who privileges her "child" becomes childish (i.e., uncivilized). As such, the possibility of civilization itself is predicated on repression. At one point, Freud (1957) defined psychoanalysis as "a prolongation of education for the purposes of overcoming the residues of childhood" (48). For this Freud, the child is still the dangerous deficit. But for the "savage" Freud and his interpreters, those very residues are our only hope of being delivered from the inhuman march of "progress," or systematization and complexification. Radical Freudians like N. O. Brown unearth Freud's latent Romanticism and honor the child as the voice of desire that will not be quelled or expunged by a rationalism infected by what it represses (Brown 1966). For modernism transitioning into the postmodern, the child is one more excluded other—along with women, the mad, the "deviant," the "native"—one more voice from the margins of Platonic patriarchal subjectivity. She takes her place with the other "privileged strangers" of standpoint epistemology, who represent, by their very liminality, our only hope for the dismantling of a notion of subjectivity based on domination and exclusion (Harding 1991, 124–31).

In the "savage" Freud, the politics of subjectivity take a turn toward dismantling hierarchy. His model creates an opening for shifting power relations, for intrigue, for transgression, and above all for dialogue between the elements of the self. In this sense he is not so much departing from Plato and Aristotle as adumbrating the relations within the community of self in their complexity and paradox. He opens the way towards what Julia Kristeva calls the "subject-in-process," or self as a pluralism of relationships rather than an "organization constituted by exclusions and hierarchies" (Kristeva 1987, 65; Kristeva 1980, 135). Childhood stands for "jouissance," the experience of pre-Oedipal "forgotten time," ecstatic moments in which the socially constructed form of the boundary line between self and external world is deconstructed in the interests of ongoing self-reconstruction (Marchak 1990, 354–63).

If Plato is right, as he argues in *The Republic*, that the state is the self writ large, what are the implications of this new model of subjectivity for the political systems of the world? As repression and domination within the community of the self are problematized and critiqued, does it lead to problematization and critique of economic and political domination and repression as well? The critical link between inner and outer politics could be child rearing and education. As the subject-in-process dialogues with infantia, the child within, she does so with the real child as well. In the ideology of postmodern child-rearing, Eros overcomes Thanatos through dialogue and integration. The adult subject-in-process recognize the voice of difference, of the other, which the real child represents. Like the artist and the genius, the child through her very imbalance suggests to us new ways to balance. The child is the naïve/native genius of the species. To return to Schiller: "The naive mode of thought can . . . be attributed only to children and to those of a childlike temperament. . . . Every true genius must be naive, or it is not genius. Only its naivety makes for its genius, and what it is intellectually and aesthetically it cannot disavow morally. . . . Only to genius is it given to be at home beyond the accustomed and to extend nature without going beyond her" (1966, 85). The child—inside and outside—is the prophet of futurity, the experimental being, who offers us intimations of how to "extend nature without going beyond her." This sounds like what Maurice Merleau-Ponty described as "the task of our century. . . . The attempt to explore the irrational and integrate it into an expanded reason" (Merleau-Ponty 1964a, 63). Others might speak of it as the recovery of the body, or non-repressive sublimation, or overcoming patriarchy, domination, or colonization from both within and without. "Our most liberating bonds," says Nandy, "can be with our undersocialized children. And the final test of our skill to live a bicultural or multicultural existence may still be our ability to live with our children in mutuality" (Nandy 1987, 75).

The Subject-in-Process and Community of Inquiry

To "live with our children in mutuality" would seem to imply that educational form, which in its modern structure perfectly mirrors impositional reason, would be transformed into a setting for child-adult dialogue. The transformation of the structure of schooling toward dialogue began with the Romantics, in the thought and practice of Johann Pestalozzi and Friedrich Froebel, and has been carried forward slowly through the formulations of Maria Montessori, John Dewey, the Progressive school movement of the first half of the twentieth century, and the theory and practice of early childhood education in general. Dewey's is perhaps the most important formulation of the theoretical ground of this transformation, in his notion of education as reconstruction. Reconstruction as a developmental process assumes a logical and sequential relationship between the child's rudimentary investigations of the world and the eventual outcome of those investigations in the structures of the disciplines. The child at play in the world is a little mathematician, historian, poet, musician, etc. If this continuity between the child's inquiry and the curriculum exists, then there is a path along which it travels, which is what education finds and enables.

If we believe and act on this assumption, it operates, as Dewey says, to "get rid of the prejudicial notion that there is some gap in kind (as distinct from degree) between the child's experience and the curriculum—the various forms of subject-matter that make up the course of study" (Dewey 1959, 96). The putative "gap in kind" is produced by the view of the child that follows on the Platonic model of subjectivity. Dewey is very critical of this understanding. To oppose one to the other, he claims, "is to oppose the infancy and maturity of the same growing life; it is to set the moving tendency and the final result of the same process over against each other; it is to hold that the nature and the destiny of the child war with each other" (Dewey 1959, 97).

The traditional school is structured around this war, in which the child represents nature and the adult civilization. The hierarchic structure of the institution is isomorphic with the Platonic structure of subjectivity: administration (reason); teacher (the spirited element); and children (appetite). The transformation of this structure into a dialogical one is both an intersubjective and an intrasubjective project; the two are mutually entraining. The focal point of the transformative process is the classroom itself, where the narratives of the adult-child relation are played out. Adult and child in dialogue in the classroom setting implies dialogue in the areas of curriculum, pedagogy, and classroom governance.

In the area of curriculum, reconstructionism assumes a concrete, viable continuity between the interests of the child and the articulation of the content areas. While it places the burden of finding and articulating the paths between the two on the adult, the child's burden is to attribute at least provisional trust to the adult's guidance along those paths when the connections are not so easily perceived by her. In the area of pedagogy, adult-child dialogue would appear to lead in the direction of individualization and diversification, and an emphasis on inquiry as the necessary prerequisite for any kind of instruction. In the area of power relations within the school community, any dialogical situation would seem to imply democratic decision-making, in curriculum as much as in classroom and school governance.

It may be a mistake to interpret the failures of the progressivist "child-centered" ideal of the first part of the twentieth century as more than the outcome of a dialectical moment in the evolution of adult-child dialogue. Dewey's critique of the progressive movement of the 1920s was focused on its inability to present anything but a reactive ideal to the traditionalist model: one that ignored what he called the "remaking of impulses and desires," which is the outcome of successful education, and which of necessity implies "inhibition of impulse in its first estate" (Dewey 1938a, 64). How this element of "inhibition" enters into an adult-child relationship that is not based on domination is the working edge of the evolution of that relationship. In a dialogical relationship, the "remaking of impulses and desires" is a mutual process, but the adult-child situation is a unique one, the remaking of which may take different forms for the two. For the child, Jerome Bruner offers the possibility that this remaking can actually result from intrinsic rather than extrinsic motivation. He speaks of "natural energies that sustain spontaneous learning," and lists them as "curiosity, a desire for competence, aspiration to emulate a model, and a deep-sensed commitment to the web of social reciprocity." These energies are intrinsic to humans, whose "specialization as a species is a specialization for learning" (Bruner 1966, 113, 128). The implication here is that, given an environment conducive to it—which includes an adult with whom a child is in dialogue—children themselves undertake that remaking of impulses and desires that so often seemed to be missing from early progressive educational experiments.

Although some may invoke a fear of chaotic irrationalism following on the deconstruction of the Platonic model of subjectivity, it seems more likely that a shift away from it would redistribute a greater balance of the reason-function onto the child. The Platonic model denies her the capacity to reason based on a narrowed image of rationality that is based on "exclusions and hierarchies," which does not recognize that the form of reason that leads to reasonableness—as opposed to rationalism—does not exclude the energies of appetite and will. The latter might well be the "natural energies" of which Bruner speaks. These energies are the engines of developmental self-organization, of increasing complexity, flexibility, and self-control, or as Heinz Werner put it, "a state of increasing differentiation, articulation, and hierarchic integration" (Werner 1957, 126). The image of reason that emerges from Werner's organismic theory—and from constructivist learning theory as well—implies an expansion of the notion of reason to include the "irrational," because it is an image of spontaneous self-organization in interaction with an environment that is itself reorganized by that interaction. Reason imbues appetite and will and is imbued by them, rather than demanding a position of dominance, because dialogue implies the mutual transformation of interlocutors.

The rise of community of philosophical inquiry (CPI) theory and practice in the last half of the twentieth century is exemplary of the effects of a transformed adult-child paradigm on education, and of a new model of subjectivity, and therefore of reason, and of the child's capacity to reason. As such, it will play a major role in this book. The broad educational implications of CPI theory and practice are a decentered classroom, an emergent form of curriculum, and a pedagogy dedicated to promoting distributive thinking. CPI reconstructs reason, not only as communal and distributive, but also as the servant of, rather than the determiner or container of, meaning (Lipman, Sharp, and Oscanyon 1980, 12–13). "Meaning" implies the participation of all the elements-in-dialogue of the subject-in-process. The critical thinking skills through which CPI functions and develops in children and adults are tools of the search for meaning through communal dialogue.

Another protagonist of this book, the educational program known as Philosophy for Children, is one major exemplification of the community of inquiry approach and operates on the assumption that these critical and interactive skills are available to children from an earlier age than mainstream developmental psychologists think they are. Philosophy for Children shifts the model of classroom discourse from a unilateral, adult-dominated, monological model to a model based on communal dialogue. When children are allowed a collaborative interactive context dedicated to meaningful inquiry, the tools of logic are allowed to emerge and develop from their basis in the structure of language. A discourse model that is based on a socially mediated, distributive, collaborative model of reason evokes reason.

The Platonic model of the child as without reason is in fact suppressing what it claims not to find. The reasons for this suppression have to do not only with the maintenance of class-based social and political form of governmentality, but also with a model of subjectivity, understood as a characteristic way of organizing our "impulses and desires." The adult in dialogue with the child is to some extent in dialogue with that adult's own childhood, and as such is involved in remaking her own impulses and desires as well. That remaking involves the development of an expanded reason through recognizing and integrating the natural energies that the child brings in relatively unmitigated form to the relationship with the adult. That remaking is never finished, but the process itself is critical both for self-actualization and for cultural evolution: for extending nature without going beyond her. The chapters that follow explore this evolutionary movement in a variety of contexts—historical, sociocultural, psychological, literary, philosophical, and biological—based on the underlying assumption that human childhood per se represents the perennial possibility of an emergent shift in human subjectivity, and that adult-child dialogue, especially in the context of the adult-child collective called "school" understood as a primary site for the reconstruction of personal and collective subjectivity, is a key locus of the epistemological change that shift implies.

Chapter Two

Neoteny, Dialogical Education, and an Emergent Psychoculture

This chapter continues the argument that children represent one vanguard of an emergent shift in Western subjectivity, and that adult-child dialogue, especially in the context of schooling, is a key locus for the epistemological change that implies. Following Marcuse's invocation of a "new sensibility," I argue that the evolutionary phenomenon of neoteny—the long formative period of human childhood and the paedomorphic (in the form of a child) character of humans across the life cycle—makes of the adult-collective of school a primary site for the reconstruction of belief. After exploring child-adult dialogue more broadly as a form of dialectical interaction between what Dewey (1922) called "impulse" and "habit," three key dimensions of dialogic schooling are identified, all of which are grounded in a fourth: the form of dialogical group discourse called community of philosophical inquiry (CPI), which is based on the problematization and reconstruction of concepts through critical argumentation. As a discourse model, CPI grounds practice in all of the dialogic school's emergent curricular spaces, whether science, mathematics, literature, art, or philosophy. Second, it opens a functional space for shared decision-making and collaborative governance, making of school an exemplary model of direct democracy. Finally, CPI as a site for critical interrogation of concepts encountered in the curriculum (e.g., "alive," "justice," "system," "biosphere") and as a site for democratic governance leads naturally to its expression in activist projects that model an emergent "new reality principle" through concrete solutions to practical problems on local and global levels.

Chapter one was concerned with tracing the genealogy of the cultural image of the human child as "prophet of futurity" and "experimental being," and as representing the possibilities evoked in Merleau-Ponty's (1964a) characterization of "the task of our century: to explore the irrational and integrate it into an expanded reason." This task was associated with the philosophical critique of the Western notion of disembodied rationality and the search for a post-Cartesian paradigm, and the phenomenon of childhood presented as one framework through which to organize this search. In paying closer attention to children, we're listening for what follows when the Platonic and Cartesian paradigms break up and begin to transform. We're listening for the (r)evolutionary emergence of what Marcuse identifies as a new form of reason, which he associates with what he calls a "new sensibility." This chapter will be dedicated to exploring the part that children may play in that emergence, particularly in the context of the school and of the educational discourse model of CPI.

There is plenty of evidence, at least in the history of Western thought and ethical culture, of epistemological change over historical time, which has led to new ontologies, new anthropologies, new values and convictions, and new scientific theories, all of which contribute to emergent forms of modal subjectivity. The last one hundred years have witnessed accelerating technological change, resulting in a still changing information environment, the subjective importance of which can be summed up in Walter Ong's (1982) observation that "intelligence is relentlessly reflective, so that even the external tools that it uses to implement its workings become 'internalized,' that is, part of its own reflexive process" (81), an observation reinforced by the recent "neurological turn" in theories of intelligence. Ong also implies (1967) that a historical form of intelligence is a dimension of a historical "sensorium," a characteristic way of experiencing the lived world:

Man's sensory perceptions are abundant and overwhelming. He cannot attend to them all at once. In great part a given culture teaches him one or another way of productive specialization. It brings him to organize his sensorium by attending to some types of perception more than others, by making an issue of certain ones while relatively neglecting other ones (6).

In his book *Eros and Civilization* (1955), Marcuse argues that the reorganized sensibility/sensorium he is proleptically summoning in the "new sensibility" is an emergent property of a culture in which it is generally recognized that scarcity can be overcome through technological advance, thereby obviating the need for "surplus repression," and making possible a "new reality principle" based on a transformed "libidinal economy" and an "aesthetic morality." The ground has been prepared for this sensorial and epistemological shift by explorations and discoveries that sow epistemic crises of boundary, scale, and visibility, and produce a sort of epistemic vertigo. Quantum physics has blurred subject-object boundaries and produced a crisis of objectivity. The exploration of inner space in psychoanalysis, of intersubjective space in cultural anthropology, of cosmic space and nanospace through new technological optics, the intervisibility resulting from accelerated planetwide human migration, which lead to a new sort of nomadism—all these factors contribute to a globalized world perhaps better described in the vocabulary of Gilles Deleuze and Felix Guattari (1987) as reflecting "intensities" and "flows," "lines of flight," de- and re-territorializations, or instances of "becoming other." And this epistemic crisis is synchronous with multiple economic, social, psychological, environmental, and political crises associated with late technocapitalist economies and their correlates: climate change, dramatic economic inequalities, perpetual war, and grave environmental degradation.

This epistemic change might be described as a dialectical evolutionary gambit. It is dialectical in the sense that it is, first of all, urged forward by contradictions within the whole system, and second, in the sense that earlier elements of the system can be restated in a "sublated" way in the emerging structure. Compare, for example, classically defined "primitive" animism, young children's animism, and the animistic tendencies of process philosophy, or the "quantum animism" of the physicist Nick Herbert (1995), Rupert Sheldrake's (2009) morphic fields, and James Lovelock's Gaia theory (1979). These could be understood as attempts to overcome our deep enculturation in mind-matter dualism, and to rethink some fundamental ontological and metaphysical issues (see Skrbina 2005 and Kennedy 1992). We can find statements of each in each of the others, and as such we might say that each is one limited response to a question based on an intuition of the unity of mind and nature that is continually restated in different historical contexts and in different discourses. As such, epistemic change is continuous discursive reconstruction. It is also psychological: it results, not just in a new episteme, but in an emergent psychoculture. It involves new forms of modal subjectivity.

An epistemic system has not changed until it changes the thinking—not just the abstract or theoretical thinking but also the intuitive insights and the practical, everyday reasoning and decision-making—of a collective. Even more it is, Marcuse (1969) insists, "aesthetic" in the etymological sense of "felt." It is embodied. It is what he calls a particular form of "human nature" or set of "needs and satisfactions," which is marked most significantly by the way we experience nature and the lived world. It operates at the perceptual level, and only from the level of perception—of what we see and touch and how we feel about it, how our body "explains" it—does it lead to the formation of different scientific and moral and ethical concepts. In his announcement of a new sensibility, Marcuse foresees a new onto-epistemological model "that replaces the bifurcated practice of separating the social from the natural, the objects from the subjects" (quoted in Pierce 2009, 148). This transformed post-Cartesian superstructure is, for Marcuse, what can save us from the culture of domination, violation, exploitation, and destruction of our own biosphere, a planetary culture from whose iron grip we are finding it difficult to extricate ourselves. It was a new form of "sensuous reason" that Marcuse, in the late 1960s and early 1970s, strove to articulate, with the admonition that "liberation presupposes changes in [the] biological dimension, that is to say, different instinctual needs, different reactions of the body as well as the mind," in which "cultural needs 'sink down' into the biology of man" (1969, 17, 10). And the goal of this is, Marcuse claims, a human being whose "second nature" has raised an "instinctual barrier against cruelty, brutality, ugliness" (21), product of a "revolution in perception which will accompany the material and intellectual reconstruction of society, creating the new aesthetic environment" (37), where "freedom [has become] a biological necessity," and we are "physically incapable of tolerating any repression other than that required for the protection and amelioration of life" (28).

Neoteny and Adult-Child Dialogue

Where might children and children's thinking—and children's thinking voiced in settings of communal philosophical inquiry in particular—fit in the dialectical emergence of a new sensibility and form of reason, and how are children potentially unique agents of its emergence? Marcuse associates its onset with what he calls the Great Refusal, an alienation against alienation, which he finds universally expressed in student and youth movements. These movements could be said to emerge from one high point of the long human childhood—adolescence—as its flower, but roots must be searched for in earlier childhood. The child is the biological and cultural representative of the new, the emergent, and a concrete, literal embodiment of futurity: a futurity, in fact, in its own image. As Ashley Montagu (1989) wrote, "The child is the forerunner of humanity—forerunner in the sense that the child is the possessor of all those traits which, when healthily developed, lead to a healthy and fulfilled human being, and thus to a fulfilled and healthy humanity" (106). But this developmental pathway, this evolutionary possibility inherent in human embodiment itself, for which childhood is a promissory note, is unimaginable apart from our species' educability.

Education is the proof of our relative freedom from instinctual determinism, and its power—either negative or positive—is based on what both Dewey and contemporary neuroscientists call the "original plasticity" of the young, which is a primary aspect of neoteny, the extraordinarily long period of relative immaturity in humans. Dewey sounded the neotenic theme in 1922, when he wrote:

> . . . the intimation never wholly deserts us that there is in the unformed activities of childhood and youth the possibilities of a better life for the community as well as for individuals here and there. This dim sense is the ground of our abiding idealization of childhood . . . [that] remains a standing proof of a life wherein growth is normal not an anomaly, activity a delight not a task, and where habit-forming is an expansion of power and not its shrinkage. (99)

As Montagu argues in his book on the biological and cultural phenomenon of neoteny, the term describes, not just our prolonged childhood and the opportunity it provides for personal and cultural reconstruction, but also the human predilection for ongoing development and learning and consequent adaptive reconstruction throughout the life cycle (1989, 106). Per neoteny theory, humans are paedomorphs. "Evolution," Montagu argues,

> has consisted of a shedding of the adult traits of our ancestral forms, and an increasing retention and development of the juvenile traits of those forms. Together with this has gone a stretching out of developmental periods, so that more time has become increasingly available for growth and development. The same processes clearly have been at work for functional and behavior traits. It would be a great step forward if we ceased to regard childhood as a phase of development which terminates

> at whatever arbitrary age we decide upon and to perceive it for what it is, an extended period of growth which slows down, if at all, only after many years. (61, 98)

The evolutionary gambit under the sign of neoteny assumes that whatever its multiple and even chaotic causal influences, a new psychoculture emerges in and through the young and those adults who retain youthful characteristics. Education is the institution that operates either to reproduce a reified psychoculture and a static modal subjectivity, or to provide a space—both temporal and experiential—for transformation in the emergence of new, more adaptive forms of intelligence and sensibility. Often, of course, we find some ambiguous mixture of these two extremes, but the advance of developmental neuroscience has at least given us several key indicators by which to evaluate change, all of them under the rubric of plasticity, or modifiability of the brain. It continues to grow through adolescence, and neuronal connections are created and modified long after they have reached a terminal state in any other species, resulting in greater cognitive and behavioral flexibility (Bjorklund 1997). Most importantly for education, the connections that neuroscientists have discovered between experience and neuronal development would suggest that the brain is as much "made" as it is found. Brain growth theorists postulate at least a working distinction between experience-expectant and experience-dependent brain growth (Johnson 2008, 2011). We may think of the intergenerational meeting place called "school" as one crucial site of the latter, a cultural space that the extraordinarily long period of childhood makes a psycho-cultural laboratory, from which the "new brain" of an altered modal sensibility promises to emerge.

Joseph Chilton Pearce, who also frames our evolutionary potential in terms of brain development during the primary neotenous period of childhood and adolescence, argues that for evolutionary change to occur, a model is necessary, that "from the beginning of our life, the characteristics of each new possibility must be demonstrated for us by someone, some thing, or an event in our immediate environment . . ." (2002, 5–6). In the case of the adult-child relation, both at home and at school, life-course neoteny theory would suggest that the model is bidirectional. If the result of successful education is—in keeping with the post-(French) revolutionary Romantic educational ideal, stated by Samuel Taylor Coleridge as "carry[ing] on the feelings of childhood into the powers of manhood" (quoted in Abrams 1971, 378)—a neotenic adult or "paedomorph," the schoolteacher, in encouraging both the "feelings" and the "powers," acts as a mediator between the two. This reconstructed role of the teacher, which could be said to characterize what is now called progressive education since its first stirrings in that same post-revolutionary Europe of the early nineteenth century, is stated at the end of the twentieth by Paulo Freire under the sign of dialogue. Freire (2005) calls for the "resolution" of the "teacher-student contradiction"—that is, the struggle between child and adult—in what he calls "problem-posing education," whereby "through dialogue, the teacher-of-the students and the students-of-the-teacher cease to exist and a new term emerges: teacher-student and students-teachers. The teacher is no longer merely the-one-who-teaches, but the one who is himself taught in dialogue with the students, who in turn while being taught also teach" (72). This form of dialogue is also suggested in Dewey's (1959) formulation, at the end of the nineteenth century, of the mediation of what he called the "gap" between the child and the curriculum. In his formulation, child stands for the original impulse to inquiry and is implicitly pre- or proto-disciplinary: the spontaneous playful inquiry of the child is pre-scientific, pre-literary, pre-mathematical, and so on. On the other side of the gap, the curriculum represents the finished product, categorized into the "disciplines," of thousands of years of that very inquiry that each child begins anew. Under the sign of dialogue, the teacher attempts to close this gap by working with the child's inquiry and not against it, and by delivering the curriculum in a form that evokes the child's "wholehearted purposeful activity" (Kilpatrick 1918).

Generally speaking, the adult models the culture: the given, the inherited, the accumulated patterns of the species, the current forms of adaptation, the episteme, and the ethical and moral superstructure. It is in the child's interactive experience with these models that the neuronal structure of each individual brain develops, through synaptic exercise and consequent myelination, which preserves the emergent neuronal architecture against the periodic hormonal purging of unused potential pathways. The "original modifiability" or neuronal plasticity of which both Dewey and the neuroscientists speak is literal: the immature brain is physically organized differently by immersion in different experiences.

While the adult models the given, the child models neotenous characteristics—among which Montagu (1989) has identified ". . . love, friendship, sensitivity, learning, curiosity, wonder, playfulness, imagination, creativity, open-mindedness, flexibility, experimental-mindedness, explorativeness, enthusiasm, joyfulness, honesty and trust, compassionate intelligence" (107) as a Novum, a utopian horizon—forms of potential social transformation, not yet fixed into patterns, which disrupt the fixed patterns of the adult and challenge them to transform. The dialogue is between emergent structure, here standing for "child," and relatively fixed structure, here standing for "adult." The assumption of dialogue is that both terms of the relation are liable to transformation through their interaction. The assumption of mutual modifiability of adult and child in relation is the key difference between traditional and neotenic forms of education.

One useful formulation of adult-child dialogue is, as we have already seen, Dewey's (1922) notion of a dialogue between "impulse" and "habit." The two are in continual interaction: whether in struggle, uneasy partnership, or some kind of conversation. Both are fundamental to individual, dyadic, and group experience. Habit represents naturalized, reified, or codified initiative and response patterns to the novelty of every situation: We use things that worked before. The problem is that every situation has irrepressible emergent characteristics; it keeps changing. If we were completely unhabituated, we would be in a fugue state—mad—to the extent that, as Dewey said, habits ". . . constitute the self. In any intelligible sense of the word will, they are will" (25). If we were completely habituated—if every response and initiative were based on a response to a past situation—we would also be mad, because our habits or habitus would no longer be adapted to an ever-changing environment; we would be responding to a projection from the past. Given that "selfhood (except as it has encased itself in a shell of routine) is in process of making, and . . . any self is capable of including within itself a number of inconsistent selves, of unharmonized dispositions" (137), intelligent behavior requires habits that are flexible—permeable constructs, capable of revision and reconstruction in adaptive response to the now—that can distinguish projection from the past from what reality there is in the open space of the present situation.

"Impulse" is Dewey's word for the spontaneous experience of the present situation, which we may associate with Charles Sanders Peirce's "firstness," with Freud's "libido" (instinctual energy or *nisus*), Henri Bergson's "élan vital" or "vital impetus," Martin Buber's "originator instinct," and George Herbert Mead's "I" as opposed to the "me" of habit—in short, *eros* or desire. It can manifest in many forms, destructive as well as constructive, but in children it is often identified with all the traits that Montagu associates with the permanent childlike characteristics of the human species—"questing, striving, questioning, seeking . . . curiosity and excitement in the enjoyment of new experience" (1989, 53). It is the energy that challenges habitual response, which acts to disrupt and transform it. In optimal situations, its effect is to loosen it, to open it up, to bring it into the present, to reconstruct it. On a larger scale, it signifies, not just the individual's "power to re-make old habits, to re-create" (Dewey 1922, 97), but also "a future new society of changed purposes and desires" (96).

Typical child-adult interaction embodies a conversation between impulse and habit. The adult brings models of habit to the table, including the habits of categorical thinking that divide the knowledge economy into fields and disciplines, which Dewey calls the "logical"; the child brings the "psychological" in the form of impulses that encounter habit as expressions of her "own vital logical movement" (1959, 97) in the desire to investigate, to make or construct things, to speak and communicate, and to express thoughts and feelings (1959, 57–61 passim), all in the interest of a highly personal inquiry. The adult brings the habitus of the age: implicit epistemological beliefs and assumptions; explicit and implicit doctrines; felt truths; spoken or unspoken proscriptions; aesthetic rules; attitudes; and relational styles; all of which imply ontological convictions, often pre-conscious, whether based on scientific or religious or cultural epistemes. As we have seen in Marcuse's formulation, these are encoded in perception itself, and have immediate implications for how we experience what is alive and what is not; about whether we feel that killing animals for food is a fundamental violation or not; about what we can be said to "own"; about what constitutes a "just war"; about the boundaries between private and public property; about whether what is right for me can always be the "right thing to do"; and so on.

The child brings, first, a quite literal "standpoint epistemology," ingeniously illustrated by Paul Ritter, a professor at the University of Nottingham, who created a papier-mâché mock-up of a domestic living room that was arranged with "furniture" two-and-a-half times actual adult scale. A papier-mâché man sitting on a papier-mâché couch is completely hidden from the observer by the newspaper he is reading. The couch has to be climbed like a cliff. The lamp on the table looms above one like the Eiffel Tower; ". . . it brought gasps of astonishment from the visitors" (Ward 1978, 23). Correlatively, from the child's standpoint, how do other animals appear? Or those psychological characteristics of adults that we adults take to be normal? Or the perceptual world of nature itself? When trees move in the wind, is it a sensuous experience for them? Is there really more than a rather superficial difference between the way humans and animals think?

The child represents what Merleau-Ponty (1964b) called a "polymorph" (110)—"not an absolute other, nor the same" as the adult—that amounts as well to a polyvocalism, which is associated with a heightened (relative to adults) capacity for mimesis, mimicry of multiple viewpoints that arises from being less "disembodied" than the adult. On this account, the child is in a more direct feeling-relation with the world and with others, and grounded in a form of temporality more closely allied with Bergson's "pure duration," or "qualitative multiplicity." Matthew Lipman, founder of the Philosophy for Children movement and applied philosopher of childhood, modeled his philosophical novels for children intuitively on the narrative fantasy that the child—in dialogue with others—is in fact capable of reproducing in some form all the major philosophical standpoints in the canon: whether Descartes's cogito, ergo sum; Plato's innatism; Locke's sensationalism; Berkeley's idealism; Kant's phenomenalism; James's radical empiricism; and so on.

The child as model for the adult is representative of a form of intentionality, a way of being-in-the-world. In fact she models, under the sign of impulse, the unsubjected subject—that "admirable indetermination" that Lyotard (1992) refers to as infantia. The child dwells in an affective and noetic space that is there before there is the Father and the Law, without predetermined categories of identity and experience, a space in continual transformation, which involves "unlocking affect in new combinations and flows" (Deleuze and Guattari 1987; Kennedy 2013a). This is indeed a Romantic formulation of the child as—not "angel" (in fact there is nothing sentimental about the Romantic child)—but "genius," in the sense of the child as emblematic of an original unity beyond good and evil, and dwelling in another form of temporality that Walter Kohan, following Heraclitus, has called "aionic," as opposed to "chronic." The power of aionic time is, in Kohan's view, its intensity, its undetermination—an "un-numbered movement, not successive, but intensive" (Kohan 2012, 173). As such "child" is, in William Wordsworth's familiar words, the "great birthright of our being," an archetype available only symbolically and, if we follow Schiller, an unconscious master of the experience of play, that "third joyous realm" that "makes man complete and displays at once his twofold [i.e., sensuous reason] nature" (Schiller 2004, 79). This ideal could also be stated, following Winnicott (1989), as an adult who is more capable of negotiating "transitional space," and following Schiller, as an adult who is more sensitive to the "play impulse," which in Marcuse's rendition is related to the emergence of a "new sensibility."

The adult—and especially the adult whose vocation involves the adult-child collective called "school"—is in dialogue with the aionic character of being through her engagement with the actual child before her, who in turn is in dialogue with the chronometric and kairotic character of being through the adult. On the other hand, this mutual engagement is a material one—located in the world as we know it—and as such as vulnerable to the deep Hobbesian shadows of "diffidence, competition and glory" as any other. The child is no less vulnerable to assuming habits of negativity than the adult: perhaps more so, given her polymorphism. "Child" in the Romantic formulation does not mean "inherent" or "natural" goodness; it means before/beyond good and evil. In addition, the contribution that childhood education may make to the new sensibility can take more than one form and will vary across historical moment and culture. What does not vary across historical moment and culture are the evolutionary possibilities of an emergent psychoculture offered by the biological facts of neoteny and the experience-dependent brain, which provide a "hard-wired" explanatory background for Arendtian natality.

I have already suggested that "progressive" or "child-centered" education is at least one emergent (counter-) tradition in the West that aspires to create the social and psychological space for the emergence of Marcuse's "new reality principle" and "new form of sensuous reason." This tradition is ever-developing: after Freire, we may call it "dialogical education," and find it inaugurated in early twentieth century anarchist educational praxis (for which see Suissa 2010, and Avrich 2006), and still under development in the contemporary Democratic Schools movement (for which see www.idenetwork.org). And as I will argue throughout, Matthew Lipman's introduction of communal philosophical dialogue as a privileged form of educational discourse adds another dimension to this emergence, in the form of a practice that involves continuous discursive reconstruction through critical inquiry, and thus acts as a platform for epistemic reconstruction.

All of these approaches assume, of course, utopian ideals—Dewey's "future new society of changed purposes and desires"—and understand the school as only one, if a highly important one, institutional element in its ongoing creation. Nor is the utopia here envisaged a "no-place," but rather a potential or virtual one that, as Marcuse put it, "is blocked from coming about by the power of established societies" (1969, 4). This utopia emerges not from without, but from within: it is rooted in what he called "a revolution in perception" (37), or what the Romantics called a "renovation of the senses" through a "marriage of mind and nature" (Abrams 1971, 113). Following Marcuse, this revolution is an evolution of perception arrived at dialectically through a resolution of the contradictions present in our historical situation, a "third thing." It is not something that is imposed on the future, but rather something that one sees "coming about" in a more paedomorphic society, which in Deweyan terms may be described as a society composed of more adults whose habit structures are more adaptive, who are more capable of ". . . utilizing impulses for formation of new habits, or what is the same thing, the modification of an old habit so that it may be adequately serviceable under novel conditions"; who recognize "the place of impulse in conduct as a pivot of re-adjustment, in a steady re-organization of habits to meet new elements in new situations" (Dewey 1922, 104). The guarantor of this reconstruction is a corresponding society that is transitioning to what Marcuse called ". . . a higher stage of development: 'higher' in the sense of a more rational and equitable use of resources, minimization of destructive conflicts, and enlargement of the realm of freedom" (1969, 3).

Certainly, this evolutionary gambit is guided by a vision, a representation of one possible future. Adults tend to be the keepers of that vision as it is enjoined; but that vision is, as I have argued elsewhere (Kennedy 2006), triggered by the encounter with childhood, and to that extent it is children who co-initiate it, and who model its neotenic possibilities. The dialogical school is a site in which that encounter takes shape as an institutional form. Such a school offers a transitional cultural space in which the vision is dramatized, codified, and performed, and its evolutionary possibilities explored. In what follows I attempt to delineate the structural characteristics of that educational space, both as a historical phenomenon—a dialogical school for this particular moment—and as a sort of platonic form or archetype: "school" as an expression of the adult-child relationship in its most dynamic aspects, and as an engine of social transformation.

Four Dimensions of Dialogical Education

The Child and the Curriculum

The most prominent arena for adult-child dialogue in the context of school is, as Dewey has argued, in the relation between child and curriculum. A direct conversation between child-initiative and adult-initiative, between impulse and habit, and between tradition and innovation is implicit here, and has concrete implications for the content and organization of the school's course of study. A dialogical curriculum is structured to engage four "instincts" identified by Dewey as "construction," "communication," "investigation," and "expression" (Dewey 1959). It frames and reframes itself in response to children's neotenic impulses: "curiosity, wonder, playfulness, imagination, creativity, open-mindedness, flexibility, experimental-mindedness, explorativeness," and so on (Montagu 1989, 107). When it does both, it adapts itself to the purposive interests of the child. This in no way implies that, in entering into dialogue with the child's interest, the curriculum must necessarily sacrifice its logical structure or its status as cultural conservator. Dialogue operates from both sides, and the adult demands of rigor and continuity are as legitimate as the child's for relevance and immediacy.

The most natural operative medium for child-curriculum dialogue is art—the aesthetic—given the expressive and constructive direction of childhood impulse, and the neotenic status of art in human culture—its role in initiating new perceptual experience through exploration and invention. Art and making of all kinds—plastic arts, music, dance, writing, theatre, crafts, cooking, sewing, building, gardening—ground the impulse-habit relation in the body. They express the creative interaction between the conceptual and the material, and so provide bridges to the more abstract inquiries of history, psychology, sociology, science, and mathematics, which the creative and resourceful teacher brings as responses to or extensions of the process of artifact-making. For example, coterminous with children's pottery making, the teacher launches a study project on ancient near-eastern archeology, with an emphasis on the use of pottery as texts through which prehistory is read. This form of curriculum development—already known and practiced for one hundred years (see Kilpatrick 1918; Rugg and Shumaker 1928; Katz and Chard 1989) as the "project method"—is the most vivid expression of the dialogical nature of emergent curriculum. It creates a situation in which initiative is shared and negotiated between teacher and students, and in which disciplinary boundaries are crossed and disrupted in the interest of new connections, and ultimately in the interest of an emergent episteme: a new way of thinking about the world.

COMMUNITY OF PHILOSOPHICAL INQUIRY (CPI)

Community of philosophical inquiry (CPI), as a form of critical group deliberation on and around the epistemological and ontological status of the concepts that "underlie" the curriculum—concepts like "alive," "fact," "justice," "measurement," "organism," "system," and so on—adds a dimension that has not been present in school practice up until now, at least in a formalized operational structure. Ideally, it is the sphere in which the epistemological reconstruction that interaction with curriculum triggers finds a discursive form. Here, the "big ideas" that are evoked and invoked through the child's interaction with materials, art, ideas, knowledge-bases, artifacts, and practices are teased out and identified, and the beliefs and assumptions that support them are interrogated. These assumptions comprise the conceptual infrastructure of the current episteme, and the critical, experimental, and transitional space of CPI encourages their deconstruction and, if only implicitly, their ongoing reconstruction. Although CPI is only one dimension of dialogical education, it is the most pervasive, in that it acts as a discursive model that frames the whole enterprise.

The assumptions that are uncovered through the child's interaction with the curriculum tend to revolve around the beliefs associated with the epistemological, ontological, and ethical concepts—"fact/opinion," "belief/knowledge," "living" or "alive," "nature," "human/animal," "individual/group," "fair," "right" (in all its senses)—that inform our "big picture." CPI is the laboratory of their reconstruction: the place where contradictions appear and the drive for reorganization is triggered. It is in this discursive space that formal schooling redeems its archetypal role as a place apart—*temenos* or *hieron*—disassociated from everyday work and production, that has, from its beginnings, distinguished the school from the intrusive, impositional "village curriculum" (Lancy 2008), which is oriented to assimilation of the "natives" by a colonialist culture rather than personal and social transformation. The difference here is that it is a space of critical questioning rather than indoctrination, of the evolutionary gambit rather than socioeconomic reproduction; it functions in the interest of the new, emergent episteme that is governed by the neotenic impulse, rather than the old, which is governed by what Montagu (1989) characterizes as gerontomorphosis, "extreme specialization . . . whose net effect is to decrease ability for further evolution and to expose species to extinction" (9, 253).

CPI is the public heart of the speech community in dialogic education, the site where deliberative reasoning as process and activity trumps personal power or manipulative skill, irrational authority, and groupthink. As a discourse-model, it grounds practice in all the school's curricular spaces, whether science or mathematics, literature, art, or philosophy tout court. Philosophy as identification and critical interrogation of concepts is this school's primary language: problematizing, hypothesizing, instantiating, connecting and distinguishing ideas, or reflecting on one's own or the group's thinking. Every school content area has a philosophical understructure: a network of concepts held together by epistemological, ontological, and axiological beliefs and assumptions about the world based on those beliefs. CPI is the site for the identification and problematization of those beliefs, and in this sense every disciplinary community of inquiry—whether math, science, literature, and so on—is by definition also a community of philosophical inquiry. CPI is the zone of confluence, the discursive space where the lineaments of our shared episteme emerge into view, and where its limits and its frangible margins, its aporias and its contradictions, and its anomalies and inassimilable counterexamples offer themselves for critique and ongoing reconstruction.

In the dialogical school, CPI guarantees children a discursive space in which they may both express their standpoints and affirm, question, and contest the received beliefs that, they discover, have been "received" differently from different sources: parents, media, peers, and the "wheels" already inside their own heads. One discovers that not everyone thinks alike—not even oneself and oneself—and that our beliefs are based on assumptions that bear examination through the giving and testing of reasons, the exploration of implications, and the challenge of thinking normatively. This epistemological skepticism is related to Marcuse's (1972) "great refusal," the "alienation from alienation" that he understood as the necessary precursor of a new form of reason, which is a response to a world in which technocapitalism has colonized our very instinctual structures, our perception, and our wants and needs. This is often perceived by adults as a dangerous space, because it overturns that very construction of the child that legitimates, as Dewey (1922) said, "an impatient, premature mechanization of impulsive activity after the fixed patterns of adult habits of thought and affection" (96). This open space of dialogue and interrogation into which adults enter themselves, not just as models and coaches of group argumentation but as interlocutors, requires them to rearrange their thinking about what they are hearing and who they are hearing it from. They should not understand children's formulations as naïve, or random, but as fragments of an emergent world view in the making. Adults, as models, coaches, and interlocutors, support a dialogical space that, in its very interactional structure, challenges the natural social-survivalist camouflage-position that children (and adults) often take in repeating the received ideas they hear from parents and other authorities, peers, and media.

DEMOCRATIC PRACTICE

A third, closely related dimension of dialogical school practice opens directly from the philosophical dialogue of CPI into the practical, ethical, and collective action-space of democratic world-making. As an approximation of an ideal speech situation, CPI offers a functional space for shared decision-making and collaborative governance within the adult-child collective. This is a direct realization of Dewey's (1959) notion of school as an "embryonic society," and is already present in the international Democratic Education movement (http://en.wikipedia.org/wiki/Democratic_education). It implies a reconstruction of the relations of power, based on the assumption of children's capacity for social self-regulation in the context of an intentional adult-child collective, for the development of habits that allow for mediating and resolving conflicts of interest, and for the reconstruction of authority, personal responsibility, and individual-group relations through "direct"—or in Benjamin Barber's (2004) term, "strong"—democracy. The reconstruction of personal and social habits related to governance, group-discipline, individual-group responsibilities, and ways of dealing with violations of group norms is a fundamental aspect of a new sensibility, because it challenges the habits—domination, exploitation, privilege, inequality, gratuitous hierarchy—that keep the old one in place. As a model of a self-governing community, the dialogical school provides a key site for the emergence of an authentic democratic subject, in whom, in Dewey's (1922) words, "habit is plastic to the transforming touch of impulse" (102), and for whom "situations into which change and the unexpected enter are a challenge to intelligence to create new principles" (239).

The degree to which children exercise influence over the curriculum itself—what is chosen to study and how that study will be carried out—is perhaps a key indicator of the dialogical character of any given school. In actual practice, we find dialogical schools arrayed across a wide range between complete child choice and decision—characteristic of those schools that count themselves as members of the Democratic Education movement—and adult choice and control in schools in which adults respond to children's interests with projects and courses of study. The issue of children's power to determine their activities through the school day tests the deep structure of adult beliefs about childhood, which in turn are connected with beliefs about authority, the human developmental process, freedom and responsibility, self- and social organization and control, and the value of tradition, among others. These adult-held beliefs and assumptions inform the quality and tone of adult-child dialogue, and directly inform the balance and interplay between adult and child initiative in any given school situation.

An Activist Collective

Finally, a fourth dimension leads from the interaction of the previous three into community expression as group production and activism. Concepts that are encountered in experiencing the curriculum—for example the concept of "life" in biological inquiry, of "just war" in social studies, or of "form and function" in art, architecture, and town planning—enter a space of interrogation in community of philosophical inquiry. As a result of that interrogation, they can be translated into an action-oriented ethical and political space, the outcome of the ultimate philosophical question, "what should we then do?" Through a process of democratic group deliberation, they are transformed into specific practical projects. The activist collective understands itself as implicitly connected with and responsible to the larger community, where projects that reflect the emergent democratic sensibility of the school enter the macrosphere of shared (and perhaps conflicting) values and conscientious action. Concrete projects dedicated to saving the biosphere, to speaking out against perpetual war and economic exploitation, to succoring the vulnerable and the marginalized, and to building relationships with other adult-child collectives around the world are natural outgrowths of an emergent sensibility that is in the process of reconstructing notions of moral responsibility at the level of the collective. They move child-adult dialogue into an expanded sphere, where the paedomorphic "embryonic society" of school encounters the often dystopic and sclerotic policies and practices of the larger, adult-dominated society, and seeks to engage them through concrete solutions to very practical problems.

To deny children knowledge of these problems or of the opportunity to address them because they are complex and dogged and seem continually to elude solutions through the best efforts of adults, is to deny knowledge to those whom adults typically invoke as those in whose name we wish to solve them: we seek a better world, we say, "for our children." Furthermore, it is children who are typically the first and most egregious victims of these problems. The school as adult-child collective is a logical space for these problems to be recognized, identified, and actively addressed, because they are problems that violate on a profound level the value structure of a sensibility that is in the process of developing, in Marcuse's words, "an instinctual barrier against cruelty, brutality, and ugliness," and for which "freedom has become a biological necessity." To argue that to invite children to study, ponder, and respond to these problems "uses," "exploits," or robs intentionality from children is to marginalize them within the human community, and as such suggests subspeciation. In fact, if we recognize the possibilities for the emergence of new perspectives that standpoint epistemology represents, children's understanding and grasp of the fundamental moral issues that these problems represent could very well provide unexpected insights.

A New Relation to Nature

The emergent reality principle that suggests a new sensibility finds, in Marcuse's account, its primary narrative in what he calls a "new relation to nature." This relation is the central element of his evolutionary thinking:

> In the established society, nature itself, ever more effectively controlled, has in turn become another dimension for the control of man: the extended arm of society and its power. Commercialized nature, polluted nature, militarized nature cut down the life environment of man, not only in an ecological but also in a very existential sense. It blocks the erotic cathexis (and transformation) of his environment: it deprives man from finding himself in nature, beyond and this side of alienation; it also prevents him from recognizing nature as subject in its own right—a subject with which to live in a common universe Liberation of nature is the recovery of the life-enhancing forces in nature, the sensuous aesthetic qualities which are foreign to a life wasted in unending competitive performances: they suggest the new qualities of freedom. No wonder then that the "spirit of capitalism" rejects or ridicules the idea of liberated nature, that it relegates this idea to the poetic imagination. Nature, if not left alone and protected as "reservation," is treated in an aggressively scientific way: it is

there for the sake of domination; it is value-free matter, material. This notion of nature is a historical a priori, pertaining to a specific form of society. A free society may well have a very different a priori and a very different object; the development of the scientific concepts may be grounded in an experience of nature as a totality of life to be protected and "cultivated," and technology would apply this science to the reconstruction of the environment of life. (1972, 235)

The dialogical school is one cultural site where—in our time and place anyway—the "historical a priori" of a free society has a place within which to emerge and grow, through a process in which both child and adult are active participants. This is in direct contrast to the historical function of schooling under capitalism and the nation state, or to any form of education which is dedicated, if not by its own nature, then by those who control it from above, to minimizing difference, creativity, and ongoing social reconstruction in the interest of gerontocratic structures of domination. This suggests that at this critical moment in our species history, our global situation of crisis encourages us to undertake a radical reevaluation of the value and role of childhood in bio-cultural (i.e., brain-based) and cultural and social evolution, a reevaluation that is summarized in the biological and psychological concept of neoteny, which in fact only emerged in the latter half of the nineteenth century. It is just the qualities of childhood that adults require in order to reverse the trend towards planetary dystopia; and it is just education in the form of the adult-child collective of school—understood as a laboratory for the germination of a form of modal subjectivity that is, in Marcuse's words, "grounded in an experience of nature as a totality of life to be protected and cultivated"—that provides the developmental niche for such an ongoing evolutionary project.

In chapter three, I carry some of these speculations to the field, in a direct look at how young children—in this case mostly five-year-olds—talk together about the "big questions." What stands out for me in their conversation, although it cannot be fully captured in a transcript, is the extent to which the rudimentary prototype of community of philosophical inquiry here on display is grounded in the fundamental discursive register of play—more specifically, play as group ritual. In this play, prosody—shared, interactive patterns of rhythm, stress, and intonation—and gesture make of the group a mimetic whole, an improvisational ensemble in which the semantical is only one level on which the players are interacting. I will explore the playful nature of group philosophical dialogue further in chapter ten. Here it is enough to recognize its fundamental connection with childhood, for which play is a primary epistemological apparatus, first among all those characteristics of childhood that Montagu identifies as neotenous, and which identify the human as the paedomorph par excellence.

Chapter Three

Young Children and Ultimate Questions
Romancing at Day Care

What follows is one section of a series of conversations that I convened with a small group of young children, the majority of kindergarten age, in a day care center where I was working as a teacher-caregiver in 1983. The children were between the ages of three and six, and we had been together long enough to speak frankly and comfortably with each other. I used small group time to ask six questions, all of them about the ultimate issues—the origins, ends, and limits of things, death, dreams, soul, spirit, self, God, evil. Taken together, the conversations we had make for a transcript of sixty-five manuscript pages. The issues raised there are many and provoke questions not only about how young children think, but also about how adults influence them to think. The issue taken up below—the origins of things—was continued past this conversation. Although the text tends to speak for itself, a few comments on the pattern of the conversation follow the transcript. The ages of the children involved (whose names have been changed) are as follows:

Charles: six years
Nat: five years
Michael: four years
Ken: five years
Kristen: five years
Jim: five years
Fred: five years
Faith: four years

First Conversation

D. K.: How did the world begin?

Nat: The dinosaurs . . . It's dinosaurs.

Charles: No, the world didn't begin with dinosaurs. . . . I know something that happened before the dinosaurs, and it's gotta be happening on the earth. . . . What just can't float in the air . . . water and mud just can't float in the air.

D. K.: No, they can't. Like you couldn't just throw them up.

Nat: The sun makes them come up into the air and turn into a cloud! It does that to rainwater . . . puddles.

Charles: Well . . . well . . . I know something that happened to the little fish. . . . And I got a fossil, that the fish got caught in my coat. . . . Well, Diane [a teacher] told me that happened before dinosaurs.

D. K.: Well, what was before that?

Michael: Babies! The first baby was born!

Charles: Uh uh! People weren't back when dinosaurs were, and I'm saying this happened before dinosaurs.

D. K.: What was . . . you're saying that before dinosaurs there was the fish. Now what was before the fish?

Ken: Nothing.

Kristen: Indians.

Jim: Just Indians.

Nat: Just water!

D. K.: Just water?

Nat: Yeah, just water and rain and clouds.

Charles: Just the earth.

D. K.: Just the earth. . . . How was the earth made? What was before the earth?

Ken: God was the very first thing.

Jim: This was the very first thing—God . . . Jesus.

D. K.: Who was before God?

Jim: Nobody.

Ken: Nobody.

Nat: Nothing. . . . God is alive every time. God never, never dies.

D. K.: So, God has always been, you mean?

JIM: God died.

Nat: God was alive when dinosaurs were down on the ground.

D. K.: OK. So, you are saying that he was first—

Michael: He died because men came and killed him. That's what my Mom said.

D. K.: Oh, you mean Jesus.

Jim: My Mom said He died and came back alive.

D. K.: Yeah, but we're talking about—

Jim: He was nailed on the cross.

D. K.: Yeah, but we're talking about the very beginning of things. How far back can we go, to when things started? How did things start? How did they begin?

Nat: We don't know!

Charles: When it began all that there was just space. There weren't any stars, there weren't any planets, there wasn't any moon, there wasn't any sun . . . Space!

Jim: Just space.

Ken: Just the universe.

D. K.: Just the universe, Ken says.

Charles: That's space.

D. K.: That's space. And how far does space go?

Nat: Way to the dark clouds.

Charles: It's all around this earth.

Ken: It never does stop.

D. K.: Ken says it never stops.

Charles: That's right. There's no end of it.

D. K.: You mean if you could take a rocket ship and go straight out into space that you would go forever, you would never come to the end of anything?

Charles: That's right.

Ken: You'd keep on going through space.

Michael: You would go up to heaven.

Kristen: No . . .

Jim: I have a spaceship story.

Nat: If you took a rocket you could only go the moon and the sun. . . . A airplane might could go to the sun.

D. K.: Well, but let's—

Nat: Airplane can go over the clouds.

D. K.: On top of the clouds, yeah. . . . So, what you're saying, Charles says at the very beginning there was just space. There was no sun, no moon, no planets, no earth.

Ken: Yeah!

D. K.: How were the sun the moon the planets and the earth made?
Fred: God made them.
D. K.: How did he do that?
Fred: He was kind of magic.
Kristen: He used his spirit.
Michael: I don't believe this.
Fred: Twinkle of an eye, and the earth was made!
D. K.: So, you say it happened suddenly.
Michael: I don't believe these people.
D. K.: Well, how do you believe it started?
Michael: I don't believe nothing.
D. K.: Oh, you don't believe anything?
Michael: Do you?
D. K.: Do I?
Michael: Do you believe what they're saying?
D. K.: Do I believe that God created the world?
Michael: How did God . . .
D. K.: How he did it, you mean?
Jim: He had a lot of power!
D. K.: Well, I'm asking you. OK. You say he had a lot of power. Fred said he was kind of magic. Charles, how do you think the world came into being?
Charles: I think . . . I think he just . . . God made the people, so I think he made one of them and when . . . and they got a baby and pretty soon—
Michael: God made everything!
Charles:—they started growing up and pretty soon everybody started having babies so there were millions of people in the world.
D. K.: Oh, OK. But I'm talking about before people.
Jim: Before people there was just space.
D. K.: OK, but what was there before space?
Ken: God.
Charles: Nothing.
D. K.: But where was God then, if there was no space, and he had to make it?
Nat: He was dead.
D. K.: At the beginning?
Ken: No.
D. K.: No.

Nat: He had to make himself.
Faith: David. . . . Do you know what first God made? God made a mud man first.
D. K.: A mud man? OK, but I'm talking about . . . Charles said, in the beginning there was only space. I'm saying, who made the space, or how did the space come into being?
Charles: Just . . . space was already there.
D. K.: Was already there from when?
Jim: [After a long pause]. The wind was there before space.
Charles: Outer space was just there.
D.K.: Was just there: nobody made it.
Charles: Right.
Ken: Wrong.
Faith: David . . . David . . . God made everything.
Michael: I want to go outside now.

Second Conversation

D. K.: We're going to go back to question number three, which we did some talking about yesterday . . . OK. Question number three is, "How did the world begin?"
Jim: There was all space.
D. K.: And you said, Charles said, somebody said there was all space. Nathaniel?
Nat: Just space.
D. K.: Just space. And I said, where did space come from?
Jim: Nobody.
Nat: Nobody.
Nat: Space is still there.
Michael: It was already there. . . . It was the first thing . . . and God was the next thing.
Ken: Uh-uh, God was the first thing, and He made the space and then He made the planets.
Nat: Yeah!
D. K.: Who made God?
Ken: Nobody. He just made Himself!
Jim: How did He?
Michael: Maybe His wife, but how did his wife get her self?

Jim: I know.
D. K.: How?
Jim: Maybe because . . . the space had magic.
D. K.: The space had magic?
Michael: Naah!
D. K.: Oh, you think the space made God or God made the space?
All: God made the space!
Nat: And the space made God.
Ken: No! God made God (laughs). God made space and the planets and us!
Jim: God made God.
Nat: He also made dinosaurs and things.
Jim: Jesus made Jesus.
Michael: Yeah, Jesus made Pacman.
[Silly sounds]
D. K.: OK. Good. Um . . .
Faith: He said Jesus made Pacman.
D. K.: Yeah, well—
[Tape cut]

Commentary

Jean Piaget (1979, 10) would probably refer to the kind of thinking and talking that the children in this transcript are doing as "romancing," by which he seems to have meant what children are doing when they are not answering a question according to his criteria of seriousness and intelligibility. It produces, he said, "fallacies," because its "mythomania" and "suggestibility" lead to "an answer which he [the child] does not really believe." The philosopher of childhood Gareth Matthews (1980) is more encouraging. He finds that often the child's "romancing answers are the most philosophically interesting," and "will not so much express the child's settled convictions as explore a conceptual connection or make a conceptual joke" (39). Matthews is suggesting what is demonstrated throughout these transcripts—that there is a fundamentally ludic element in logic, and that often young children first discover its operative patterns through joking and playing with language.

Language play has a strong aesthetic element; when it is working, it works because it sounds right, the way music works. It is aesthetic elements—prosodic rhythms that capitalize on phonological echoes and interplays, on pitch, juncture, and stress ("Nothing . . . Indians . . . Just Indians . . . Just water! . . . Just water? . . . Yeah, just water and rain and clouds"), and syntactical and semantic repeating or reversible patterns ("God made the space . . . And the space made God . . . No! God made God")—which guide the emergence of meaning. On the other hand, the issues being talked about in these conversations are ones that are considered serious—when adults talk about them, they typically do not do so in a joking manner. They tend, in fact to present their opinions about the being-status of things such as the origins of the universe, the earth or God—whether in the church or in the classroom—with utter certainty. Hence the atmosphere of serious, even passionate negotiation going on in these conversations. But even this passionate negotiation is an aesthetic form; it is a way of singing together. This is what adults do too in these kinds of conversations, but they are taught to ignore the elements of play and song in the interests of the cognitive data, the truth claims and their implications. But it seems to me that the two systems—the aesthetic play of the Argument and the series of logical moves—are symbiotic and mutually regulatory. Logic is grounded and expressed in the body, and the body is grounded and expressed in an interactive web of social relations. It is the musical "jamming" of the individual elements of this web which drives the Argument, as much as it is driven by it.

Next, I would like to suggest that the conversation transcribed here has a structure, composed of certain essential characteristics that operate in the community of philosophical inquiry wherever we find it. First, there is the gathering of information at the beginning in response to a question—in this case fossils, babies, Indians, dinosaurs, rain, sun, and clouds. The initial framing of an answer to any question emerges, that is, from the knowledge and interests of the participants. Then there is the movement forward through the statement of generalities or principles, which are then challenged by concrete counterexamples (e.g., "God is alive every time. God never, never dies. . . . God died"), followed in turn by an extended search for a resolution of contradictions through the making of connections ("God was alive when dinosaurs were down on the ground") and distinctions.

As always in the function of CPI, there is the taking of roles, the positioning of oneself within the conversation, a positioning determined by philosophical experience and authority structure—Michael's mother, for example, is quite consciously not a Christian; Fred's family is very active in a fundamentalist, participatory, Christian group; by age and training, Charles, at age six, is the oldest, and actually goes to kindergarten in the mornings—and by personality; Nat is dramatic, zany, and poetic, and Michael, at age four, is the youngest, but also highly verbal and very assertive. Then there is the matter of individual leadership, which irrevocably determines the course of the conversation. So, after Nat says, "We don't know!" there is a slight pause; then Charles, the eldest and most authoritative, introduces the space-as-receptacle theory (cf. Plato's *Timaeus*), which sets the course for the rest of the conversation.

There is the element of self-correction characteristic of community of inquiry: a working backwards and forwards through the splitting (analysis) and the joining (synthesis) process of the dialectic, the continual reconstruction of the material according to the play (or is it the working?) of the collective mind, which is this group of children in interaction. The interplay of individuals in the conversation is an "intra-play" of the one mind that they represent together, and it is this shape of the whole that has the character of song. Also characteristically, there is the introduction of new explanatory concepts or principles, in response to the challenges posed by the Argument as it progresses: so here the concept of "magic" as the function of God's "power." But when the notion of space as the receptacle, or first thing, coequal with God, emerges, then it is suggested that "maybe the space had magic." It is not far from there to introducing the notion of space as God, which is in fact a position explored in early modernity by Henry More and his followers, for whom, as Alexandre Koyre, in his history of cosmology, has described it, "the infinite extension must be truly and really, and not only metaphorically, attributed to the First Cause" (1957, 199). But that idea is rejected, and it is in this apparent deadlock with which this part of the conversation ends. This is in keeping with the movement—sometimes slow, sometimes fast—characteristic of CPI towards the edge of a conceptual cliff, an *aporia* that requires an expansion or contraction of noetic horizons—either the re-covering of ground already covered in search of another clue, or the leap into the unknown. In this case, the *aporia* has to do with the possibility of something coming from nothing, and the idea of the necessity of a first cause.

As these children approach the cliff, they do not shrink from thinking the unthinkable: "God made himself," for example, or "Space was already there," or "What was there before space? . . . Nothing." Then the *aporia*, discovered to be unsolvable, for the moment anyway, becomes the occasion for the explosion (indeed the final explosion, since it ended there) of the conversation in a round of joking, using as elements of the joke the very logical structures that have reached the end of their rope, and are spinning their wheels against the mystery of the real. So: "God made the space. . . . And the space made God . . . God made God . . . Jesus made Jesus . . . Jesus made Pacman" . . . at which point the whole thing collapsed in hilarious nonsense sounds, and soon after everyone went outside. The reductio ad absurdum is not just a way of breaking off, however, but also a way of summing up and expressing, if only as an absence, the distant goal toward which the dialectic is striving: the ultimate synchronization of all the individual elements of the collective mind, the height of their mutual regulation.

Catherine Garvey, in her discussion of language play, speaks of it in just these terms—as "ritualized play," in which "each child controls very precisely the behavior of the other, and this regulation is in itself satisfying, a form of mastery play where what is mastered is the control of one's own and one's partner's actions" (1977, 120). This is the implicit telos of the dialectic, the truth that beckons on the horizon—the last horizon, which promises to justify the rigors and tortuous twists and turns of the conversation. Young children, being "aesthetes," have it already in play. Their reductio ad absurdum reveals, only incompletely and prophetically it is true, the goal that the dialectic of the community of philosophical inquiry promises. They demonstrate it to be a coordination of bodies—in rhythm, pitch, juncture, and gesture—as much of minds. They show us that the ideal communicative state, which is implicit in any conversation (even the most frustrating), is somatic as well as noetic—that, indeed, the two are inseparable.

In this conversation, as in the operation of communal inquiry in general, there are many opportunities for turns that are either missed or deliberately ignored. An example of the latter is the question about how God could die, which is implicit in the phenomenon of Jesus, and which I brushed past, anxious not to get entangled too soon in straight theology. There is the question of the first people; and there are some fairly sophisticated ideas about physics stated right at the beginning ("the sun makes them come up into the air and turn into a cloud! It does that to rainwater—puddles"). Each of these might have been a turn that led us on a better path than the one we took, or a worse one. There is no unambiguously best or worst turn in the conversation, except in hindsight.

Finally, the operation of the community of philosophical inquiry is a power struggle, in the sense that this group, like any group, is a complex of forces—personal, developmental, ideological, and even biological, locked in the *agon* of the dialectics of existence. The historical struggle between the belief systems of theism and atheism, a struggle deeply ingrained in late-twentieth-century American life, is already implicit in the conversation of these four-to-six-year-olds. In addition, the relations of power between children and adults are clearly marked here. I, the adult, act almost as an interrogator, holding everyone's feet to the fire of a question—the origins of everything—which these children may already have decided to be unanswerable, and not worth pursuing ("How did things start? How did they begin?" . . . "We don't know!"). In addition, I am already framing the terms of the discourse with phrases like "What was before that?," which assumes that there has to be a first cause, some ultimate "beginning." And it seems inevitable to me that, although I do my best to suppress personal beliefs and ideas, my gestural and prosodic reactions, as well as my repetitions and restatements, discourage certain expressions of beliefs and ideas, and encourage others. In fact, young children, because they are "aesthetes," often have a very sharp, if unconscious, sensitivity to gestural and prosodic cues. Michael's wavering between affirmation and denial of God is only partly because he has just turned four and is new to this kind of talk. It is also because he is attempting to read my ideas and beliefs, in order to compare them to those of another authority figure in his life, his mother, and compare these with what his peers are saying. At one point he comes right out and asks me what I believe. My attempts to evade the question, although they are sincere, lead into an assumption of the argument he is questioning—that God is a necessary concept for positing a beginning of things. Now, apart from lack of training and/or inherent clumsiness, I might have been less likely to make this mistake if I myself were not a theist of sorts. So, the grounding patterns of the conversation in the community of inquiry are often out of sight—large framework theories, or systems of belief that it is the function of the dialectic to uncover, so that they can encounter each other "in the light," so to speak, and thereby become interlocutive. We might say, then, that one of the goals of the CPI is to clarify the ground of power relations, and thereby work for their ultimate resolution in an ideal community of intersubjective mutuality, that vanishing point at which personal and collective goals are harmonized.

In fact, all decisive action within the CPI is a tropism of one sort or another, or even more, an error (and each one, potentially, a necessary one), in the sense that to move in any one direction is not to move in another, which might have been a better one. Inevitably the community of philosophical inquiry moves by taking positions, and by the clash and negotiation of realms of influence. We can only be consoled by the fact that the process is self-correcting, but certainly situations can be more or less tangled, and take longer or shorter times to self-correct.

This transcript of young children in conversation offers, beneath its apparent chaos, an insight into the phenomenology of what might be called the deep structure of community of philosophical inquiry—its grounding in the body—in the tonal, in the rhythmic, the dramatic, the mimetic, the poetic and the playful, revealing it as group ritual, or "living" theatre. In the next chapter, I identify the origins of this form of experience directly with childhood, understood as a form of life characteristic of what has already been identified in the last chapter as *infantia*, and explore further why Schiller would call it a "representation to us of the ideal . . . not as it is fulfilled, but as it is enjoined," leading to the perennial question already raised here: what do we have to learn from children?

Chapter Four

Becoming Child

Wild Being and the Post-Human

> Time held me green and dying.
> Though I sang in my chains like the sea.
>
> —Dylan Thomas, "Fern Hill"

What do children have to teach adults? I want to revisit the often trivialized and clichéd trope, perhaps first articulated in Lao Tzu—"He who is in harmony with the Tao is like a newborn child" (2006, chapter 55) and more recently in Friedrich Schiller—"They are what we were; they are what we should once again become (1966, 85)—of child as "unconscious master" and prophet of a new humanity. This mastery is a virtual one: it is never actualized, although it is present in what we call *infantia*, which signifies more than biological or even psychological infancy, but rather a form of life distinct from normative adulthood. In the same way that the form of lived time that characterizes *infantia* and that we call *aion*, does not appear until it is cut and bound into *kronos*, or fixed sequential segmented time; just so the child's mastery does not appear until it is bound and negated by the *mancipium*, or the power and control of the Father and the Law (*mancipium*: the status of a freeman subject to the power and control of the head of a Roman family similar to that of a slave except that he could not be abused or killed without legal cause [See Lyotard 1992]). As such, the form of life of *infantia* is always a virtuality, a becoming, but it is no less real for all that. In this chapter, I want to explore the lived temporal experience of embodiment, in the interest of finding that transitional zone between the virtual and the actual that is the space of becoming other, and which, paradoxically, is also the space of self-actualization, or singularity. Is this the space of mastery? If so, it is a negative ideal, in that we typically associate mastery with seizing, controlling, determining, whereas this is a letting go, even a forgetting.

Timebody

As Flesh, in pre-reflective experience, as wild being (Merleau-Ponty 1968), we are not "in" time; rather, we are time. We are duration, desire, living ground, the matrix of embodied mind, or minded body. Before thought, after thought, apart from thought in its instantaneity, before individuality—as singularity—mind and body are one in the sensible: the primal rhythm of the heart, the rivers of blood pulsing and streaming through the veins, the neural cells firing together in electrical charges across the plasma membrane. Here there is nothing beyond endless, instant, originary sensation, existential matrix and flow of biological, organic, organismic duration, cellular desire that is the conatus. Here there is no such thing as past and future except vaguely felt—a residue and a faint anticipation, and only a perpetually emergent "me," a system of self-organizing tensions and potentialities emerging towards an open future of becoming; and becoming is always becoming other.

Felt time is like weather—continually transforming, emerging into new states, atmospheres, moods. We move constantly into a new time, and thus an otherness, where everything is the same but different, different but the same. Novelty is guaranteed by the structure of time—is wrapped into it. There is always an emergent now that is different from any other. Time's body is mood, and mood is shift, transition, and flow. There are multiple temporalities of mood, whether in background or foreground of awareness: the felt time of boredom, loneliness, waiting, delay, fear, sorrow, anxiety, joy, relief, abandon, suffering, grief, agon, *voluptas*, creation, birthing, performance, grief, romance, argument, conversation, dream, intoxication. Each has its immediate felt rhythm, color, weight, resistance, consistency, flights, and perchings. In becoming other, we are continually losing and finding ourselves. As reason confronts madness and life confronts death, time confronts oblivion—the loss of measure, the possibility of losing the thin thread of my identity in my continual becoming. But it is that very movement of becoming other—the creative deconstruction of that identity—that promises realization as a singularity—which, in turn, is invisible to me because that realization would shatter the mirror of virtual becoming in sheer actuality.

Aion

Is it the case that the felt subjective ideal of full attention, utter mindfulness, enlightenment, the state of being fully awake, consciousness sub specie aeternitatis—every cell open to experience, unified with the world in full perceptual chiasm that is love—is so deep in time that it is outside of time? Perhaps this is what the Greeks meant by *aion*, for which the word "eternity" is only a partial and indeed a misleading translation because of its religious connotations. *Aion* is the originary self-sensing, where sensing and sense are one and the same. Deleuze and Guattari describe it as "the indefinite time of the event, the floating line that knows only speeds and continually divides that which transpires into an already-there that is at the same time not-yet-here, a simultaneous too-late and too-early, a something that is going to happen and has just happened" (1987, 262). Philosopher of alterity Emmanuel Levinas (Levinas/Cohen 1987, 5) refers to it as the "atomic instant," the time of the ancients, where "only pure unity of being is affirmed, since future and past are not present, thus are not" (12), Einstein's "Now." As we have seen, *aion* is associated since Heraclitus with childhood and with play: αἰὼν παῖς ἐστι παίζων πεττεύων παιδὸς ἡ βασιληίη: "Aion is child playing ["childing"] at draughts [i.e., a board game]; the kingdom is a child's" (Heraclitus 2003, fragment 52). *Pais* = child, *paizein* = to play. Play is the manifest activity of *aion*. The power of the kingdom (*basileus*) is "ecstatic self-presence of an existential or ontological unity" in "prepredicative forestructure of understanding" (Levinas/Cohen 1987, 13), an ontology of wild being. *Aion*, the kingly power, is *infantia*, ecstatic self-presence in implicit resistance to the *mancipium*, the controlling hand of Father Time or Kronos, the Law and Kafka's Apparatus, which inscribes the Law in our very flesh (Kafka 1971; Lyotard 1992; Lyotard and Larochelle 1994). It is also the cruel and inevitable mechanism of individuation, which carves out ego in the throes of chronological time.

Kronos

Kronos names what we usually associate with that experience of time in which past and future become visible in retension and pretension (Husserl 1990/1928). *Kronos* is not just linear clock time but is also the time of cosmos as organismic totality—birth, growth, and death; the seasons and cycles; cause and effect—planting, harvesting, storing, blooming, and shriveling; making it through for a time, then dying in one way or another. *Kronos* is the law of the excluded middle: the "plane of organization" (Deleuze and Guattari 1987), of coding, stratification, congealment, and territorialization: hierarchies and distributions, sectors, connections and disconnections, cuts and demarcations, records and predictions, power, police, inevitable violence. It is the time of necessity—water, food, clothing, shelter—of planning and decision-making; of exigency in the face of a harsh and fundamental materiality; of surplus repression; the "reality principle" and the inevitability of war. One thing comes after another, this leads to that, death, violation, disfiguration is always just around the corner; clear and strategic judgment—*krisis*—keeps us alive for a time. It is the time in which we are captives, slaves, sunk in it, asleep, though we struggle to awaken. *Kronos* is body and cosmos itself as radical finitude, being-toward-death, an organic life-machine with its demise already programmed into it, in a universe in which chance—*tyche*—is servant of a larger necessity.

The original god Kronos, in castrating and killing his father Uranus—Freud's "primal transgression" (Freud 2010)—made a cut that created a space between earth and heaven, which separated them, thus opening a hermeneutical space, a between where being and becoming are separated, thereby creating the virtual. Uranus's genitals fell into the sea, and from the foam they generated emerged Aphrodite: blinding, spellbinding beauty and love of beauty, concupiscence, the exigencies of desire, the illusion of perfection, emancipatory striving for the unattainable through pleasure, earth as a garden of delights; the lovers, the artists, the musicians, the poets and dreamers who sing in their chains like the sea. This elemental world of becoming other that has been opened through Kronos's cut is Nature, the world of Generation: sex, birth, eating and being eaten; Anaximander's Opposites, Heraclitus's Strife, Blake's Contraries, Freud's Eros and Thanatos, Nietzsche's will to power, and Deleuze's and Guattari's desiring-production. It is neither completely divine nor completely profane—a world where animals, gods, and the human animal encounter and mingle in becomings. The semi-divine muses—nymphs—daughters of Harmonia, herself the daughter of Aphrodite and Ares—bring *mousike*—music, dance, song, poetry—as engines of transfiguration, expressions of *kronos*' pathos, its hidden longing for transformation into *aion*. In the aesthetic, the cruel boundaries of the law of duality become the seams that connect, that lead to transformation in art and cult.

Kronos is also Saturn, who is associated with ego-crystallization over time, with slow maturation, with being tested and judged according to the implacable rules of the game—with labors and trials, tenacity, patience, endurance, eternally put to the test by the arbitrary objectivity, the uneasy, temporary safety of the prison-house of the Law. *Kronos* is the time of the body politic and the body economic, of the ethical and the moral body—ethos, value, custom, formation, training, including the training of perception itself. Through the grinding experience of *kronos* as naked logical contingency, life stripped bare of all but its lessons for an uncertain future, Saturn carves out in the ego an executive office in the bureaucracy of selfhood, a putative control center, and with that, a "me" who, because he presumes to bind time to his will, stands outside of time. In Eastern doctrine, the ego is a ghost in the machine, a full-time denizen of Samsara and Plato's Cave, a little god in fear of death. But in fact this "me" is all we have. It is the self-construct in which, through which we climb out of *kronos* and become other to ourselves. Once exposed to its own dramatic limitations, the ego seeks the bliss of its own annihilation: "If the doors of perception were cleansed everything would appear to man as it is, Infinite. For man has closed himself up, till he sees all things thro' narrow chinks of his cavern" (Blake 1966). It is *kronos* itself that equips us, that builds a structure of awareness whereby we escape it.

Kairos

Kairos is interruption of *kronos*, not in a break or cut, but in a spontaneous culmination, as in epiphany, celebration, feast, festival—sacred time, another lived, perceptual modality. Usually translated as "opportunity" or "appropriate moment," "appointed" or "proper" or "suitable" or "fulfillment" of time, time come to a head in fruition, *kairos* is visible manifestation, and hence time on the mountaintop—glory: *shekinah*, *kabod*: the appearance of the god, whether Apollo or Dionysius. *Kairos* interrupts *kronos* as the always improbable lifting of its endless labor—in the revelation of the work of art, the extraordinary conversation, the encounter of soulmates, of lovers, carnival, song, the revel, the spontaneous dance, the sudden appearance of musicians or commedia dell'arte, the flashmob or the rave: the beautiful surprise. *Kairos* stops time through momentarily completing it, and manifesting *kronos*' hidden and repressed drive for realization through annihilation in play (*paizein*, "childing"), which is the "clue to ontological explanation," the "transformation into structure," being as self-representation, *theoria*, total presentness (*ek-stasis*) (Gadamer 1975)—that is, the vehicle for transformation into *aion*. In its association with *tyche* its appearance is guarantor of a universe of chance and novelty (Peirce 1966)—of natality (Arendt 1958), which challenges *kronos*' law of necessity, its ominous suggestion of a closed universe policed by the law of cause and effect. *Kairos* announces (but does not deliver) the "last days," the "end time," millenarian time, the dissolution of the law in its fulfillment—beyond good and evil, the form of subjectivity for which the Resurrection has come. *Kairos* announces the "third joyous kingdom" of play, Schiller's sensuous reason in the *spieltrieb*, or "play-drive" (Schiller 2004): παιδὸς ἡ βασιληίη, "the kingly power is a child's." In *kairos*, this kingdom is announced in the "event" (Badiou 2013), which emerges *ex nihilo*, making visible what official discourse tries to suppress, and announces, through the rupture of an old order, the emergence of a new.

Time and the Other: Veritable Time

In *kronos*, the time of the other and my time do not occur at the same time (Levinas/Cohen 1987). The time of the other disrupts my temporality. The temporality of relation is neither the other's nor mine—it is ours; but we are singularities, marked by radical alterity and unalterable difference, although we are also mirrors for each other and of the same flesh, signature expressions of the human genome: essential sameness and incommensurable difference. Our heart vibrations automatically synch when we are together, and our mirror neurons duplicate each other's inner thoughts and feelings, but finally we cannot share the same space or time. Relationships based on fusion, like the sleep of reason, breed monsters.

"It is this upset, this insertion of the other's time into mine, that establishes the alterity of veritable time, which is neither the Other's time nor mine," and which makes me "responsible to respond to the very alterity of the Other, to an alterity which is always on the verge of presence but never comes to presence . . . which is never present though infinitely close to the present" (Levinas/Cohen 1987, 12,18). Time in the face of the Other, "veritable time," is the time of ethical coexistence, whether easy or uneasy: of harmony, disharmony, synchrony, diachrony, symmetry or asymmetry, cacophony, homophony, polyphony, dysphony, anachronism, rhythm or arrhythmia. But there is also the promise in any encounter of mediating veritable time, not just in the sudden flourishing of *kairos* but in *pathos*, and *storge*, *philia*, *eros* and *agape*—the various forms of love. As each of us lives time in a style, a rhythm, and a mood. In the presence of the Other we enter the ethical rigors of veritable time in our own way, coloring it like a tincture in water. Even in what Levinas/Cohen refer to as "the impossibility of the dispersion of time to assemble itself in the present, the insurmountable diachrony of time" (21), in the "irreducible alterity of the other person" (13), even in the throes of *kronos* the *spieltrieb* or "play instinct" persists. The kairotic drive for transformation into structure—total presentness, being as self-representation, the synthesis of the formal and the sensuous, the actual and the virtual, freedom and inevitability—deep play—lives to overcome veritable time, if only momentarily, in the event.

Infantia and the Aesthetic State

The very etymology of *infantia*—in-fans, "not speaking"—betrays an implicit adultomorphism in that it already associates childhood with lack, absence, deficit, incapacity. This indicates the deep problem of childhood for patriarchal West at least from Greeks to modernity, which has acted, through gender identification and child-rearing patterns based on fear, exclusion, hierarchy, and domination, to betray the evolutionary potential of human development made possible by the long human childhood—particularly in the relationships between emotional and rational neural systems in the brain (Pearce 2002)—a potential that promises the advent of a form of subjectivity characterized by greater emotional intelligence than is now the norm. *Infans* as wild being, being before the reification of the subject-object split, is associated in historical narrative with the "wild man" of the repressed Euro-colonial imagination (Dudley and Novak 1972)—the noble savage or Caliban, or both at once. Child has consistently been identified with "primitive" and with animal and madness and divine—at the liminal margins of "human"—because as wild being, pure immanence, aionic subjectivity, it embodies the force of unrepressed affect, which represents danger to an adult culture and economy based on surplus repression. Child is in this sense the enemy within the gates—the wild man in the heart of the Oedipal family—which must be disciplined and tamed in a process of formation through coding and normalization.

Now, with the turn toward childhood that began in West in the eighteenth century, prophetically announced in 1763 by Jean-Jacques Rousseau in *Emile* (1979), and in hidden correspondence with the queering of conventional gender identities as prophetically announced by Mary Wollstonecraft (1996/1799), child emerges as agent, influence, symbol, and prophet of post-human deterritorialization, of wild being in aion as a cultural force (Kennedy 2006). Both *infans*-theory (Lyotard 1992; Deleuze and Guattari 1987; Agamben 1993; Kohan 2014) and queer theory are emancipatory cultural evolutionary movements whose fundamental impulse is the deconstruction of patriarchy and domination that is an implicit undercurrent in *Aufklarung* and Romanticism, revolution, democracy, anarchism, and socialism, in freedom of conscience, the rule of law, and universal welfare economies.

In psychoanalysis, Freud announced the identity of child and adult in the vicissitudes of psychological growth, and thus the interlocution of child and adult throughout the lifespan: childhood does not disappear, but simply repositions itself in adulthood. And from Pestalozzi to Froebel, to Montessori, Dewey, Freire, Lipman, and Malaguzzi, and among countless other progressive educators, the principle of adult-child dialogue has in the last two hundred years been gradually built into Western educational thinking, and the principle of formation replaced by the principle of emergence and ongoing reorganization.

The promise of adult-child dialogue is the reappropriation of wild being, the advent of the "kingly power" of childhood across the lifespan in revolutionary eros and non-repressive sublimation (Marcuse 1955) and the lifting of the surplus repression that haunts *kronos* in its social and cultural manifestations. *Infantia* is the kingdom of transitional space-time—the timespace of chiasmic perception (Merleau-Ponty 1968), of a creative ambiguity between the subjective and the objective, of the *spielraum* or "play space"—and a "third joyous kingdom of play and semblance" (Schiller 2004; Abrams 1971)—of the "aesthetic state" (pun intended) in a new sensibility (Marcuse 1969) and an emergent social order whose "fundamental law" is "to bestow freedom by means of freedom"(Abrams 1971, 351), where "no privilege, no autocracy of any kind is tolerated."

We are offered a new, invented language for the operation of the aesthetic state in the Deleuzian-Guattarian vocabularies of assemblage, deterritorialization and reterritorialization, rhizome, and becoming-other—in particular the concept of "becoming child"—which clarify the source of the "kingly power" of *infans*, and intensify the evolutionary implications of an era in which childhood is recognized as a form of life and specific children as interlocutors, with a corresponding change in the cultural institution of education. The temporality of *aion*/child is, on Deleuze's and Guattari's account, "a force through which 'the double affirmation of becoming and the being of becoming' occurs . . . and as the vehicle through which old value systems are dismantled and new ones built" (Deleuze and Guattari 1987, 23). Here Child is the very source of eternal resistance to the *mancipium*—the repressive force of the Father and of Law (Lyotard 1992), and to the tyranny of mutually exclusive, reified, "molar," "majoritarian" categories. Child exemplifies the power of affect. This power, which is libidinal, polymorphous, "non-linguistic, asubjective, impersonal" (Gill-Peterson 2013, 6), acts at the "molecular" level to pass through the poles of binary oppositions in "lines of flight"—to blur clear categories, to marry the virtual and the actual (transitional spacetime) to "struggle against and aim to overcome (not oppose) the impositions of parents, of a normalizing social order, of an oedipal narrative of sexuality, and a schoolyard of hylomorphic pedagogy" (ibid., 6). Here child is not "father to the man" but the virtual site of lines of flight that break up rigid, hierarchical, and dualistic molar assemblages and lead to "productive assemblages" in new means of expression, new behavior, new realizations—the production of a new reality (Parr 2010,18).

As Anna Hickey-Moody put it, *infantia*'s "experiential, pre-genital, polymorphous eros produces an affective flow capable of deterritorializing majoritarian libidinal systems, a power that is expressive and generative rather than controlling." *Infantia* is the "corporeal model of experimental life and subjectivity," and the child a "potentially revolutionary body," "a model of power from below," a "fleshy pedagogue, building getaway routes and opening sensory realms through which one might escape stratification" (Hickey-Moody 2103, 279–81 passim). Transitional spacetime, the spacetime time of "childing," is the space of *aion*, where *spieltrieb* emerges in *kairos*, or the event: where subject and object, potentiality and impotentiality, enter a spacetime of the virtual. So for Deleuze and Guattari "becoming-child," as a general movement of becoming is a disruption of the molar and the "majoritarian"—the plane of organization, which is dominated by social stratification and fixed knowledge, fixed categories, the classifications that swallow singularity, that codify and enforce surplus repression. In the "lines of flight" towards the "minoritarian," where the emergence of new assemblages appear on the plane of "pure immanence"—the molecular level below/before the level of individuality or monological identity—(Deleuze and Guattari 1987, 291) we recognize each other as singularities in time. There we are becoming-individualities, shaped by no hylomorphic or teleological principle, but by the principle of affective thriving, connection, and creativity in the emergence of new assemblages, new connections—which, as an affective capacity or capacity to be affected, both positively and to grow and connect in new ways, can be activated at any stage of life. As such, all becomings—becoming-woman, becoming-child; becoming-animal, -vegetable, or -mineral—are traversed by becoming-child, an "iteration of the affective register and a wonder at worldly surrounds: a new awareness" (272). Childhood is a configuration of a frontier that registers experientially as the capacity to be affected. The affective capacities of the child are part of the deep mixtures that unfold to constitute our mobile limits of becoming (and being) in the world. Or, in other words, virtual possibilities for change will always have "childhood" parts, or affects, which may be mobilized in processes of becoming (261).

In the journey into the molecular and the minoritarian, becoming child is becoming-post-human, where we experience the deconstruction of unitary or developmental discourses of subjectivity, identity, and ethics—the standard identifiers of humanism and historical ideals of self-actualization. In dwelling on the aionic plane of immanence, "we know only relations of movement and rest, of speed and slowness, between unformed, or relatively unformed, elements, molecules or particles borne away by fluxes. It knows nothing of subjects, but rather what are called 'haecceities,'" which "are simply degrees of power which combine, to which correspond a power to affect or be affected, active or passive affects, intensities. . . . In fact, no individuation takes place in the manner of a subject or even of a thing" (Deleuze and Parnet 2007, 92).

Becoming child breaks open and reorganizes the plane of organization, not just in the queering of dualistically organized notions of gender, but in the suspension of the distinction at the ontological level between organic and inorganic, animate and inanimate—in the discovery of a "multi-tiered ontology in which there is no definitive break between sentient and nonsentient entities or between material and spiritual phenomena"

(Coole and Frost 2010, 9–10), in affirmation of Spinoza's "single substance" and the realization that matter and energy are not ontologically separate (Gill-Peterson 2013). As such, the advent of the post-human results, perhaps paradoxically, in a humanization of the natural world to the extent it breaks down those distinctions and understands Spinoza's single substance as also characterized by affect, lines of flight, deterritorialization and territorialization, ever new assemblages, arrived at through a rhizomatic rather than a linear movement—that is, with "human" qualities. As such, becoming-animal and—insect and vegetable and mineral—is about the becoming, not just of the human but of the whole world, and participates in the aionic, transitional time and space of planet and cosmos.

Child time, wild time, body time, aionic time, is time at the juncture of all becomings: the time that signifies the pathos, the erotic longing of the desiring body of *kronos*. Plagued by reification, the god Kronos dreams of perfect symmetries and correspondences, and broods over the plane of organization with visions of mathematical perfection, while half-secretly, fearfully even, in desiring-love with the broad sea of becoming, with the world of generation that his original bloody transgression opened between earth and sky. There, Aphrodite emerges continually from the foam in multiple becomings, and the *spieltrieb* drives the worlding of the world forward in flows and intensities, "relations of movement and rest, of speed and slowness," in the "floating times, the floating lines of Aion," among "elements, molecules or particles borne away by fluxes" (Deleuze and Parnet 2007, 92), where the royal child plays at draughts: παιδὸς ἡ βασιληίη; the kingdom belongs to the child. The child is regal by birth—from Old French *roial* "royal, regal; splendid, magnificent." But it is a paradoxical royalty, directed as it is by deregulatory impulses, affects and intensities, and dedicated as it is to becoming other. But it is, finally, the species' only hope.

In keeping with the characterization of the child as "prophet of futurity" and "experimental being" explored here and in previous chapters, and on the conviction that the politics of subjectivity is directly linked with politics per se, the following chapters revisit Marcuse's "new sensibility" in its suggestion of a form of subjectivity—collectively understood as a "psychoclass"—that cultivates the habits of what John Dewey called "social democracy," without which, he argued, authentic political democracy is impossible. He defined social democracy as a particular "mode of associated living, of conjoint communicated experience" (Dewey 1916, 87) that acts as both cause and effect of what Erich Fromm (1994, 2013) called the democratic "social character," and characterized the latter as a normative form or style of subjectivity open to difference, tolerant of complexity and ambiguity, autonomous and self-organizing.

Both concepts—a new sensibility and the democratic social character—when considered in the historical context of the proliferating cultural and political boundary-crossings that result from the ever-increasing interface of globalization and localization on a planetary level, suggest a revised, postmodern understanding of human subjectivity itself. One expression of this emergent revision can be found in the notion of a "dialogical" self, offered by Dutch psychologist Hubert Hermans and outlined in the next chapter, as an ontological formulation that moves beyond the isolated, highly boundaried Cartesian form of modernist subjectivity. This historical shift may be understood as a dialectical response to the dramatic cultural, social, political, and personal intervisibility and interdependence created by the postmodern information environment, and a consequent deconstruction of boundaries that, I will argue, creates the conditions for the emergence of the democratic social character, the increasing practice of social democracy, and the promise of a new sensibility. These evolutionary potentialities invoke, in turn, the notion of *skholé* as an educational form adapted to their emergence, along with community of philosophical inquiry as an ur-pedagogy. All depend, to a greater or lesser degree, on the evolutionary emergence of a dialogical relation between children and adults, expressed both in widely practiced child-rearing modes and in educational forms, the theory and practice of schooling in particular. As such, the next chapter will also be devoted to the historical evolution of the adult-child chiasmic relation, and to its educational implications.

Chapter Five

Paths in Utopia

School as Holding Environment for the Dialogical Self

By way of tracing the genealogy of Dewey's "social democracy," Fromm's democratic "social character," and Marcuse's "new sensibility," all would seem to suggest a form of subjectivity that is implicitly committed to the experience of living both individually and collectively in what Hubert Hermans (2018), founder of dialogical self theory, has termed the "challenge" zone of "the dynamic interplay of I-positions"—the various narrative voices—within the self, and is practiced in negotiating the proliferating boundary-crossings that result from the ever-increasing interaction of globalization and localization that is the postmodern situation. The historical appearance of a democratic psychoclass may also be linked, after Marcuse and Bookchin, with the promise of an emergent form of culturally mediated subjectivity that acts to recover the continuum between our "first nature" and our "second nature," our natural world and our social world, our biological being and our rationality. Here I want to further explore a form of education that has been present in latent or manifest form as long as democratic values and aspirations have been present in the Western social and political imaginary, and argue that it is intimately linked to the same impulse that this new reality principle represents. Its evolutionary potential is fed by what psychohistorian Lloyd DeMause identified as a dialectical advance in child-rearing "modes," whereby adults enter into dialogue with childhood forms of intentionality, resulting in the invention of school as an adult-child collective that acts as a facilitating environment for the emergence of a psychoclass dedicated to dialogue, democracy, and ongoing personal and social reconstruction.

Social Democracy and the Democratic Social Character

Dewey (1916) argued that, apart from that form of collective intelligence that cultivates the habits of social democracy, authentic political democracy is impossible. Social democracy emerges, he suggests, with ". . . the increase in the number of individuals who participate in an interest so that each has to refer his own action to that of others, and to consider the action of others to give point and direction to his own, [which] breaks down barriers of class, race, and nationality," leading to "more numerous and more varied points of contact," and as such, "greater diversity of stimuli to which an individual has to respond, which puts a premium on variation in our actions," which is linked in turn to the "liberation of a greater diversity of personal capacities," a "widening area of shared concerns," and "greater individualization and a broader community of interest" (87).

As a relative newcomer in the history of Western subjectivity, the democratic social character or psychoclass has emerged in the interstices of a dialectical process of deconstruction of three broad forms of self-understanding: Plato's hierarchical tripartite self with its clear both internal and external class positions; Descartes's discrete, isolated subject—*homo clausus*—as a function of the radical individualism of the modernist rising bourgeoisie and the capitalist ethos; and Freud's queering of the Platonic hierarchy, reflecting the crisis of Enlightenment—the revenge of the unconscious, and the post-Freudian project, albeit tragically hampered, of the emancipation of Eros. The form of subjectivity that makes the democratic social character possible acts to decenter and democratize all those "parts of the soul"—whether reason, passion, appetite, id, ego, superego—to give them voices and put them in dialogue, and as such represents an act of faith in human nature itself: the faith that the "healthy" self can navigate around the black holes of the various forms of dissociative disorder that are possible when the multiple elements of the self are decentered and democratized, and to endure the uncertainty of the lived experience of continual repositioning of elements in a relational field.

The democratic, dialogical self has in fact been announced in numerous formulations over Western historical time, and it has always been present as a human possibility, an archetype of a form of lived experience. As a normative ideal, it represents the dialectical impulse that drives us forward—the negation of the structures of hierarchy and domination that have ever shaped the apparatus of capture that is the state. The democratic impulse affirms the possibilities in human nature that the ominous Hobbesian formulation (bellum omnium contra omnes, "the war of all against all") precludes. It represents a clear evolutionary bio-social potential in the human brain for a certain organization of the relations between the prefrontal cortex and the limbic system—reason and feeling and desire—that is promised in every human infant, and the development of which, as evolutionary philosopher Joseph Chilton Pearce (2002) argued, is only interrupted by toxic culture and bad education. As such, it represents what the eco-philosopher Murray Bookchin (2005) identified as an emergent normative form of culturally mediated subjectivity that acts to "recover the continuum between our 'first nature' and our 'second nature,' our natural world and our social world, our biological being and our rationality" (369). In fact, Charles Taylor (1989) identifies this emergence as an expression of the perennial impulse in the history of Western subjectivity to forge "a new synthesis of reason and desire," to "overcome the barrier between reason and the instinctual depths," and thereby to "escape from the restrictions of the unitary self" (386, 471).

As we have seen, one recent formulation of an ever-emergent "second nature" that grounds the dialogical, democratic self is found in Marcuse's "new sensibility," an emergent organization of the relation between reason and desire that accompanies a "revolutionizing of instinctual structure," a change in the system of needs" (1978, 17), leading to "a society organized under a new reality principle" (29). Marcuse's formulation, inspired by Ernst Bloch's (1995) notion of the *Novum*, also resonates with the anarchist Peter Kropotkin's (1902) argument that successful evolutionary adaptation follows from cooperation rather than competition, and that "mutual aid" is a fundamental characteristic of all successful species. It also suggests a new relationship to "first nature"—the natural world that is both outside us and within us.

Our present default reality principle is based on repression, commodification, extreme superego demands, hierarchy, and domination, and encourages dissociative splitting such that first nature and the other become objects outside us. This way of framing the world is connected with the corporate capitalist mode of production, which is grounded on the unlimited exploitation of nonrenewable natural and human resources, and is expected, if things continue at current levels, to bring the planet to or over the brink of ecological disaster by some time in the 2030s. As such, the evolutionary step in the history of subjectivity that Marcuse is invoking may be understood as an adaptive response to an extreme threat and poses the question whether the species that has radically altered the fundamental physical dynamics of the planet can survive the unintended consequences of the alterations it has made. Is it too late for the species to self-enculturate in a new relationship between prefrontal cortex and limbic system—a new organization of desire—and as such, a new, healing relationship with first nature?

Marcuse's vision of a "new relation to nature and to man" involves a "different formation of scientific concepts, and new values between humans and their technological and scientific objects," which is grounded in a relational onto-epistemological model "that replaces the bifurcated practice of separating the social from the natural, the objects from the subjects" (1972 148). A new "libidinal rationality" or "sensual reason" is necessary, the actual felt "liberation of the mind, and of the body from aggressive and repressive needs" (Marcuse 2009, 35; and see 1978) and it emerges, on his account, through the experience of art and sexuality, play and social experiment, inquiry, reflection and dialogue—those formative experiences through which the new sensibility is educated in its etymological sense of "led forth." It evokes not only Bookchin's notion of "second nature" as an ongoing reconstruction of "first nature," but also recent philosophical theory in the realm of post-humanism and vital materialism (Bennett 2001, 2010; Coole and Frost 2010), as well as the perennial tradition of neo-animist and vitalist theory. As Peter Marshall (2010) put it, "the second nature of human society would help actualize the potentiality of first nature" (612), and act to foster a "technological imagination which considers matter as an active substance developing meaningful patterns and not a dead collection of atoms" (614).

For vital materialist theory, matter itself is "lively," and exhibits agency at the ontological level; it refuses the exclusionary distinction between the inorganic and the organic, animate and inanimate, between sentient and nonsentient entities, and between material and spiritual phenomena. As such, it implies an emergent philosophy of nature that represents a dialectical recovery of a form of the relation between first and second nature that is characteristic, not only of some indigenous cultures and of young children's "philosophies" (Piaget 1931), but of the perennial tradition of panpsychism in Western philosophical thought (Skrbina 2005). It may be argued as well that it represents a response, not just to the crisis of the Anthropocene—the radical existential alienation from first nature that has resulted from its degradation and disfigurement in the hands of *homo technologicus*—but also a corresponding shift in the direction of the "posthuman," understood as a form of subjectivity that has consciously renounced an attitude of hierarchy and domination and embraced dialogue, not just in its inter- and intrapersonal, but in its interspecies relations as well.

The New Sensibility and the Dialogical Self

The new sensibility is, then, both an evolutionary phenomenon—a potential next step in the history of human subjectivity—and a dialectical one. It is based on a reorganization of the desiring economy and the emergence of a new reality principle for which splitting, repression, and projection are no longer requirements for survival: it is based, in short, on a new form of reason, which follows on what, as we have seen in chapter one, Maurice Merleau-Ponty (1964a) called "the attempt to explore the irrational and integrate it into an expanded reason" (63). As an emergent form or style of subjectivity, it implies the ongoing reconstruction of boundaries both within the self and in relations with others—including the other of "first nature." In terms offered by Deleuze and Guattari (1987) it is the product of a deterritorializing "flow," a decentering movement—a "line of flight" that escapes the overcoding of the dominant signifying regime and seeks to reterritorialize on a new plane of consistency. As an assemblage, the dialogical self as a normative ideal renounces its solipsistic, totalizing, and hierarchical impulses—what Hermans would call its tendency to "over-positioning"—and understands itself as an ever-shifting and repositioning psychic field of dynamic relations that extends across the boundaries between inside and outside, self and others; for which, in fact, boundaries are context-dependent and ever-shifting. Above all, it comes to understand psychological success ("mental health"), not as a product of forced unification under one overcoded persona, but as an open conversation, however fraught, between multiple archetypal I-positions in the self—"I" as child, adult, mystic, hedonist, success, failure, activist, follower, hidden, open, mortal, immortal, free, addict, male, female, sexual, asexual, etc. On a more operational level, "I" as son, daughter, parent, friend, worker, colleague, or rival interact with internalized significant others, living or dead, who most often position themselves as superego figures within my psychic constellation: spouse, father, mother, siblings and other relatives, mentors, lovers, and colleagues.

The dialogical self is intrinsically dialectical in that as a subject-in-process and as an event rather than a substance, it is involved in continual reconstruction through the repositioning and ongoing resolution of emergent contradictions between the multiple both intra- and intersubjective elements of the field of the self, whether we call those elements personae, identities, self-objects, introjections, voices, or I-positions. Dialogue is only possible when, multiplicity and polyphony, singularity and difference are recognized and affirmed, and when every voice—whether within the self or in the larger, virtual self of the collective, and however dark—is heard. The dialogical self as normative ideal has not only recognized internal multiplicity; it has also renounced on principle the totalitarian impulse and the logic of the excluded middle. The latter seeks by nature to categorize, classify, centralize, to construct hierarchies—arboreal structures based on binaries—in the interest of control, which, in turn, is driven by the unconscious phantasm of a univocal Identity, of a becoming-god. On the other hand, the dialogical sensibility is, as a normative ideal of being-in-the-world, committed to the executive "meta-position" of tolerating doubt, uncertainty, and ambiguity, and to living with the existential tension between I-positions. Self understood as event rather than substance implies an ongoing process of mutual interrogation and repositioning in dynamic relations of power, oriented towards ongoing systemic reconstellation. Above all it recognizes and acknowledges its own shadow material—abjection, rejection, narcissism, sadomasochism, envy, jealousy, greed—a recognition that the Jungian psychologist Erich Neumann (1973a) has argued is fundamental to what he calls the emergence of a "new ethic." Until the dark materials of the unconscious are integrated into conscious awareness, he argues, they are projected onto the other, and in particular the unfamiliar other.

A Genealogy of Dialogical Education

Are the new sensibility and the dialogical self outcomes of education? In fact, the causal networks that generate human psychoclasses would appear to be hopelessly overdetermined, and each of the major paradigms of self-understanding in the West is a broad evolutionary gambit, triggered by complex historical factors (Kennedy 2013a). What set of relations between Marxian base and superstructure, for example, created a space for the ascendancy of the Platonic tripartite self in fourth-century BC, or the Cartesian discreet self in the seventeenth, or the inherently conflicted Freudian self of the twentieth? What amalgam of material conditions—climatic patterns and events, technological innovation, exploration, trade, conquest, colonization, class conflict, demographic flows, cultural invention, religion, epidemiological patterns, and events—contributed to their emergence and their passing? However, we certainly can identify education as a major factor in the formation of social character if we understand the former in the broad sense of Bildung, which includes the individual's encounter with the reproductive forces at work in the everyday life of material culture; the dominant discourses and regimes of knowledge that underlie and reinforce patterns of construing self and world; and the organization and interactions of the microsystems in which the individual identified as "student" or "learner" is placed—family, religious institution, information environment and socioeconomic, racial, ethnic, and gender class niches. However, one particular microsystem—the "school"—has become dominant over the course of the last two hundred years in the West and is in fact dedicated specifically and more or less consciously to subjectification.

As an ideological state apparatus, universal compulsory schooling—not just in its more recent neoliberal incarnation but from its beginnings in association with the ever-increasing hegemony of the centralized nation state—has functioned to indoctrinate its subjects into a form of subjectivity and self-understanding as an isolated unit in a particular plane of socioeconomic and governmental organization, now clearly identified as global capitalism. As such, the school functions as a something like a penal colony, or reeducation camp dedicated to the rehabilitation of "children" through instruction and formation such that they can be released into the greater society and economy as "adults." The reproductive function of mass schooling in its rawest, most basic dimension reinforces the Cartesian paradigm of selfhood to the extent that it understands itself as preparing the future worker/citizen/consumer for individual survival in a collective jungle of huge, virtually uncontrollable market forces, metastasizing hierarchies, and ever-deepening inequalities.

We might ask then, is there a form of "school" that is dedicated to the emergence of the democratic psychoclass—of individuals and groups for whom social democracy has become a normative way of being in the world—for whom dialogical encounter, cooperation, self-regulation and ongoing personal and social reconstruction have begun to replace personal and social reproduction on a purely economic model? Of a discursive space in which the fundamental concepts that underlie any given philosophy of nature—"nature" itself and its relation to "culture," "life" or "alive," "matter," "goal" or telos, and their interaction with scientific and psychological concepts—come under interrogation and undergo transformation? Indeed, can a school be implicitly dedicated to clearing a discursive, philosophical, ideological space for the emergence of a psychoclass dedicated to dialogue, critique, reconstruction, and the reconciliation of first and second nature—and if so, how?

I have suggested that there is indeed such a form of schooling, that it has been present in latent or manifest form as long as democratic values and aspirations have been present in the Western social and political imaginary, and that it is intimately linked to the same evolutionary impulse that the new sensibility represents. What I will call dialogical schooling in its modern incarnation emerged over the course of the nineteenth and twentieth centuries as an antithesis or counterpoint to state-provided universal compulsory schooling in forms now broadly termed "progressive." It has roots in left-libertarian (anarchist) and liberal reformist Enlightenment ideologies—roots that are clearly discernable, not just in the beliefs and practices of "child-centered" educators, but also in the contemporary "democratic education" or "free school" movement. Moreover, those roots are fed by what the psychohistorian Lloyd DeMause identified as an evolutionary advance in childrearing "modes."

The Rise of the Empathic Child-Rearing Mode and the Hermeneutical Turn

DeMause (1975) identified six historical modes—Infanticidal, Abandoning, Ambivalent, Intrusive, Socializing, and Empathic—each of which represents an evolutionary advance on the previous mode. In the moment of its historical ascendancy, each represented a widely accepted set of beliefs about the nature, significance, and value of childhood, and a set of corresponding educational practices, whether in the home or the school. We may also assume that, although one mode is accepted as "normal" at any one time, all are represented in every age: there have always been parents operating all or in part in the Empathic mode, just as there are Infanticidal and Abandoning parents today—just, for that matter, as there have always been individuals and even groups living, all or in part, in the dialogical and democratic sensibility. In fact it is the presence of the latter minoritarian psychoclass that make broadly distributed evolutionary change imaginable.

DeMause's theory is based on the notion that there are two broad forms of reaction when parents are faced by a child's need—the "empathic reaction" and the "projective reaction." The latter is adult-centered: the child is felt as an extension of the adult, whether negative or positive (devil or angel). The adult projects the dangerous, inferior, abject contents of their own unconscious—their "shadow" material—onto their children, who function as a sort of blank screen, and then become objects of those parents' attempts to eradicate or discipline those same contents. So, for example when J. Sulzer, a German child-rearing "expert" writes in 1748 "it is impossible to reason with young children; thus, willfulness must be driven out in a methodical manner. If one gives in to their willfulness once, the second time it will be more pronounced and more difficult to drive out," etc. (quoted in Miller 1990) he is projecting his own dangerous aggressive and narcissistic impulses onto the child.

Sulzer's discourse reflects what DeMause has termed the Intrusive child-rearing mode, which he dates roughly to the eighteenth century, and thus corresponds with the rise of universal compulsory education in Europe. The Intrusive mode is an advance on the previous Ambivalent mode in the extent to which it is now thought possible to forcefully transform the child's "evil" nature rather than suppress it. In the Intrusive mode,

> . . . parents shifted from trying to stop children's growth to trying to control them: their minds, their insides, their anger and the lives they led. [They are] more involved in their children's upbringing. Rather than physically controlling the child they tried to conquer their minds, controlling the child's insides, his anger, his needs and his will. Children were nursed by the mother, not swaddled, neither played with nor beaten. They were made to obey promptly with threats, guilt and other punishments such as being shut up in dark closets for hours. (DeMause 1975)

The evolutionary advance in the modes is driven by the "empathic reaction," a corresponding capacity of adults to become conscious of and "withdraw" or "own" their shadow projection. In what might seem a paradox, this is made possible by a growing distance between child and adult: recognized as a separate individual, the child is no longer a container for the adult's projections, but rather an individual, a singularity, a person. The evolutionary impulse that drives this advance is no doubt nourished by multiple causal threads—for example levels of affluence, the rise of the nuclear family as a new form of intimacy, and a decrease in child mortality (Aries 1962). They are also institutional, for example the Roman Church's official condemnation of infanticide and child-abandonment beginning in 379 AD. The Socializing mode, which is the "normal" of our day—the mode that contemporary child-rearing manuals tend to reflect—represents a shift from stern, cold disciplinary control to warmer, soft behaviorism or covert manipulation. The general transition into the empathic mode began after WWII, as reflected in the huge influence in the US (fifty million copies sold, in seven editions) of Benjamin Spock's *The Common Sense Book of Baby and Child Care* (1946). It is currently represented by a variety of vanguard movements such as attachment parenting, slow parenting, free-range parenting, positive parenting, gentle parenting, not to speak of the growth of the unschooling and the Democratic Education movements.

According to DeMause, the signifying moment of the psychodynamic shift represented by the empathic reaction occurs when "the adult is face to face with a child who needs something," and the adult is "able to regress to the level of a child's need and correctly identify it without imposing an admixture of the adult's own projections" (1975, 6, 7). Children of the past were most commonly subject to the projective reaction where they were seen as evil or animalistic or impulse-ridden. Here they are regarded as individuals separate from their parents, who deserve the same respect and tolerance and care as adults. As such, the empathic reaction may be understood as a form of what psychoanalysts call "therapeutic regression," and has significant implications both for Marcuse's "revolutionizing of instinctual structure" (which could also be termed "revolutionizing of pre-frontal cortex-amygdala relations") and for its realization in child-rearing practices in general, including the institutionalized encounter between children and adults that we call school.

The emergence and ascendance of empathic parenting as "standard practice" in the West may also be described as a hermeneutical process in the relation between adulthood and childhood, and therefore between specific adults and children as well. The projective reaction is one of psychological both splitting and fusion: the child is felt as an extension of the adult, and her behavior is interpreted in terms of the adult's unconscious contents, which he or she does not recognize as her own (splitting). The empathic reaction—the ability to feel what the child is feeling—although it is based on sympathy or feeling-with, is empathic to the extent that the adult is not hijacked by that feeling, is able to maintain a distance from it, and thus avoids fusion and mutual contamination. As such, the empathic process begins with a separation, a distanciation, what Martin Buber (1965) characterized as a "putting at a distance," without which what he calls "entering relation" is impossible.

In a parallel development, the psychodynamic distancing between "adult" and "child" reached its apogee in the rise of *homo clausus*, the normative bourgeois, Cartesian subject—the radically field-independent, strictly self-controlled, discreet (in both senses of the term) rationalistic, Western "grown up"—the not-child, the subject for whom childhood has become an illegible "text." Psychohistorically speaking, the "invention of childhood" that Philippe Aries (1962) documented in early modern Europe is inseparable from the "invention of adulthood" of the same historical moment, described by Norbert Elias (1994) as the "civilizing process." As the white, western, male adult comes to represent all that is strictly boundaried, rational, civilized, and repressed, "child" becomes all that he is not—affect-centered, spontaneous, and expressive. This sense of separation between adult and child is both a driver of the Intrusive mode—the attempt, through strict discipline and regimentation in the form of schooling to "correct" these socially censured tendencies—and, for those capable of "withdrawing the projection," the recognition that the child's emotional immediacy is index of another form of life in which they once participated, and which is lost to them.

The hermeneutical turn in the Western adult-child relation begins in this moment of distanciation and incomprehension. It is first articulated in Jean-Jacques Rousseau's prophetic axiom in the opening lines of the hugely influential *Emile, Or on Education*, published in 1764: "Childhood is unknown. Starting from the false idea one has of it, the farther one goes, the more one loses one's way. Begin, then, by studying your pupils better. For most assuredly you do not know them at all" (Rousseau 1979, 34). The counter-movement in Western education that we identify as dialogical schooling begins here as well, in an *aporia*, and the result—the outcome of the interpretive process that follows this moment of distanciation—holds the promise of personal and cultural reconstruction in a new understanding of both forms of lived experience (child and adult), and the emergence of a form of social character grounded in the principle of dialogue that is implicit in the principles and practices of empathic child-rearing.

In the hermeneutical moment of distanciation, the "text" that is "child" has become strange and distant and can be approached only through an act of interpretation, which entails withdrawing the projection. "Adult" enters into dialogue with "child," and the interpretive moment that Hans-Georg Gadamer (1975) called "fusion of horizons," Paul Ricoeur (1981) "appropriation," and Buber (1965) "entering into relation," becomes an act of self-interpretation as well. As Ricoeur put it, "In the last analysis the text [child] is the mediation by which we understand ourselves" (1973, 141); and "the interpretation of the text [child] culminates in the self-interpretation of a subject who thenceforth understands himself better, understands himself differently, or simply begins to understand himself" (1981, 158); or, finally, "To understand is not to project oneself into the text [child]; it is to receive an enlarged self from the apprehension of proposed worlds which are the genuine object of interpretation" (182).

It is that "enlarged self"—a self that has reconnected with the experience of childhood on the level of self-understanding—that is the implicit telos in committing to the adult-child encounter that is dialogical parenting and, in a larger social context, dialogical schooling. For the adult, the child is now recognized as the lived representation of "natality"—the felt understanding that each birth represents the introduction of novelty into the world and the corresponding capacity for "beginning something anew, that is, of acting" (Arendt 1958, 9)—which is the subjective ground of freedom and agency, and as such represents the potential for personal and collective reconstruction. The "enlarged self" that results from understanding oneself anew in the encounter with childhood represents a recovery of natality, in the sense described by Deleuze and Guattari (1987) as "becoming child," which represents, as we have seen, "an affective capacity or capacity to be affected, both positively and to grow and connect in new ways, [which] can be activated at any stage of life" (282). From the point of view of evolutionary psychology, natality, and the unending process of "becoming child" are affirmations of the fact that humans are paedomorphs—the species that remains in "the form of the child" throughout the life cycle (Montagu 1989; Bjorklund 1997). To come to this understanding of the role of childhood in one's own life and in the life of the species means to encounter actual children differently. As such, working with children—whether in parenting or teaching—becomes a form of self-work, fundamental to the individuation process, a crucial element of which is the practice of withdrawing—or at least resisting—the projection.

On the side of the child, we may say that the implicit goal of the encounter with adults is not a historically determined one. In comparison with the adult, the child experiences the interaction between "inside" me and "outside" me as liminal and labile, shifting and transforming. As such, she is Merleau-Ponty's (1964b) "polymorph," whose lived experience is characterized by what Alfred Schutz (1973) called a different "tension of consciousness." In the language of dialogical self theory, she lives in a world in which internal and external I-positions are relatively undifferentiated, and even intertwined and where in Jungian terms, conscious and unconscious dimensions of the psyche are fluid—the *nigredo* of the alchemists (Jung 2014). For the Romantic imagination, which historically represents the first hermeneutical appropriation of childhood, this *unio naturalis* is Thomas Traherne's "Infant-Ey" (Traherne 1965), one univocal I-position. The *conatus* of the child is growth, in the sense of continual developmental interplay of differentiation, hierarchization, and centralization of functions in the interest of "competence" or "mastery" of one's immediate environment (Werner 1957), an environment to which the distinction between animate and inanimate does not yet fully apply. As such, the child is engrossed in the discovery and invention of I-positions, and with negotiating the dynamic interplay between those emergent positions. She is drawn involuntarily to those internalized "promoter positions" that facilitate this process, which are represented by significant others, usually (but not always) adults.

In addition, the child is in a physiological state of continual neuronal transformation such that her interaction with her world—especially when it is experienced as a form of deeply felt inquiry—contributes directly to the form and function of ongoing synaptic reorganization. The developmental organization of the brain is to a great extent determined by her actual concrete, existential experience, which is driven by a search for optimal experience, or flow. In accordance with Yerkes-Dodson theory (quoted in Hermans 2018, 291), and with Piaget's theory of cognitive equilibration (for which see Bjorklund 1995), optimal experience involves a level of cognitive arousal—of interest—that is not too high such as to create anxiety, or too low such as to create boredom. The child instinctively seeks to remain in what Hermans calls the "challenge zone," which is intrinsically playful, in the sense described by Gadamer (1975) when he writes, "The players are not the subjects of play; instead play . . . reaches presentation through the players" (92).

Lineaments of Dialogical Schooling

We may ask, then, whether there is a particular form of schooling—broadly understood as an intentional community dedicated to intergenerational encounter—that is organized so as to nurture the child's intrinsic search for meaning, so as to create a safe psychological space for the child's (and the adult's) challenge zones, and so as to model a form of community, referred to by Dewey as an "embryonic society," which is grounded in principles of dialogue. For the adult, this space is dedicated, not just to the facilitation of the child's intrinsically driven developmental project, but also to resisting the projective reaction in the interest of the "enlarged self" that is implicit in her—the adult's—individuation process. For the child, such a space is dedicated to the emergence of possible I-positions and the forging of their internal and external dialogical relations, organized by a metaposition—a coherent ensemble of all her I-positions—that Iannaccone, Marsico, and Tateo (2013, 220) characterize as the "educational self." As such, the adult project of enlargement and unification that is "becoming child" is put in the service of the child's project of differentiation and putting-in-relation that is "becoming adult." The teacher's role is an exemplar of the promoter position. She sees possibilities that child only feels, and organizes a material environment that acts as a lure and stimulus for the discovery and exercise of those possibilities—a "prepared environment" that organizes space, time, objects, ideas, activities, and interhuman relations so as to encourage a continual movement between the child's comfort and the challenge zones, with an eye, as Hermans (2018, 288) puts it, to "widening" the latter.

The infant psychoanalyst and philosopher of human development D. W. Winnicott (1965) introduced us to the idea of what he called a "holding" or "facilitating" environment, which he considered necessary for the emergence over the course of early childhood of a form of subjectivity for which, in the language of dialogical self theory, self's I-positions are distributed optimally—which is to say dialogically—across inner and outer boundaries. In Winnicott's construct, "good enough" parenting maintains a place for the emergence of a psychological space that he calls, variously, "transitional," or a "third" or "potential" space—a space between inner and outer, subject and object, self and other, the individual and the world. As we have seen, this space is associated with creativity, the imagination, and with deep both personal and relational experience, whether it be in the form of art, inquiry, or emotional experience. It is a zone of experience associated by play theorists with "flow," a ground of becoming on which the metastatic equilibrium between the virtual and the actual is pointed and clarified. Implicit in Winnicott's maturational theory is the assumption that the deep experience of relational ontological structure, when nurtured and protected in a facilitating environment of family, informs a process that leads to "relational autonomy," or the capacity of self—understood by Hermans (2018) as a "dynamic multiplicity of I-positions involved in mutual communication"—to be "ultimately the leader of itself."

We might extend the concept of holding environment from the sphere of child and family and apply it to the next Western institution organized for the cultural and social mediation of the long human childhood, the school. In theorizing "dialogical schooling," I ignore the historical phenomenon of school in its Foucaultian incarnation as disciplinary institution and ideological state apparatus and return to its first statement as a democratic institution, associated with the "invention" of democracy in fifth-century-BC Periclean Athens. There *skholé* (from which "school"), per its literal meaning—"free time"—as formulated by Jan Masschelein and Maarten Simons (2013), identified itself as a form of gathering that sets itself apart from the world of production, discipline, economic "skilling" and ideological indoctrination, and devotes itself to inquiry and dialogue, cultivating a form of attention that can be summed up in the word *studium*, with its etymological connotations of passion, eagerness, wonder and enthusiasm.

Skholé represents a founding archetypal statement of an adult-child collective dedicated to dialogical inquiry, and by implication to ongoing epistemological reconstruction. As such, it may be characterized as a neotenic shelter—a holding environment for the optimal developmental potential of the human brain. It is a site for opening a future, a transitional zone in which the new forms, meanings, interests, and understandings that childhood carries in potentia are nourished, in the perennial evolutionary hope of an emergent psychoclass dedicated to dialogue, democracy, and ongoing social reconstruction in the interest of shalom, or human thriving. In its albeit never perfect but "good enough" iterations in the contemporary democratic schools movement and progressive education in general, *skholé* suggests an embryonic community in which communal dialogue is the fundamental discursive form, whether it be in the practice of disciplinary inquiry or school governance. As such, it plays a key role in, as Marcuse (1969) put it, "the strategy of those who, within the existing society, work for the new one" in the form of "projects of a new social morality and of new institutions of freedom" (88, 30).

Skholé is based on the intuitive understanding—attested to by its genealogical identification with the historical emergence of political democracy—that social democracy depends on the rise of a form of intentional community that the philosopher Robert Corrington (1992), after

Josiah Royce, calls "community of interpretation" as opposed to "natural" community. The latter remains opaque to itself, uninterested in—in fact resistant to—interrogating its own deeper assumptions and examining its own values. On Corrington's account, communities of interpretation are latent within natural communities; they are dedicated to self-reflection and an openness to the "not yet," or what Ernst Bloch (1995) called the *Novum*, which makes of them "communities of expectation," or hope, and as such breeding grounds for a form of social character based on, in John Dewey's (1922) formulation, new relations between "impulse and habit." As he put it: "What is necessary is that habits be formed which are more intelligent, more sensitively percipient, more informed with foresight, more aware of what they are about, more direct and sincere, more flexibly responsive than those now current. Then they will meet their own problems and propose their own solutions" (128). Understood as a community of interpretation, *skholé* is an interactive space that is set apart for and governed intrinsically by what, as we have seen, Friedrich Schiller (2004) called the "play drive" or "play instinct" (Germ. *spieltrieb*). On his account, the *spieltrieb* is dedicated to mediating the relations between mind and body, the learned and the instinctual, emotion and reason, sense and sensibility, conscious and unconscious, impulse and habit. Here *skholé* as a form of gathering is understood as a space organized for the play of sociability, the play of ideas, the play of investigation and discovery, the play of artistic creation, the play of ritual and performance, and the play of collective decision-making, or direct democratic practice. Above all, what distinguishes *skholé* as a community of interpretation is the centrality of the play of communal dialogue, or what, as we have seen, has recently come to be called community of philosophical inquiry (Lipman 2003, Kennedy 2017).

The first educational implication of child and adult entering dialogue in the transitional space of *skholé* is in the interruption of what Paulo Freire (2005) called "the banking method" or "transmission" model that dominates conventional monological pedagogy. In what Freire called "problem-posing" education on the other hand, student and teacher roles are decentered and de-hierarchized. Implicit here is a reorganization of power and authority in the deconstruction of fixed, hierarchical forms of control; a shift from closed to open-system organization in the identification and performance of roles and in the power dynamics of a collective within the small community of *skholé*. As an intentional intergenerational community dedicated to dialogue and encounter, *skholé* understands itself broadly as an autopoietic or self-organizing system, a "chaosmos" in which order is an emergent dimension of a system in which chaos is always present as the virtual dimension of the actual.

This understanding is based on a set of critically examined beliefs, not just about children, childhood and human development, but about order, authority, and agency—all of which are fundamental to our beliefs about the possibility of democratically organized self-governance of autonomous individuals in relatively small communities, dedicated to mutual aid and to the creation and maintenance of what Plato called *dikaiosune* and Aristotle *nomos*, broadly translated as "justice." *Skholé* as an intentional community understands itself as a place apart, where society "puts itself at a distance from itself" (Masschelein and Simons 2013) in the interest of the ongoing reconstruction of social character (Dewey's "habit") or second nature—of opening a future in which authentic democracy has become a fundamental human disposition. It is consciously dedicated to this evolutionary project and constructs itself as space dedicated to the interruption of the natural order of production (pressures of work, state, society) and of the instrumentalism that is the hallmark of school understood as ideological state apparatus.

As a site dedicated to inquiry and dialogue, *skholé* cultivates a different kind of time. It suspends the machinic, self-reproducing time of *kronos*—a time that cultivates the illusion of repetition without difference, which generates the Same ad infinitum. Rather, *skholé* cultivates "non-productive" time: *kairos*, the time of event, meeting, appearance, manifestation, singularity, epiphany, synchronicity—the "just in time" and "the right time"—and *aion*, the time of the eternal present, the temporality of deep play, "flow," which is associated with the lines of flight, the flows and intensities of becoming other; or, as Elizabeth Grosz (2005) has put it, "the inevitable force of differentiation and elaboration, which is also another name for becoming. . . . Duration is the 'field' in which difference lives and plays itself out" (4).

As a transitional or "potential" space, a "between," a "third area of cultural experience," *skholé* is a space of serious play, where new forms are encouraged through investigation, inquiry, study, group dialogue and deliberation, teamwork, project, performance, and reflection. This suggests an emergent, negotiated curriculum that is rhizomatic, interest-driven, partially individualized, thoroughly multidisciplinary and poly-signifying, drawing into play what the founder of Reggio Emilia preschool Loris Malaguzzi referred to as "the 100 languages" of children (Edwards,

Gandini, and Forman 1993): poetry, narrative, languages, drawing, painting, sculpting, craft, dance and movement, music, drama, nature study, and scientific experiment. It also suggests a pedagogy that creates a space and an atmosphere for ongoing social and emotional counseling, on the understanding that life in community is ever vulnerable to our shadow material—feelings of envy, inferiority, competitiveness, and emotional greed that, through splitting and projection, can hinder the formation of both internal and external democracy, and of the ongoing negotiation of the boundaries between the two.

Given its identity as a community dedicated to epistemological reconstruction, the ur- discourse of *skholé* is in the regular practice of communal philosophical inquiry. As an interpretive community of ongoing reflection, theory, deliberation, and judgment, the practice of CPI values the question over the statement, and is implicitly dedicated to the communal interrogation and ongoing reconstruction of the concepts that underlie and inform our beliefs and assumptions, actions and reactions in the world (friendship, justice, happiness, beauty, person, self, animal, mind, body, etc.); and as already pointed out, it makes a place, not just for interdisciplinary inquiry, but also for the interrogation of those concepts that underlie disciplinary knowledge—concepts like matter, cause, chance, change, measurement fact, freedom, possibility, truth, power, and so on. These and related concepts form the understructure of our commonly held philosophical anthropology and our philosophy of nature, and their problematization represents the first step in their ongoing reconstruction.

As an ideal speech community, CPI provides *skholé* with a model, not just for epistemological inquiry, but for shared governance as well; the two are related, in that both involve communal deliberation and judgment. Like philosophical discourse, direct democratic practice insists on the metacognitive. It maintains a reflective stance on its own functioning, and is dedicated to continually evaluating itself as a thinking group on rules and principles of formal and informal logic—exemplification, analogy, classification (syllogism), conditionals—in addition to what Cannon and Weinstein (1993) have called "interpersonal" and "philosophical" reasoning: identifying multiple perspectives, constant clarification through restatement and summarization, clarifying basic concepts in their relations with each other, searching for criteria. This collectively self-imposed form of epistemological discipline acts as a pedagogical form when applied in a given academic inquiry—a group discussion, for example, about what we mean when we say something is a "fact," or what can be measured and how, or on the nature of friendship. Even there, extended group inquiry, whatever the topic, tends towards the deontological, or ethical imperative: how should we then live? And that tendency is fully exemplified in *skholé*'s governing process, the clearest most recent example being the "weekly meeting" that is the one consistent feature of all those schools that identify themselves as part of the Democratic Education movement.

In the case of the latter, the regular practice of collaborative self-governance functions as a holding environment for the emergence of a what Hermans calls the "democratically organized self." He characterizes the latter as "a micro-society giving space to the free expression and development of different, opposing, and contradicting I-positions with the possibility of mutual dialogical relationships so that they may learn from each other in the service of their further development" (2018, 354). In the weekly meeting, the boundaries between internal and external democracy are crossed and re-crossed, and—again Hermans—". . . a diversity of communicating people and a diversity of I-positions in the self meet and feed each other via open communication channels" (320). Decisions about matters of rules of conduct and of disciplinary issues, of scheduling, of individual responsibilities within the group, of curriculum, and of forms of activism (community projects) are made by the community as a whole, and the dynamic balances and tensions that exist both within self and within group, when manifested in the procedural context of group deliberation, are given a space that is both safe and challenges transformation.

Skholé creates a space for a culture in the making that is grounded in an awareness of relational ontology, and as such, is dedicated to dialogue in the form of encounter, cooperation, self-regulation, mutual aid, and ongoing adaptive transformation. It has been made possible in the West, I have argued, by a historical shift in child-rearing modes that allows for understanding the adult-child relation as one of interlocution and dialogue, rather than one of monological formation and control. This follows from the recognition of childhood as a neotenic zone that is charged with futurity—with the production of new meanings, and with the potential for the formation of habits that are "more intelligent, percipient, informed with foresight, aware of what they are about, direct, sincere, flexibly responsive . . ." (Dewey 1922, 128). It is also made possible, as is suggested by its historical emergence as an educational form in Periclean Athens, by the perdurance of the democratic impulse, for which the human hunger for autonomy, self-regulation, cooperation, rational authority, and participatory governance is a fundamental evolutionary drive. That drive is implicit in the ongoing historical reconstruction of human subjectivity in the image of polyphony, dialogue and difference that dialogical self theory is concerned to map; and that drive is energized, I would suggest, by the hermeneutical turn to childhood, which acts to realize those paedomorphic characteristics that are our evolutionary heritage.

For Deleuze and Guattari (1987), a "block of childhood" represents an affective and noetic space "without predetermined categories of identity and experience," which is in continual transformation, and involves "unlocking affect in new combinations and flows." So understood, "child" is emblematic of an emergent "post-human" style of subjectivity, more attuned to the play of the world itself, and an exemplification of the "child" of Nietzsche's (1999) "three metamorphoses" or stages/states of human development, whereby "the spirit shall become a camel, and the camel a lion, and the lion at last a child"—the latter understood as a creator of new values—a "a new synthesis of reason and desire"—and as such a central actor in human evolutionary possibilities. It is these possibilities to which *skholé* is dedicated.

In the next chapter, I argue that the primary prerequisite for effective teaching in the environment of *skholé*, which includes the facilitation of communal philosophical inquiry on the three levels mentioned above—that is, the philosophical concepts underlying the curriculum, philosophical dialogue tout court, and collaborative governmental decision-making—is the capacity to listen to children. This capacity is enhanced in the regular practice of dialogue among teachers themselves around the concepts that preoccupy *philosophy of childhood*, which may be described as an ongoing critical and reflective interrogation of one's own and others' beliefs and assumptions about children and childhood, which adults tend to project onto real children. I will argue that the most effective way for teachers to explore these assumptions is in their own community of philosophical inquiry, where we encounter the same underlying concepts in thinking about the phenomenon of childhood—nature, person, good and evil, innocence, etc.—that underlie more general philosophical inquiry. The regular practice of philosophy of childhood in community of inquiry among teachers, together with the regular practice of CPI among children, offers us a grounded, integrated form of ongoing "in house" professional development for schools dedicated to adult-child dialogue and to school as a site for cultural reconstruction.

Chapter Six

Practicing Philosophy of Childhood

Teaching in the (R)evolutionary Mode

In this chapter, I suggest that a primary form of teacher preparation for doing community of philosophical inquiry (CPI) with children should be in the form of teachers doing CPI with each other on an ongoing basis and devoting that inquiry—or at least one major dimension of it—specifically to philosophy of childhood (POC). I will argue that the natural training that teachers receive through doing shared philosophical inquiry into and around the concept "child" prepares them in an exemplary way to become facilitators of CPI among children, because that natural training is presumed to lead to a recognition, deconstruction, and ongoing reconstruction of their implicit, preconscious beliefs about childhood in general and children in particular, which thereby allows them to listen more openly, more carefully, more intelligently to children's reasoning. I argue further that the teacher's self-understanding as a philosopher of childhood involves an openness to the child-adult chiasm that has emancipatory potential, not just for their vocational self-understanding, but also for our understanding of school as a site for adult-child dialogue. The teacher in dialogue with children is also an adult in dialogue with childhood, and hence with the evolutionary possibilities expressed in the Arendtian concept of natality for which the school, as a space of creative possibility for the joint production of new meaning and of value, is a privileged zone, and for which CPI, as a paradigmatic form of communicative action, is a master discourse. Finally, I offer an example, in a brief review of the work of the philosopher-educator Patricia Carini, of another form of applied philosophy of childhood in her Descriptive Review process. This process approaches the assessment and evaluation of children from a reflective, phenomenological perspective, through which what she calls the "disciplined student of childhood" endeavors to become the "seer of children" and, as such, complements and enhances the practice of CPI by means of a structured meditation on the lived worlds of individual children.

What Makes for a Good Facilitator?

What is it that equips and enables a teacher to converse ably with children in a group setting about philosophical themes in such a way that there is (a fair percentage of the time anyway) substantive development of ideas, and new meaning is generated? Is it something that comes naturally to some people and not to others (a genetic form of intelligence); some predilection to dialogue that one's parents' communicative values and style imbue in the first three or four years of life; a hard-won result of constant exposure and practice, or some incalculable mixture of the three? Can it be anything but idle conversation if the facilitator has no academic philosophical preparation, or even autodidactic preparation in philosophy? Can it be learned through talking and listening to adults about philosophical themes? What is it that leads to the formation of a teacher as a competent facilitator of a community of philosophical inquiry among groups of children?

Given that schoolteachers are adults whose vocation entails spending long periods of time in the company of children, which naturally involves spending long periods of time conversing with children, both individually and in groups, it would seem that they would be the kinds of adults most likely to be successful facilitators. However, we generally do not find this to be the case. Rather, those skills and dispositions that make for a good facilitator do not seem to be the necessary result of study or training either in the field of education or in the field of philosophy. I would hypothesize that, whatever the balance of the multiple causes and conditions that make for a good CPI facilitator, there is one particular basic skill that is indispensable, and that is the capacity for and the motivation to listen, whether to children or adults. In the case of children, the capacity to listen is influenced by the fact that many adults carry around with them a set of beliefs and assumptions about children and childhood that they project onto real children, which can dramatically affect how seriously or accurately they listen to them, if at all (the analogy with racism, ethnocentrism, ageism, etc., is obvious). As such, one first and fundamental step, not just in preparing facilitators but also in preparing teachers of children in general, should be in identifying and interrogating those beliefs and assumptions, which make up their own (and others') implicit philosophy of childhood.

Interrogating Our Own Philosophies of Childhood

Interrogating beliefs and assumptions together in a group, in a conscious, reflective, and at least semi-methodical way, is the primary activity of a community of philosophical inquiry. Typically it begins with identifying one or more philosophical concepts in response to some stimulus—whether it be a story, a film, a newspaper article, a poem, a picture, or just a list of questions—and engaging together in a dialogical discussion that seeks to give an account of that concept or concepts—justice, for example, or friendship, or happiness—that satisfies (generates new meaning for) the participants in the discussion. And what we find when we do philosophy of something—whether art or history or science or technology—in this way, is that the conversation tends to gravitate towards certain key concepts that are common to various fields of inquiry. The concept "person," for example, may be relevant, if in different ways, whether we are talking about history, technology, psychology, or literature; the concept "fact" in doing philosophy of history and of both hard and soft sciences; the concept "power" in psychology, history, both soft and hard sciences, and so on.

The field of inquiry that is philosophy of childhood both upholds and is upheld by many of these same key concepts—of nature, human nature, persons, animals, time, innocence, good and evil, sexuality and aggression, growth and transformation, autonomy and heteronomy, normality, authority, identity, and so on—that form a continual subtext or pretext whenever we say "child." For example, "child" very often acts for adults as a proof text for one's beliefs about "human nature," which in turn are connected with beliefs about the nature of persons, which in turn are connected with beliefs about the nature of animals, which in turn are connected with beliefs about nature itself, which in turn are connected with beliefs about growth and development, which in turn are connected with beliefs about intrinsic and extrinsic motivation, which in turn are connected with beliefs about autonomy and heteronomy, which in turn are connected with beliefs about freedom, which in turn are connected with beliefs about good and evil, and so on. One adult, for example, may say with Rousseau:

> He wants to touch everything, handle everything. Do not oppose yourself to this restlessness. It is suggestive to him of a very necessary apprenticeship. It is thus that he learns to feel the hotness, the coldness, the hardness, the softness, the heaviness, the lightness, of bodies, and to judge their size, their shapes, and all their sensible qualities, by looking, feeling, listening, particularly by comparing sight to touch, by estimating with the eye the sensation that they would make on his finger. (Rousseau 1979, 64)

Another might say, with another eighteenth-century child-rearing "expert,"

> One of the traits in children that border on abnormality is exuberance, which can take many forms but usually begins with exceptionally agitated activity of the voluntary muscles, followed to a greater or lesser degree by other manifestations, should an aroused desire not be immediately satisfied. Children who are just beginning to learn to talk and whose dexterity is still limited to reaching for nearby objects need only be unable to grasp an object or not be allowed to keep it; if they have an excitable disposition, they will then start to scream and make unrestrained movements. Malice develops quite naturally in this child . . . (quoted in Miller 1990, 29–30)

Both of these observers trust the evidence of their senses, which each interprets differently based on a set of core beliefs about human nature, good and evil, selfhood and human will, the nature of learning, the nature of habit, and so on. The very perceptions of the children before them and the evaluation of their behavior are informed by these beliefs.

I would suggest that a primary ongoing task to be undertaken by schoolteachers whether they have aspirations to facilitate specifically philosophical conversations or not, is philosophical self-examination of a particular sort—specifically the practice of philosophy of childhood (POC), in a community of inquiry setting. In addition to making teachers more aware of their own beliefs and assumptions about childhood, doing

POC as an applied practice in a CPI format acts to prepare teachers to be CPI facilitators tout court, in that POC as a conceptual zone opens out, as we have seen, onto the major philosophical concepts in our tradition. In this hands-on, learning-by-doing form of facilitator preparation, we teachers enter philosophy from the ground up; we become aware of the major concepts in our tradition—self, knowledge, the other, beauty, justice—as philosophical elements of our lifeworld, before we have even heard of Plato, Aristotle, et al. And if, in order to deepen and enliven our familiarity with these concepts, we turn to the written works of philosophers, we do so with some level of prior thematic and even conceptual background knowledge that acts as a scaffold.

POC-CPI is then one dimension of applied philosophy of childhood practiced as a form of professional development among schoolteachers, whether we plan to facilitate straight CPI with children or not. We might kick off a weekly series of POC-CPI sessions among our fellow teachers, for example, by posing the question, "What is childhood 'innocence'?" which is likely to lead us to a consideration of the concept of innocence and its different connotations, its relationship to experience, whether it is even thinkable without other concepts like guilt, and so on. In other words, the concept is broached through its application to and reflection on children and childhood, but its interrogation leads beyond the child to the concept in its broader senses and uses and its relations with other concepts—then, in a circle of interpretation, reflects back on the way we see the real children with whom we are in relation as we facilitate philosophy discussions with/among them.

For teachers, this kind of communal critical inquiry challenges stereotypes and habitual interpretive misunderstandings of children's motives and understandings. Once the concept of innocence, for example, is problematized and deconstructed through the dialectical play of intragroup argumentation, we tend to apply the concept to real people and situations in more nuanced, more complex, more ambiguous ways. The concept loses the one-size-fits-all quality that leads to the sort of profiling that unexamined assumptions and beliefs tend to produce. So, when we sit among children, we do less polarizing and automatic classifying of children's responses. We are better able to listen, and to help them clarify their own thinking through our efforts to understand that thinking. We become more adept at "translating" in the sense of restating a person's idea in such a way that it makes it clearer, both to themselves and to others. And we are better able to do this because we start to hear all conversation—any conversation—with a more philosophical ear. Having talked and listened critically and searchingly and with care to our peers about the concepts for which childhood is a sort of magic lens—innocence, human nature, autonomy, authority, growth, development, and so on—we start listening for and "outing" assumptions, noting the logical order and articulation of premises and conclusions in a given argument, or judging the rightness of an analogy or a part-whole relationship. Our goal then becomes not to teach this heightened critical capacity to children so much as to notice children exercising it when they do, calling attention to it and encouraging it. Indeed, we might just notice that some children are doing it better than we are—that their ear is already more philosophical.

As philosophers of childhood, we see children better, but we recognize that we are also seeing adults, to the extent that children are often saying things that an adult would say, and they are doing so quite consciously and without mimicking. On the other hand, the difference between us becomes more poignant because the concept "child," after this work, is no longer monological and unitary: we start to see individuals before we see children. This does not mean, however, that we treat children like adults, even though we may accord to this or that individual child every right and privilege that we would to an adult. The difference between us remains, and it is in this insistent fold of difference between child and adult that we start to listen and to hear seriously—not as a confirmation of our adultist psychological, developmental, pathological, pedagogical, and so on theories of about children and childhood, but for something new, some fresh way of seeing the world, of understanding self and relationship, of understanding nature, or freedom, or justice. Once we awaken to their voices, children become our genuine interlocutors, and we expect new meaning to develop between ourselves and them as much as we expect it when we talk seriously with adults.

In brief summary, I have tried to make the case that a primary form of teacher preparation for doing philosophy with children should be in the form of doing community of philosophical inquiry among themselves on an ongoing basis and devoting it—or the first phase of it—specifically to applied philosophy of childhood. I have further argued that the natural training that teachers receive through doing POC-CPI prepares them to become facilitators of CPI among children. For example, when issues of personhood are raised in a discussion of friendship among fifth graders, teachers have probably already discussed both these concepts in their weekly faculty-CPI-POC, and so already have some familiarity with different ways the concept may be approached, and their philosophical ear better recognizes the cadences offered by students.

The Descriptive Review of the Child: Philosophy of Childhood in Everyday Practice

For the second and last part of this chapter, I introduce another teacher practice/exercise that I consider to be a form of applied philosophy of childhood which, in combination with the practice of POC-CPI, offers us a grounded, integrated methodology for schools. This practice might be categorized on first glance as an instance of typical adult behaviors in an institution in which the child becomes an object of scrutiny and even an inherently problematic element in a smooth-running school—one that must be observed and monitored, indoctrinated, managed, rewarded or punished, tested, medicated, and so on. But in fact when we look more closely at the child observation protocol that the American educator-philosopher Patricia Carini developed in the 1960s as the Descriptive Review of the Child—for which see Himley and Carini 2000; Carini 2001; Carini and Himley 2010; and Himley 2011—we see the double power of its practice: while it is structured as a specific practice designed to yield thick, phenomenological description of individual children, it is in fact a form of self-observation and self-questioning by adults, an earnest interrogation of one's own perceptions of the children with whom one is in relationship in the classroom or the home, and an exercise in seeing. As such it is complementary to the conceptual work that POC in community of philosophical inquiry represents.

Carini cofounded the Prospect School in Vermont, USA in 1965, where she developed the Descriptive Review process, a simple but profoundly innovative dialogical protocol based on phenomenological observation and description of children in classroom and home settings. Her method has been introduced in a variety of both public and private schools throughout the US and is supported through a national network of yearly conferences and workshops. Her teaching and writing represent a philosophy of childhood fully incarnated in practice, based on, as she says, the "definition of the person as active maker of works, the dialogic inter-animation of person and world, and the world itself as plural, ambiguous, and always larger than the systematized readings of it" (Carini 2001,

10). The aim of the Descriptive Review process is to recognize and work to understand a particular child's strength and style as a person, learner, and thinker, using her art, writing, and other artifacts as "texts," in a language that eschews the toxic vocabulary of ranking, labeling, and deficit diagnosis that pervades contemporary educational discourse. Her practice offers teachers, not just another emergent language, but a concrete method based on dialogue and collaborative deliberation as well, which opens a clear and vivid space in schools for teacher community of inquiry focused on the review process, a space in which adult assumptions about children are exposed and transformed in the process of looking closely, carefully, and caringly at real children. This process identifies the teacher as what Carini calls a "seer of children," and thereby a "teacher in the revolutionary mode." What follows is a very short overview of the Descriptive Review process, which is in fact an adult community of pedagogical inquiry centered on a particular child, as well as, by implication a practical case study of applied POC-CPI.

Although not a necessity, the Descriptive Review of the Child protocol is congruent with what used to be called an "open" classroom setting, by which is implied an "emergent curriculum"—one that is the product of adult and child in dialogue, and in which the "basics"—reading, writing, and math—are taught through projects that are of interest to students. Teachers who practice emergent curriculum play, in Elizabeth Jones and Gretchen Reynolds's (1992) classic formulation of a play-based curriculum, seven roles: "stage manager" (preparing an interactive environment), "scribe" (transcribing, recording and collecting students' artifacts), "planner" (of projects and activities), "mediator" (between students, and between students' interests and curriculum), "interrupter" (introducing new concepts in media res), "assessor" (as part of planning), and "communicator" (with parents and other adults).

On the Descriptive Review model, teachers as scribes and assessors keep daily track of children's choices, and finish each day or week by writing "four or five sentences for each child describing what the child did that week, with whom, and any other observations the teacher may have made" (Himley and Carini 2000, 10). Teachers also collect children's work—writing, drawing, constructions, and so on, At least once a year, one meeting, including a small group of teachers involved in the student's school life, is devoted to each child, which would represent roughly one meeting per week. The student's classroom teacher prepares a narrative reflection in which she or he describes the child, using ordinary language and illustrated by samples she has collected of the child's work—whether artwork, poetry, papers, letters, or some other collection of representative artifacts. This narration is preceded by the teacher posing a question, typically a question to herself—again, put as simply and directly as possible. It might be a question, for example, like, "How is it . . . that this child seems always to slip by me. How can a get a clearer picture of where she is making her presence felt in the group?" (Himley and Carini 2000, 13). The question leads to a reflection on the key words in the question—in this case "visible/invisible" and "presence" are rendered down to "slips," and the facilitator/chair of the meeting "invites everyone in the review circle to write down words, images, and phrases that these words—slip or slips—call to mind" (Himley and Carini 2000, 13).

Then the teacher presents her narrative, dividing her description into five categories of observation: (1) physical presence and gesture; (2) disposition and temperament; (3) connections with others (both children and adults); (4) strong interests and preferences; (5) modes of thinking and learning. All of these descriptions are set in a descriptive, anecdotal context, completely free of theoretical or clinical jargon, and of educational or psychological classificatory grouping. When she is finished, the chair summarizes and offers the opportunity for others in the circle to offer insights into what they have heard. This same process is sometimes also used through an exclusive focus on one drawing or painting, letter or other artifact.

The deep goal of this process is not to come up with new ideas for teaching the child in the classroom, or to rank the child in some sort of hierarchy of skills, intelligence, or achievement, or to place the child in this group or that, but to understand the child as, in Deleuze and Guattari's (1987) compelling formulation, a "desiring machine," a dynamic set of affects and intensities in a process of becoming, an energy-picture, a singularity. It is to feel the child as Carini says, as person under the sign of what she calls "ideas key at Prospect," which she lists as follows: "The importance of the child's or any person's uniqueness, complexity, and integrity. The role of description in representing these. The attentiveness to the manner in which, for any person, dynamic polarities, seemingly contradictory, enact that person's expressiveness and complexity. The assumption of human capacity, widely distributed, as the taproot value nurturing all these ideas" (Himley and Carini 2000, 4).

School, the Child-Adult Chiasm, and Becoming-Child

I would suggest that the accomplished facilitator of philosophical dialogue among children is by definition also what Carini calls "a disciplined student of childhood" (Himley and Carini 2000, 16)—one who observes and listens with as much concentration and internal stillness as she can muster for what has not been heard before. And from the other side, philosophical dialogue with children finds a completely natural home in Carini's methodology, because the latter implicitly enables and encourages children both to voice (or write, or paint, or dance) their own emergent philosophies and to enter into dialogue with adult philosophies, thus activating the transformative dimension of the adult-child relationship. This is the dimension within which the particular balance of identity and difference that is the adult-child chiasm—both within each person and between persons—creates a transformative space, a space of creative possibility for the joint production of new meaning and of value. It is this dimension that the practicing philosopher of childhood is always in search of in her or his day-to-day life with children.

The teacher's vocational identity as a philosopher of childhood is of great importance to the possibilities that schooling offers for cultural evolution in any given society, because of its power either to attempt to domesticate the next generation or to encourage its emancipatory tendencies. School is the space where two generations meet, in a place specifically designed for that meeting. In a school in which that meeting happens consciously and mindfully, and where dialogue is the normative discourse, "child" and "adult" are folded into each other in the mutuality of lived experience, in a chiasm where there is difference, but one doesn't know exactly where it begins and where it leaves off.

Following John Dewey's (1916, 1938) broad formulation, educative experience is above all an experience of "growth," which is the result of a form of experience that makes further, equally or more significant experience possible. In an ideal school, both child and adult are undergoing educative experience—are growing. The school is the experimental and experiential zone of that chiasmic growth, where the adult models for the child a form of adulthood that is deeply influenced by living and talking with children. This is what Deleuze and Guattari (1987) refer to as "becoming child," and what Dewey (1922) identifies as a form of ongoing individuation that retains a childlike flexibility of schemes and habit structures. Even children, Deleuze and Guattari argued, need to be "becoming child," to retain or develop or stay in touch with the virtual dimension of self—that dimension in which self is always forming and never quite realized, and which, when it is foreclosed in adulthood for cultural or personal reasons or both, betrays our human possibility. As such, school is a social-emotional laboratory in which the interaction of children and adults encourages new forms of subjectivity.

In imagining the normative ideal of school as a territory of cultural evolutionary advance, in which the adult-child chiasm produces new meanings and even new sensibilities—an experimental zone governed at its base by the principle of adult child dialogue—I have identified three specific practices that I associate with a practice of applied philosophy of childhood: (1) POC-CPI, where teachers engage in group dialogue in which they explore and interrogate their own beliefs and assumptions about the nature of childhood, the nature of the adult-child relation, and the process of childhood learning and development; (2) the Descriptive Review process, in which adults work, through what Carini calls the "discipline of description," to "make the child more visible as a full and complex person through the language the teachers develop in their efforts to do justice to that complexity" (Himley and Carini 2000, 21); and finally, (3) CPI with children, where children identify, explore, and work to reconstruct, in ordinary language, the concepts that we typically call "philosophical"—that is, concepts that touch on epistemological, ontological, axiological, logical, and metaphysical problems.

Perhaps neither Matthew Lipman nor Ann Sharp, founders of Philosophy for Children and early promoters of the pedagogy of community of inquiry, quite grasped—at least on an operational level—the broader (r)evolutionary implications of the post-colonial emancipatory discursive movement they were part of, which shares genealogical roots with the cultural revolution of the 1960s, driven as it is psychologically by the search for a new sensibility, politically by a global impulse toward authentic democracy, and educationally by a search for a truly dialogical pedagogy. Part of the energy of this movement is towards a reconstruction of philosophy, which, we might argue, is central to the emergence of a new global emancipatory discourse. This reconstructive impulse is fed by both the introduction of genuine communal dialogue into philosophical practice—which is a fulfillment of the Socratic promise—and by a new attention to children and their philosophies, which represents a challenge to philosophical practice as a white adult male domain governed by a narrow view of human reason. As Merleau-Ponty (1964a) pointed out, the construction of reason itself is under interrogation in the post-modern West, and it is this common evolutionary project to which children have finally been called to participate. It is those who spend the most time with the most children—classroom teachers—who are best positioned to develop the capacity to see beyond the multiple ideological and theoretical constructs of childhood and its capacities that block our view, to become "disciplined students of childhood," and to act maieutically in the service of philosophical reconstruction.

In the next chapter, I switch the narrative discourse, and offer a selection from a philosophical novel for children written specifically for use in a CPI context. This pedagogical genre was in fact Matthew Lipman's first innovation, followed by the formulation of a communal dialogical setting in which to explore the concepts that are embedded in the text and voiced by the novel's protagonists. Embodied as these concepts are in a narrative of the lived experience of its characters, the philosophical novel acts as a receptacle, a field of meaning in which they beckon, openly, inchoately, or otherwise, for the reader's attention, and as they enter the space of dialogue, even call forth new concepts in the process of de- and reconstruction, and evoke new possibilities of experience and understanding.

Chapter Seven

Intermezzo One

My Name Is Myshkin

The Philosophical Novel for Children

The genealogy of the philosophical novel for children is difficult to trace, and that difficulty begins with the character of the genre itself. Novels are, after all, written for children in the sense that we tend to approach reading one like a child ready for a bedtime story; to enter it is to enter an imaginary world, however literal and realistic its plot and tone. We might also claim that the genre is inherently philosophical, in the sense that it presents an "as if" narrative, a transitional universe in which we play with possible worlds, implicitly entertaining hypotheses, analogies, conditionals, and counterfactuals, and in which fundamental philosophical questions—what is real, what is possible, what is good, what is human—undergo implicit interrogation through the unfolding of both plot and character.

Nor is it easy to decide what makes a novel more or less philosophical. To name just a handful, are *The Man without Qualities* or *The Brothers Karamazov* more philosophical than *The Stranger* or *Lord of the Flies*? And in the realm of novels written explicitly for children, what common denominator can we find in *Alice in Wonderland*, *Sophie's World*, the Harry Potter series, and *The Phantom Tollbooth*? However, starting in the 1970s this situation of healthy indeterminacy took a new course with the introduction by Matthew Lipman, creator of the Philosophy for Children curriculum, a series of novels written explicitly for young readers, whose express goal was to find a new, dynamic balance between, as Darryl DeMarzio (2011) has put it, fictional narrative and philosophical exposition, rationality and creativity, and to translate into ordinary language—comprehensible to elementary school readers—central themes from the history of philosophy. Lipman's intention was not to deposit the wisdom of the philosophers into young minds, but to create texts that act as stimuli to their own inquiry, and that trigger the questions and puzzles that lead to doing philosophy—to "philosophizing"—in this case in a communal setting. Hence the second pillar of Lipman's curriculum: community of philosophical inquiry (CPI), a post-Socratic pedagogy that combines elements of active listening and formal and informal argumentation, in which participants learn through participating in the inquiry circle to interrogate together concepts like justice, friendship, intelligence, truth, animal, human, identity, time, rules, mind and body, knowledge and belief, freedom, obligation, and so on.

Lipman held that, in this process of focused, reflective inquiry grounded in children's life worlds, the skills and dispositions of critical thinking were acquired through mutual modeling and internalization—metacognitive habits such as offering definitions, working with criteria, classifying, making distinctions, identifying contradictions, identifying hidden assumptions, exemplifying, reasoning hypothetically, reasoning inductively and deductively, seeking consistency, grasping part-whole relationships, identifying alternatives, and so on. Above all, the result was a heightened sensitivity to the philosophical questions that lie just below the surface of everyday life, and a deeper sense of existential wonder.

Lipman's initiative resulted in seven novels, each roughly geared for a different readership ranging from seven to fifteen years old, and designed to be read aloud in short segments in the classroom, with the understanding that the reading is followed by students posing their own questions in reaction to the text, choosing one of them to start with, and entering into an extended dialogue. Lipman and his colleges also created lengthy "manuals" or guides for each novel, replete with philosophical exercises and discussion plans organized according to the philosophical topics or "leading ideas" discussed or reflected on throughout the text. As a writer of philosophical fiction, his rule of thumb is best expressed in his admonition to avoid both "all story and no philosophy" and "all philosophy and no story." "Some," he quipped, "bury the philosophy so deeply into the narrative that it would take a Derrida to ferret it out, while others sprinkle it on the surface so that it could hardly be missed by a first grader with reading disabilities" (Lipman 2002, 12). And indeed, to strike this balance remains the self-imposed imperative of several generations of CPI practitioners and theorizers, of which there is a large, international contingent; over the past thirty-five years, Philosophy for Children has come to be practiced in schools, community centers, prisons, and other venues in approximately sixty countries, and a number of practitioners have written and published philosophical novels in the Lipmanian vein.

As DeMarzio (2011) suggests, this movement to democratize philosophy through the use of a text that blends narrative and expository elements returns it to its ancient roots as "care of the self," and represents a "project for the future." He writes,

> . . . this notion of the text as model [of philosophizing] . . . connects to a lost tradition of philosophy in which the role of the text was recognized as performing a transformative function. This tradition, covered over for many centuries, but which has now been rekindled over the last half-century through some important work in the history of ideas, understands the philosophical text as reflecting—in the terms of Michel Foucault and Pierre Hadot respectively—a "technology of the self" and "spiritual exercise," in which the reader assimilates the text's manner of thinking so as to transform their own. (33)

My Name Is Myshkin

The philosophical novel for children sampled here (Kennedy 2012a) begins on the far side of the critique most often leveled at Lipman's fictional oeuvre—that his novels lack a literary quality and demonstrate a certain cultural localism that tends to date them, to no good effect. In response to this critique, *My Name Is Myshkin* features a fantasy adventure plot line that interplays with its philosophical material, which emerges in dialogue between the characters: whether one "is" or is not one's body; how we can tell what is real, animals, and humans; what is alive; the origins of evil; whether there is a true "objective" account of anything; whether one can fully know or be known by another person; the suffering and injustice in the world and one's responsibility for it; and broader themes in philosophy of science, mythology, religion, and eco-philosophy.

The story takes place in some near future time, when the full effects of global warming are beginning to be felt in an interminable summer heat wave and drought, in a small city in the foothills of a mountainous region. Myshkin, the narrator of the story, engages in numerous conversations with three school friends, who during their summer vacation frequently visit a wooded park in the city. The park features a large fountain, built by the wife of a wealthy Italian industrialist thirty years before, which is distinguished by seven larger-than-life bronze statues of ancient Greek nymphs, half-mortal goddesses of nature who were thought to coexist with rivers, springs, mountains, or any type of natural life-form, and whose death or removal elsewhere was caused by the destruction of those life-forms.

Nixie is Myshkin's next-door neighbor and best friend, and Myshkin's dog Dolphius is his constant companion, and plays an important part in the narrative. When Myshkin and Nixie fall asleep on the bus one day on their way back from the swimming pool and wake up in the city bus yard, they find themselves thrust into an adventure that leads them deep into the woods, where they discover a villa inhabited by the same woman—now a widow and a hermit—who had hired an Italian architect to build the fountain many years ago. Mrs. Epistemi undertook this project to honor the blue-haired Mediterranean sea nymphs called Naiads that she once consorted with as a girl growing up on an island off the coast of Sicily. Myshkin and Nixie eventually glimpse the wood nymphs who inhabit the forest where Mrs. Epistemi lives alone, in a caretaker's hut behind the still-furnished but empty villa, and discover a cave of the nymphs nearby. The story intersperses their three momentous visits into the deep woods with numerous conversations—with each other, their friends, the old woman, their classroom teacher, and their parents—and their actual encounter with the nymphs themselves, who are soon to disappear as the forest is progressively decimated by real estate developers. An excerpt from the novel follows.

Some Silly Questions

My name is Myshkin. My father said he and my mother named me after a prince in a famous book. I asked him how they could name me after someone who wasn't even real, whom he didn't even know. He said he felt like he knew this Prince Myshkin better than he knows lots of real people. Then he asked me what I meant by "real," and what I meant by "know." I didn't answer, because I wasn't sure. My father is always asking me questions like that.

My father said that this Prince Myshkin from the story—he showed me the book—it's very fat, and I couldn't read it at all, even though I'm actually a pretty good reader—was a gentle man, "too gentle," he said. I don't know if I'm gentle. Sometimes I get very mad. Sometimes I feel wild, like I'm going crazy with energy, and have to break something, or bite someone or wrestle with someone, or kick something, or bounce bounce bounce a ball, or roll around in the grass, or stuff like that. Dolphius likes to do that too. He's the best at that. He's kind of like my teacher—because he's a dog I guess, and dogs are really good at that, if you're friends with them.

I'll tell you more about Dolphius later, because he's a big part of this story, but for right now I'll just tell you that he's part Irish Setter and part Chocolate Lab with a beautiful curly dark red-brown coat, and that he came to live with me when he was a tiny puppy, just three weeks old, and I was only seven, and I took care of him all by myself. I house-trained him, and taught him to heel and to sit (except that he never did those things very well, I guess because he never really wanted to), and to come when I blow on one of those silent dog whistles that I have. Actually, he was my best friend. Or maybe I was like his father, or his older brother. Then, when he grew up—it took him just two years!—sometimes he was like my older brother. Dolphius is gone now—no, I mean he's still alive (I think), but he's not with me (he's with the Beautiful Old Woman), and I'm sad but I'm not sad about it. I'll tell you about all that later.

Some people tell me I don't talk very much. I don't know if that's true or not, because I'm always talking in my head. If it is true that I don't talk very much, I don't know why—I guess I just don't see any reason for it. I guess I like more just watching and listening and feeling things and people and places. And I don't like it when adults ask me questions and try to get me to talk, like I was some kind of different creature from them, or like an animal they were training or something. But I do like it when people—I don't care if they are kids or grownup—are really talking, I mean really trying to make sense, and to hear and to be heard. I like that a lot.

And sometimes, like I said, I get crazy, and sometimes I even get mean, and sometimes I get angry when grownups stop me from doing something, or other kids mess up what I'm doing. And other times I feel so peaceful, like the sun shining on a beautiful day, and there's really no reason for it at all. My Mom notices it, and she always looks at me and says, with that nice smile of hers and her eyebrows raised a little, "The simple joy of existence?" I don't know exactly what that means, but it sounds nice.

In other words, sometimes I don't even know who I am! But I don't know who it could be who doesn't know who he is, because who else could it be but me? That's one problem. The other is, if I know who I am, then it seems like I'm two people—the one who is and the one who knows he is. It's kind of like those dreams where you're watching yourself do something as if it were another person you're watching. Or like when you feel a hand touching your hand and then you realize that it's your own hand touching the other one.

If I can watch myself, then who is watching? Am I just one person or many? How could just one being have so many ways of being? Am I me when I'm happiest? I think that's what people think—that they are most themselves when they are happiest—but is it really true? Is it important to know who I am? Does it make any difference? Am I anything? Aren't I just someone who wants to be something? Aren't I just whatever is happening right now, at this very moment?

Nixie thinks those are silly questions. "Why can't you be the same person with a lot of different ways of acting and feeling and thinking, and even being?" she says. "You're just making up rules about what can't be and what can be, but that doesn't stop it from being what it is. Why can't I be as many people as I want to be and still be me?"

"As you want to be?" I repeated.

"Well, or as I am," she answered.

Nixie lives in the house next door to us with her mother, and she's my best friend. She's a different kind of best friend from Dolphius. Sometimes I want so badly to be just like her—even to be her—but I don't think I ever could. I'm not sure why. Is it because she's a girl and I'm a boy? Or is it something else? Actually I've known her almost all my life. It's funny, I know she looks different from how she looked when we were five, and me too, but I don't see any difference.

Once we looked at both of our families' pictures together, and we could see how different we looked when we were babies and then two, then three, and right on up to now—I'm ten and she's eleven—but it was like looking at someone else. It makes me wonder whether I have anything to do with this body that seems to be part of me—that seems to be me. And what if I had a body like Dolphius? Or the body of a girl? Or of an old man, or an old woman? Or somebody in a wheelchair who could hardly talk or move? Sometimes I feel so much like myself that it seems like I could be in any kind of body—even a tree or something, even a rock, or a worm, or bird or even a chair—and still be me. That's crazy, I know, but maybe it won't seem so crazy after I tell you about what happened to me and Nixie and Dolphius, when we met the Beautiful Old Woman (that's not her name, but it's what I call her).

Nixie is Bulgarian. Before I knew her, I didn't even know there was such a thing as Bulgaria. She has very very dark hair and dark eyes and darker skin than me—mine is kind of sandy looking. I guess nobody would ever take us for brother and sister. Sometimes she looks like she's dreaming. Then her mouth kind of turns down on one side, and her eyes go sort of blank and shiny, and she stares straight ahead, or looks around really slowly, and even if she's looking right at me, it's as if she's imagining me rather than seeing me. When I ask her what she's thinking, she usually says "nothing." I don't see how that's possible. Or sometimes she says "I'm just seeing everything." It's almost as if she's in a secret place, but she's right there in front of me.

Actually, we do have a real secret place, but I'm not ready to tell you about that, because when I do it won't be secret anymore. Or maybe it will, but just more people will know about it. But then how many people would have to know about it before it wasn't a secret? Could everybody know about something and it still be a secret? I know, I sound just like my father!

Is there anything that's not real?

I told my other friends about what my father said about "real"—about how this Prince Myshkin was just as real as you or me, and even more real for him than some people are. Tracey said—quickly, the way he always does—"Then everything is real!" We were in the park near Nixie's house, walking kind of slowly towards the huge fountain in the middle. It was summer. It was very hot—the hottest summer ever recorded, they said. Dolphius was with us too. He was running up ahead of us and to either side, sniffing things. When he would pass another dog he would move aside, and put his head in the air that way he does, kind of looking sideways at the other dog, keeping an eye on it.

But then Nixie said, slowly, "But then why is there even a word 'real'? It has to have a contrary, doesn't it? If we can say 'real,' there must be something that's not real."

I leaned over and picked up a small, smooth stone from the ground. It was flat, dark grey, and oval-shaped, and had a white ring around the middle. I still have that stone, sitting on my dresser. "What about a stone?" I said. "This is real. Does it have a contrary?"

"A not-stone!" said Tracey.

We all stood there for a minute, thinking I guess. Then Nixie said, "How about the sky?"

"Why the sky?"

"Because a stone is all thick and tight and the sky is all open," she said.

"But those are ideas about stones and sky, not real stones and sky," Beth said. Beth is Nixie's friend, and mine too I guess. Except sometimes she's jealous. Or maybe I am. I'm not sure which.

"A stone is just an idea anyway," Tracey said. "How could it be anything else?"

"What do you mean an idea?" I held out the stone in my hand. "Do you call this an idea?"

"O.K.!" said Beth. She always says "O.K." like that when she gets excited. "Close your eyes and think of a stone." We all closed our eyes (actually I don't know that we all closed our eyes for sure, because my eyes were closed, so how could I know?) and I thought of a stone. It was a huge boulder, on a mountainside, like one I'd seen in a picture once.

"Now open them." I opened my eyes. "Now. . . ." Beth stopped talking for a minute, like she was confused, or thinking, or something. "Now . . . how is . . . how is this stone"—she reached out her hand toward me and I put the stone in her open palm—"anything at all like the stone you thought about? I mean, you just had the idea of a stone, and here is a stone in my hand. Are you going to tell me that this stone in my hand is just an idea, like the one you were thinking of?" Just then, Dolphius came crashing out of the woods next to the path and trotted up to us, sniffing each of us in that polite friendly way of his, and looking up into my eyes. Then he turned and disappeared again.

"But I thought of a real stone," I said. "I saw it in a picture. A huge stone. A boulder."

"How do you know the picture isn't a fake?" Tracey said. "Or that the boulder is still there? Maybe somebody came and blew it up."

"O.K. O.K.!" said Beth, more excited than ever. "What if the boulder really is there and let's pretend we're standing right next to it now. Our eyes are closed and we're picturing it in our minds. How . . . How . . ." Then she seemed to lose her idea.

"The idea is a copy of the real stone," suggested Nixie. "Like a photograph or a painting or something. It comes from remembering seeing the real stone. It's some kind of memory."

"But I can think of a stone—just any old stone of any kind, big or little, whatever color or shape, sitting somewhere or flying or talking or glowing or appearing or disappearing or anything—without thinking of a real one. I mean I can just make one up in my mind," said Tracey.

"Yeah!" Beth said. "I agree. And when I think of the stone, even if it's a real one, I don't see anything like a picture or a photograph. I don't see anything, now that I really think about it. I think it. My mind is kind of all over it, but my mind is not a camera."

I remembered my father's question. "So, what do we mean by 'real'?" I said.

"It's simple," Tracey said. "If you can touch it it's real. Everything else is a copy, like Nixie said. Everything else could turn out not to be real. Like you might be having a hallucination."

"What about my grandmother who died?" I said. I can't touch her anymore. Is she real?"

"She was real. Now she's not."

"What about yesterday, when I went to the supermarket with my mother?"

"Nope, it's not real anymore. Now it's just a copy. You might just even be imagining that it happened. Maybe in a parallel universe it wouldn't be happening, or it would happen differently."

"What about Prince Myshkin and my father?"

"Nope, your father is wrong. The prince isn't real, no way."

"What about Dolphius? We can't see him or touch him right now. Is he real?"

"Nope, not real right now. All that's real is right now, right here, that I can touch or that I can feel touching me, like the sun. Everything else is not-real."

"That's dumb!" Beth said.

"Well, I don't know," Nixie said. "Maybe he's right. 'Cause otherwise everything would have to be real—thoughts, and feelings and dreams and memories and everything—and there wouldn't be anything that's not-real, so what would real mean?"

Then there was a silence. I think none of us knew what we thought anymore—except maybe Tracey, who was smiling in that way of his, like he always knew what he thought, and was pretty happy with it. Just then Dolphius came crashing out of the woods again, panting and kind of grinning. For some reason, we all laughed, then kept walking towards the big fountain.

Can Someone Know You Better Than You Know Yourself?

Beth is my friend because Nixie is both our friends. Sometimes I wonder if Beth would be my friend if it weren't for Nixie. One time a few weeks ago the three of us were supposed to meet at the park, and Beth and I were on time but Nixie was late. She was at the grocery store with her mom, and they took longer than they expected to.

First we were just kind of shy, like we hardly knew each other, even though we'd been together with Nixie lots of times. All we could seem to talk about was when Nixie was going to show up, and then, as it got later, whether she would show up at all. Then, when it started really getting later, I guess Beth decided that she really needed to try to talk, and she started asking me questions about my family, and vacations and hobbies, and things like that. I felt like a stranger she'd just met. When Dolphius would come back to check on us from his running around in the woods she would fall all over him like a mother with her baby or something. And when Nixie finally showed up, Beth started talking to her a mile a minute and didn't even look at me. Nixie looked a little confused, like she wasn't sure what was going on.

As we got closer to the big fountain, I saw the park police in their white car and their uniforms. They looked like lego-men. We could already hear the water roaring and splashing. I took out the silent dog-whistle that I have for Dolphius—it's set to a certain frequency that only dogs can hear—and blew on it. It's a really good whistle. My father ordered it for me from Germany. You can blow on it really hard and all that people can hear is a soft little high squeak, but Dolphius hears it like a huge blast—well I guess he does, but how would I really know? Because Dolphius always comes, I guess. My father showed me how to always blow it the same way and for the same length of time.

"That's so weird when you do that," Beth said. I didn't say anything back.

Dolphius came very quickly, because he always stays pretty much close by, and I put him on the leash. He understands when I have to do it, he never tries to pull away or anything. When we got to the fountain, I sat down on one of the benches that were in a huge circle around it, on the outside rim of a very wide stone pavilion that could fit lots and lots of people. Beth and Nixie kept walking around the stone rim of the fountain. Dolphius sat next to the bench, with his tongue hanging out of the side of his mouth in the heat, watching the water surging and leaping and splashing in all kinds of different ways. The sound of it was huge and beautiful.

Everybody loves the fountain—especially dogs (well, most dogs). It's called the Epistemi Fountain because it was built fifty years ago by a rich businessman named Epistemi. Actually, it was his wife who did it, with his money. She's from Italy. I have a lot to tell about her—in fact she's probably the most important person in this story. Anyway, the fountain is huge and round, and it has seven bigger-than-real-size bronze statues of nymphs that the water spurts and splashes through and over and around in different ways. I did a project on the fountain last year for school, so I know a lot about it.

In my school project, I discovered that nymphs are spirits—except they have real bodies, so I don't know if you should call them spirits—of lakes and rivers and trees and oceans and meadows and mountains and springs and fountains and marshes. They're like nature goddesses, except they're not goddesses, because they're not immortal. Nymphs lived for a long time but they didn't live forever. Some wood nymphs would die if you cut down the tree they were the spirit of. The Nereids were sea nymphs. They had blue hair, but you can't see that on the statues. They helped sailors in storms. My favorites are the Naiads, nymphs of fresh waters and forests. Nixie and I actually saw some nymphs—but I'll tell you about that later too. One problem about them is that you can't tell whether a nature spirit like a nymph is in the thing—a lake or a tree or a mountain or whatever—or whether she is the thing. It can get a bit confusing.

Of course Dolphius loves the fountain, and if I don't keep him on a leash when we're next to it and if it's really hot like it has been all this summer, he just goes and jumps in, and splashes and swims around with this crazy grin on his face. Then the park police come and yell at me and tell me to get him out of there. It's really strange how some adults yell at kids they don't even know, like they never would with an adult, or if you were with another adult. They treat you like you don't know anything, or like you're this stupid person who's trying to get away with something. They seem to feel like they have to give you a lecture, or warn you about something, and of course they make you tell them who your parents are, where you live, where you go to school, and blah blah blah. Sometimes you wonder if they think kids are even persons. Sometimes I try to imagine them as kids themselves, and it seems that if they were kids, they would just be bullies. On the other hand, I can think of a lot of adults who are really nice, too. And some grownups are really beautiful and powerful—so beautiful and powerful it's kind of scary. Mrs. Epistemi is like that. Actually, she is the Beautiful Old Woman I mentioned before. Anyway, I keep Dolphius on a leash when we're near the fountain now.

There was a little breeze, and I could feel some very fine spray from the crashing fountain water every once and a while. Beth and Nixie walked around it lots of times, close to the edge, even closer to the spray, which was making rainbows in the sunshine. It seemed like Beth was doing most of the talking. Each time they passed Nixie looked over at me and smiled and waved, the way she does. Nixie is a very kind person.

The fountain makes my body happy. When I watch it and listen to it, it's like the water is shooting and bubbling up inside me the way it is in the statues. Sometimes I think my body is who I am. Nothing else. That's enough. Because if my body is happy, I'm happy. And if I'm happy, my body is happy. But when I said this to Nixie and Beth one time, Nixie said, "But your body doesn't matter in the end. It's what you do. What you do and say to people. Because your body will die, but what you do or say to people won't. It will go on and on."

"But it's the body that feels good or not," I said. "It's the body that's sad or happy, or free or in prison, like a dog who can go wherever he wants or a dog who's on a chain all the time, and gets desperate and crazy."

"I have no idea what you're talking about," said Beth.

Beth never understands me. Is it because she's smarter than me, or not as smart? Sometimes I think we're from different planets. How can people be so different? But I do like her. Maybe if Nixie wasn't my best friend, Beth and I would be better friends. But why can't I be friends in the same way with both of them?

I like Tracey too—I like him a lot—but I don't want to be like him, the way I want to be like Nixie sometimes. I think it's because Nixie understands me. She likes everything about me. Well, there are some things she doesn't like, but they don't change the way she feels about me. I think she likes me better than I like myself. That might mean that she knows me better than I know myself. But how could that be? How could anyone know me better than I know myself? That just seems impossible to me. But I might be wrong.

An old woman came onto the huge stone pavilion around the fountain and walked up close to it. She was carrying a big black plastic bag, and she didn't look like she was going anywhere in particular. She didn't look like she was sick or anything either, in fact she looked strong—her back was straight, her hair all white, and her skin very wrinkled but kind of tan. Even though it was a hot day, she was dressed in an old threadbare sweater and a long, full skirt that was kind of ragged at the bottom, and old shoes that looked like men's shoes. She was talking to herself. I couldn't hear what she was saying because the water was loud, but I could see her mouth moving. She looked over at me as she passed, and our eyes met. That's when I realized that no one else who had walked by me—and there were lots of people there, walking around on the smooth stone pavement—had met my eyes at all, not even kids, except Nixie of course, when she passed. And when I met the eyes of the old woman, it was like I couldn't look away, our eyes were locked, and she wasn't smiling or anything, and she had stopped talking to herself, and after a second it was a little scary, but I didn't look away. She kept walking—a strong, slow walk—and started going round the circle, and then she just nodded at me and turned her strong wrinkled old face forward and she was gone. It was so weird. I felt that I knew exactly who she was, and that she knew exactly who I was. It didn't seem to make any difference that she was so old and I was so young, or that she was a woman and I was a boy. It didn't matter what I knew about her life or she about mine, or whether I could have said what she was feeling or thinking. It didn't matter what she looked like. It was just . . . a connection. And I don't think Dolphius noticed anything at all. He was just sitting there next to my leg, on the leash, kind of panting and looking dreamily at the bursting, spouting, splashing water.

Finally, after about their fifth time around the fountain, Nixie kind of tugged on Beth's arm and they came over to the bench and sat down. Nixie was in the middle. "You look happy," she said. When she said it, I felt kind of happy, even though I hadn't been thinking about whether I was happy or not before.

"Did you see that old woman?" I asked.

"Ick!" Beth said. "She's so strange. She talks to herself. My Mom says she was probably in a mental hospital. She gives me the creeps. My mom says she must be homeless." Beth made a shuddering kind of movement.

I didn't know what to say. I couldn't really explain what had happened, except maybe to Nixie, or to my mom or dad. Maybe it was nothing anyway. "I wonder why she's like that," Nixie said. "I mean if something happened to her, or if she just kind of got that way as she got older."

"I can't even think of what it would be like to be that old," Beth said.

"I don't know if it would be any different," I said.

"But think of all the things that would have happened to you," said Nixie. "How could you not be different?"

"Do you think you would be a different person?" Beth asked. "What if you looked at her baby picture? How can the same body be so different? I mean, how much can a thing change before it turns into something else?"

"But she's always been in the same body," I answered.

"I don't think I'm in my body," Nixie said. "I think I am my body."

"Then how can you be two things at once?"

"What do you mean?"

"If you are your body, then there's you and there's your body. They're not the same thing."

"Why can't they be the same thing?" said Nixie.

"O.K.!" said Beth. She was getting excited again. I like that about her, though it annoys me sometimes. "I mean, how could you look at your body, or touch your body with your hand and know that you're touching if they're the same thing?"

Nobody said anything for awhile. We all stared at the fountain.

"What about Dolphius?" I said. Dolphius heard his name and looked up at me, waiting. When I didn't say anything more, he looked back at the fountain. I love the way he holds his head.

"Right," Nixie said. "That's what I mean. He's just his body—like us, but more. More than us, I mean."

"That doesn't make sense. Either we are or we aren't our bodies. Anyway, what would make us less our bodies than Dolphius is?"

" 'Cause our brains are different—that's all. Your brain is like a mirror. It makes everything double. And it's like a recorder too—it makes it so you hear yourself. But all you're hearing and seeing and feeling and thinking is yourself. It's just yourself hearing and seeing and feeling and thinking yourself."

"What about when you're asleep, and dream?"

"It's just your brain," Nixie said. "It's like it never goes to sleep, even though the rest of you does."

Beth shook her head, slowly, and said "I just don't believe it—that we're only our bodies, I mean. My grandma doesn't either. I'm not sure about my parents. My grandma says that when her body dies she's going to go somewhere else. And I think maybe she's right. I mean, how could I—me I mean—not be anymore? I just don't see how it's possible. I mean, how could you not go on, the same way everything goes on forever?"

Just then a woman in a long fancy skirt walked by with two dogs—two tiny Pekinese with long tan and silvery hair. They looked like twins—or clones. When they saw Dolphius, they both leaped toward him and began yapping and growling and tugging at their leashes. They seem to have caught the woman by surprise, and even pulled her forward a few feet, to where they were almost under Dolphius' nose. He was standing now, his tail wagging a bit but looking concerned. They were screeching and showing their teeth and lunging at him. Then Dolphius started a low growl, deep in his throat—suddenly he looked very mean!—and they backed up, but started yapping even louder. I held on tight to the leash, and the woman began ordering the dogs to stop in a loud voice and pulling at their leashes. Then she began dragging them both away. They slid and skittered, their little legs flailing, falling down under the pull of the leash and getting up again, still yapping and growling and straining their necks to look backwards, like two crazy little cartoon characters. She gave us one last apologetic smile as she pulled them away. We all started laughing, and Dolphius looked up at us and watched us for a while, as if he didn't quite know what was so funny, but didn't mind us laughing.

Chapter Eight

Anarchism and Education

In Search of a New Reality Principle

Previous chapters have invoked the term *democracy* under the assumption that we know what it is, as if it were self-explanatory. Beyond the principle of "one person one vote," we tend to ignore the distinction between "direct" and "representative" democracy, whereby in the former, the people make all the decisions, and in the latter, the people elect individuals who make all the decisions. Where is the balance between these two ways of governing? Those who call themselves "anarchist" are dissatisfied with the levels of greed, hegemonic class domination, and corruption that tend to infest the representative democratic process such that it is often more appropriately renamed polyarchy, plutocracy, oligarchy, or kleptocracy.

Anarchism may be understood as a philosophical, social, and political movement in search of a working form of "direct," "deep," or "strong" democracy. Its theorists and practitioners, beginning around the turn of the nineteenth century, made arguments from human nature that deny Hobbesian pessimism and are even evocative of Marcuse's "new sensibility." Their claims as to the evolutionary potential of human nature for cooperativeness and peacefulness in general are implicitly reflected, as we have seen, in Dewey's (1916) concept of "social democracy." In his classic formulation, "A democracy is more than a form of government; it is primarily a mode of associated living, of conjoint communicated experience," he identifies it, as we have seen, as "greater individualization on the one hand and a broader community of interest on the other," and also identifies it with education: "Since a democratic society repudiates the principle of external authority, it must find a substitute in voluntary disposition and interest; these can be created only by education . . . a society which is mobile, which is full of channels for the distribution of change occurring anywhere, must see to it that its members are educated to personal initiative and adaptability" (1916, 72). In identifying social democracy with education, Dewey also identifies it implicitly as reflecting a form of social character or "second nature," an ensemble of social and personal habits that are made as well as found—products of gene-cultural evolution, an evolutionary dynamic involving the interaction of genes and culture over long time periods, and responsible, as Herbert Gintis (2011,1) puts it, for the emergence of "such other-regarding values as a taste for cooperation, fairness, the capacity to empathize, and the ability to value such character virtues as honesty, hard work, piety and loyalty."

The notion of social democracy as a form of life, an ensemble of relational habits that embody both "greater individuation" and "a broader community of interest" is directly related to some form of direct, or in social philosopher Benjamin Barber's (2004) terms, "strong" political democracy. At the very least, it allows us to imagine a form of political organization more true to the ideals it attempts to implement. And as regards education, it asks what form of democracy is best exemplified and encouraged in the vision of schooling identified as *skholé*? This chapter argues that we can find direct democratic principles exemplified there and in the contemporary democratic school movement, and that these principals are in fact fundamental to philosophical anarchism. As such, the anarchist impulse is at the root of authentic participatory democracy, and anarchist educational theory and practice are at the root of that form of schooling exemplified in *skholé*. In its connection with the historical inauguration of democracy in fifth-century-BC Athens, it provides a space for the exploration of its emancipatory potentialities, and for the emergence of a form of subjectivity in a psychoclass that values individual freedom and cooperation and an ethos of mutual aid above the toxic combination of radical individualism, conformism, and universal commodification that characterizes a world dominated by corporate capitalism.

Forever true to its name, anarchist theory and practice stubbornly resist any *arche*, any arboreal hierarchy of principles or practices, any final codification, any definitive territorialization, any "state" that rules, orders, or organizes its emergent and rhizomatic exfoliation. Nevertheless, I would like to try to identify some general philosophical themes that I understand as fundamental to the anarchist vision. I present them as binaries, albeit with the understanding that experience tends to confound binaries and binaries tend to distort experience. My hope is that these thematics may help us to reflect on and to explore how the anarchist vision—which I understand as inherently prophetic—applies to education.

The first has to do with the distinction between state and community, and correlatively, the relation between political and social reality. The anarchist community is not a little state, nor can it become a state without losing its identity as a community. It is ontologically distinguished in its power structure from the state, which is hierarchical and centralized, in which power exerts its *mancipium* from above, codifies its practices in laws and regulations, and above all reserves the exclusive right to act violently to the point of death toward those who refuse its claim to sovereignty, as well as to exclude those it chooses to, thereby rendering them "stateless," "bare life," *homo sacer* and as such, profoundly vulnerable. This is a principal of state whether it is found in a vast nation state, an independent city, or a micro-institution like school.

The principle of community, on the other hand, is based on direct, participatory, democratic process, and an understanding of power as local and horizontal, as fluid, shifting, and inherently relational, and its ever-potential pathologies best contained through decentralized, rhizomatic, and federated rather than arboreal social and political organization. The success of a community—that is, its capacity to thrive in all the senses of the Hebrew word *shalom* (peace, harmony, wholeness, completeness, prosperity, welfare, tranquility) and the Greek word *eudaimonia* (well-being, happiness, flourishing)—follows from its capacity to create, follow, and recreate governing practices that manifest "power with" rather than "power over." Its rules and regulations are emergent and pragmatic—responses to the requirements and opportunities of the present moment in the life of the particular collective, which understands itself implicitly as engaged in an ongoing process of reconstruction—an ontological process inherent in temporality and in embodiment in general. On the pragmatist account, this process entails both adaptation to the emergent exigencies of the lived environment and reconstruction of that environment in the act of adapting to it—an ideal of optimal "experience" in the Deweyan (1938a) sense, and indicative of a fundamental dimension of dialogue present in lived experience itself, whether of the individual or the collective.

A second, related principle holds that political change alone, to the extent that it is not based on social and cultural change, is no change at all; and furthermore, that social change which does not emerge from or lead to—more often than not the causal chains are mutual—a majority of individuals with changed sensibilities is like arranging the deck chairs on the Titanic, whether we call the ensemble of those sensibilities social character, modal personality, collective subjectivity, socialization, "interpellation," or something else. Put differently, given the present state of what we call "human nature" we are stuck with the inherently compromised politics that we must endure. Another politics would require another form of sociability on another level—the level of subjectivity, including deep dimensions of the psyche like sexuality; hence the importance for many early twentieth-century anarchists of Reichian theory, and more specifically the notion of body "armoring," which is correlated with a tolerance or intolerance for cruelty and violence, whether individual or social (Reich 1946). So, Marcuse, in his invocations of a new sensibility, prophecies what Gianni Vattimo, describing Marcuse's vision, calls "the aesthetic (sensory and sensuous) rehabilitation of existence as a whole" (1992, 63). As self-identified anarchist Bookchin (2005) argued, "human nature" is always a "second nature," product of a "natural history" of subjectivity. As such, this rehabilitation process is in the evolutionary interest of "an ecological society and sensibility" (369).

This prophetic vision has been around awhile—in our epoch since the Romantics, whose call for a "renovation of the senses" (Abrams 1971) arose on the ruins of the cataclysmic failure of the French Revolution, but that is present in countercultural Christianity throughout Western history (see Marshall 2010, chapter 6; Landauer 2010), and even, post-Holocaust, enjoys a half-life in Walter Benjamin's (1940, II) "weak messianism." In Marcuse's formulation, it presupposes "freedom as a biological necessity," and the human organism as "physically incapable of tolerating any repression other than that required for the protection and amelioration of life" (1969, 28). As such, his "new sensibility" is an intrinsic human telos, which to realize would represent both a *novum* and a dialectical return. It registers a change in instinctual structure, or what John Dewey (1922) would characterize more pragmatically as a change in the dialectical relation between "impulse" and "habit."

The change in question here represents a new reality principle that follows on a changed sensorium—a revolution in perception, and as such a new form of reason (Marcuse 1969, 37). It implies a revolt on a visceral level against structural violence, the cruelty of the everyday, exploitation and oppression, universal commodification and alienation—a revolt that reaches into "second nature," into the "ingrown patterns of behavior and aspirations" that, given "the malleability of 'human nature,' reaches into the depths of man's instinctual structure . . . which 'sinks down' into the "biological dimensions and modifies organic behavior" (1969, 10–11 passim). To the extent that human nature is always a second nature (". . . the world of the senses," he argues (29), "is a historical world"), Marcuse sees the searing injustices and structures of domination and exploitation of late capitalism as a trigger for what he calls the "Great Revolt," and the emergence of a shared morality that—"prior to all ideological expression," "this side of all values," based on "a 'disposition' of the organism . . . rooted in the erotic drive to counter aggressiveness, to create and preserve 'ever greater unities' of life—represents an instinctual foundation for solidarity among human beings" (1969, 10).

In response to the obvious characterization of Marcuse's formulation of profound change on the level of "instinct" as utopian, he identifies utopia, as we have seen, not as "that which has 'no place' and cannot have any place in the historical universe, but rather that which is blocked from coming about by the power of the established societies"; and he also invokes those "utopian possibilities that are inherent in the technological forces of advanced capitalism and socialism" (1969, 4). But even more to the point, we may call on the testimony of major figures (among many, many unsung others) in anarchist thought and practice such as William Godwin, Peter Kropotkin, Élisée Reclus, Gustav Landauer, Colin Ward, George Woodcock, and Pierre Clastres, and to the testimony of our own experience to the effect that the new sensibility is in fact not new but, in Landauer's well-known words, "the actualization and reconstitution of something that has always been present, which exists alongside the state, albeit buried and laid waste" (quoted in Marshall 2010, 34); a sensibility that carries an inherent conviction rooted in human experience that, as Pierre-Joseph Proudhon put it, "liberty is not the daughter but the mother of order" (Marshall 2010, 92). The anarchist remnant, most recently evoked in Antonio Negri and Michael Hardt's (after Baruch Spinoza) "multitude" (Hardt and Negri, 2004) represents a psychoclass that is already here among us, and, to some degree, always has been. As Woodcock put it, "The anarchists have always valued the endurance of natural social impulses and the voluntary institutions they create, and it is to liberating the great network of human co-operation that even now spreads through all levels of our lives rather than to creating or even imagining brave new worlds. . . . [T]hey have always believed that human social instincts, once set free, could be trusted to adapt society in desirable and practical ways without plans" (quoted in Ward and Goodway 2003, 11). On this account, the anarchist habit-impulse relation is a virtual dimension of all social experience that, when allowed to, is always becoming actual in the "metastable equilibrium" that characterizes the process of individuation and socialization, and that, in that it is virtual, is never completely actualized. As such, Marcuse's new sensibility and Bookchin's second nature have always been potentialities of human experience that, given the material conditions—of which, I would suggest, the leisure ("free time," Gk. *skholé*) made possible by an economic "irreducible minimum" and well-developed laws of the commons are the essentials—will become actualizable. Of course we encounter a vicious circle here: in our present "actual," the irreducible minimum can only be guaranteed by the state apparatus, which, in the present epoch of aggressive corporate, global capitalism, goaded forward by reactionary, right-wing libertarian and protofascist ideology, effectively "buries and lays waste" the anarchist impulse, turning it into an impotent utopian fantasy, or, as Colin Ward and David Goodway (2003) characterized it, at best "a series of running engagements" with the state.

We are not, in short, living in "the best of all possible worlds." The reality is that solipsism, delusion, greed, fear, and narcissism in individuals, and, correspondingly, authoritarianism, group pathology, and plain bigotry in human collectives is as much the rule as its exception. The youth of our species is as vulnerable to the social pathologies of the culture of rugged individualism, social indifference, and cruelty as were the indigenous peoples to the diseases of the invading colonialists. As Kropotkin's (1902) influential account of human nature suggests, the struggle between what Jewish thought calls the yetzer hara and the *yetzer harov and yetzer hatov* (the good and the evil "inclinations"), is a fundamental one, and perhaps even necessary to the dialectic of human development; albeit in Kropotkin's grand narrative, cooperation and mutual aid hold the evolutionary advantage.

We appear to be living in an epochal moment in which Kropotkin's faith in that advantage is being sorely tested, hovering as we are on the verge of the planetary apocalypse that is global warming in combination with global corporate capitalism. Not surprisingly, it is the anarchists who are first responders, whether it be Occupy Wall Street, G-7 protests, animal liberation, squat communities, autonomous zones, and cooperatives of all kinds—all the various contemporary prefigurative anarchist "transfer cultures," which should certainly not be excluded from a larger discussion of anarchism and education. They are prime examples of educational deterritorialization—of, after Deleuze and Guattari (1987), a "nomadic war machine" engaged in "lines of flight" acting to deconstruct the state's ideological and repressive apparatuses. Indeed, "street" activism and informal education—in the form of reading groups, public lectures, demonstrations, neighborhood cooperatives, and small press publications—have been the modus operandi of European and American anarchist practice ever since the late nineteenth century, in which such unsung (and vilified by the mainstream) heroes as Voltairine de Cleyre, Errico Malatesta, Emma Goldman, Louise Michel, and Colin Ward, worked tirelessly in an atmosphere of unrelenting hostility from state, law enforcement and the press (Avrich 1974).

While these "running engagements" are fundamental to the anarchist educational project, my primary interest here is in anarchist schooling, understanding "school" as, in Jan Masschelein and Maarten Simons's (2013) phrase, a "form of gathering and action" in the more or less conventional sense of an organized (which, on the anarchist account, would mean self-organizing) intergenerational encounter within a dedicated space, involving a regularly attending group of students and teachers, and committed to a "curriculum," or course of study.

As we have seen, Masschelein and Simons understand the basic model of the "school" as we know it—albeit they see this model as being "tamed" and "neutralized" in its conventional contemporary form—as an invention of the ancient Athenian polis that accompanied the "invention" of democracy. They also understand it in its original form and impulse as a result of the drive to, first, create an institution that acts to suspend the "so-called natural, unequal order." The school, they argue, "is the materialization of the belief that humans have no natural destination. It is the materialization of the refusal of natural destiny and of the confirmation of *homo educandus*" (180). This principle corresponds with the anarchist persuasion that there is no given "human nature"—that every form of subjectivity is the reflection of a second nature—and identifies the "form of gathering and action" of that intentional community called school as a crucial site in the emergence of a form of social character or modal subjectivity for which freedom—freedom from domination and freedom to inquire—is fundamental. Masschelein and Simons connect this project with the historical construction of *skholé*, a "time and space that was in a sense detached and separated from the time and space of both society (polis) and the household (oikos)," which they characterize as the site of an "emancipatory rupture" (181). *Skholé*'s etymological association with "free time" also suggests "holding back, keeping clear"—in this case from the domination of the "so-called natural" cultural, social, political, economic, and religious order that the state, in all its forms, codifies and enforces.

As a communicative, noetic, and discursive system that holds back and keeps clear of the world of production and the inexorable pressures of *kronos*, *skholé* is dedicated to "study," whose etymological root *studium* denotes "passion, enthusiasm, zeal"—that is, the deep play of cognitive arousal and emergent, self-organizing inquiry—a concept articulated by Giorgio Agamben and recently explored in depth by Tyson Lewis (2015). As such its form of temporality is characterized by *kairos*—the time of epiphany, manifestation, event—and by *aion*, or the time of pure presence, of release from the small world of everyday consciousness, the push-me-pull-you of retention and protection, into a noetic state in which the interplay of past, present, and future approach simultaneity. I would argue that such an institution, especially when constructed as an intentional community dedicated to intergenerational encounter, is an archetypical "counter-signifying" or "nomadic regime" (Deleuze and Guattari 1987), which acts to create lines of flight that deterritorialize the ideological underpinnings of the state—or, as Masschelein and Simons put it, provide "a time and a space for study, exercise and thought in order to give the young generation the opportunity to renew society" (183). Just as *skholé* accompanies the invention of democracy, it provides a space for the exploration of the radical, anarchistic potentialities of that form of life, and for the emergence of a form of subjectivity in a psychoclass that is intrinsically oriented toward values of individual freedom, creativity, dialogue, cooperation, and an ethos of mutual aid.

The current neoliberal construction of "school" profoundly belies the vision of *skholé*. In fact, mainstream schooling as we know it—and have known it since the rise and consolidation of the monolithic industrial nation-state in early-nineteenth-century post-revolutionary reactionary Europe—presents us with a painfully clear example of an "ideological state apparatus" (Althusser 2008) dedicated to the universal reproduction of hierarchy, inequality, and domination, first for the nation-state and now for corporate capitalism. In fact, contemporary public school policy represents, in its rhetoric of "accountability," its mythology of "data driven" practice and its entrenched transmissionist pedagogy, a catalogue of capitalism's most egregious violations of anarchist principles, and even in professedly democratic countries acts as a primary incubator of "soft" or "inverted" totalitarianism (Wolin 2010).

It is also the case, however, that the taming and neutralizing of *skholé* and the co-opting of the school as a radical democratic institution by a hegemonic dispositif that "flips" it from a site dedicated to adult-child dialogue and social reconstruction to one of social reproduction and normalization, has been contested from the beginning. The rise of progressive schooling also begins in post-revolutionary nineteenth-century Europe, and its emergent articulations are typically associated with libertarian and socialist impulses, whether in Pestalozzi, Froebel, Montessori, Dewey, or the more radical Francisco Ferrer, Sébastien Faure, Paul Gobin, Louise Michel, and others (Marshall 2010). Furthermore, as I have already suggested, those impulses were provided the cultural and social space in which to emerge and grow in the context of a psychohistorical shift connected to what some would call the "invention" of childhood, but which I would prefer to call the recognition of childhood, or the becoming-aware of childhood, or the entering-dialogue with childhood—or, in Deleuzian/Guattarian terms, "becoming child," which first reaches the level of public discourse in Rousseau's (1979) explosive pre-revolutionary manifesto *Emile*.

The slow rise over the course of the nineteenth and twentieth centuries of the empathic child-rearing psychoclass is in my view closely associated with the evolutionary impulse of which anarchist theory and practice are the vanguard. The new sensibility is, as I have already argued, paedomorphic—that is, characteristic of an organism that retains juvenile characteristics in the adult form. On this principle, new species emerge from the form of the young of the evolving species; the hominids arose from the bonobo or chimpanzee stage because their young remained experimental, playful longer. Paedomorphism, on this account, is the hallmark of the human species. In addition, humans are the neotenous (neos "new" + teinein "extend") species: we experience the longest period of immaturity of any creature on earth, during which time there is a continual construction of neuronal synaptic structures as a result of unique individual experience. Experience-dependent neurons are in continual development, building and refining existing structures, thus rendering each brain a singular organization of synapses (Montagu 1989; Bjorklund 1997; Gould 1977).

The recognition of the paedomorph by evolutionary biologists in the twentieth century is, it seems to me, of a piece with the gradual evolution in child-rearing modes that DeMause traces over millennia, in its recognition of the radical potential that "child" and childhood per se represent in species evolution. The psychology of the empathic mode is identified broadly with the "withdrawal of projection" of parental shadow material onto their children, and the recognition of the child, not just as a dynamic locus of natality but also as a singularity, and thus as worthy of interlocution and dialogue as any adult. It acts to initiate a deconstruction of the contrastive pair "adult/child,"—a process that we may attribute initially to Freud, in whose theory and practice "child" remains as an interior interlocutor, an I-position in each adult. That Freud's formulation involved a pessimistic account of "successful" adult development as involving a renunciation of child's "infantile narcissism"—"where id was, there ego shall be"—is material for another discussion.

The result of this evolutionary passage from the "intrusive" (eighteenth century) to the "socializing" (nineteenth century) to the "empathic" (twentieth century) child-rearing mode is, in DeMause's formulation, the emergence of a new psychoclass, or "second nature," or "sensibility"—characterized not only by increased psychological paedomorphism, but also by a recognition and honoring of the long, experience-dependent neurological journey of childhood. It is also, by implication, a recognition of the time and space of childhood as an evolutionary frontier: a site keyed for the emergence of new forms of understanding, new solutions to the problems posed by human finitude, new (or renewed) forms of communication; new forms of interaction between impulse and habit, newly configured brains in fact (for which see Pearce 2002); a site where Spinoza's famous question—"who knows what a body can do?"—becomes the question put to education both as theory and as practice. And the ancient Greek model of *skholé*, we may say, is an apparatus designed for the exploration of this evolutionary frontier in an archetypal space of intergenerational encounter. As an assemblage comprised of child, adult, place, cultural information and emergent self-organization, *skholé* is a zone of adult-child intensity, an open space of dialogue; a paedomorphic laboratory in which, as Dewey (1922) put it, the dialectical relation between impulse and habit is explored under the educational aegis of "growth" and "experience." As such it is an apparatus dedicated to epistemic, psychological, cultural, social, political, and material transformation.

The dedicated struggle to manifest, develop and maintain the educational archetype of *skholé* in the face of widespread official and public nescience was implicit in the spread of progressive educational theory and practice in the first half of the twentieth century by educators and philosophers such as Dewey, William Heard Kilpatrick, George Counts, and Caroline Pratt, among countless unsung others. But it was avowed anarchist practitioners and activists such as Leo Tolstoy, Francisco Ferrer, Célestin Freinet, Herbert Read, Colin Ward—and again, many, many others—who carried the counter-traditional banner. A. S. Neill's Summerhill school, founded in 1921, introduced a model of direct democratic school governance, operationalized in the "weekly meeting," which, with the reemergence of anarchist energies in the 1960s, inspired and continues to inspire a growing number of small independent schools that operate on the Summerhill model, and have led to the development of a worldwide network of democratic schools—the International Democratic Education Network (https://www.idenetwork.org/).

It may be inappropriate, in ours or any historical period, to search for the basic lineaments of *skholé* such that they can be stated as fundamental principles. The anarchist school is typically a response to a specific historical social situation, and more often than not emerges in the context of an intentional community for which, as children appear in its midst, the school is a natural outgrowth. Anarchist theory eschews centralization, and values the rhizomatic over the arboreal, lines of flight over over-positioning. As such, the borderline between school and a host of other educational projects, whether cooperatives of "unschoolers," the Nomadic University, or that form of "incidental education" in which the walls of the schoolhouse disappear and the city itself becomes the campus—may appear to challenge the primacy of the *skholé* archetype. The development of the anarchist project is, to be sure, linked to spontaneous, emergent historical events, moments of deterritorialization, whether the Prague Spring, the Paris Commune or Paris 1968, Occupy Wall Street, the Arab Spring, Iran's Green Revolution, or the outbreaks, uprisings, and protracted protests that have swept the planet from Hong Kong to Chile in recent decades. All are temporarily liberated (or at least contested) spaces that testify to the emancipatory force of the anarchist vision, and act as prefigurations of a possible world to come.

If we understand education in its etymological sense (*educare*, to lead forth) as a fundamental dimension of all anarchist theory and practice, implicit in whatever form the emancipatory impulse takes, it could be argued that the intergenerational intentional community dedicated to dialogue, open inquiry and *studium* called *skholé* is too specific a form to contain all the manifestations of the anarchist impulse, which runs a broad gamut, from self-governing school collectives to incidental "descholarizing" education that seek to take down the walls between the school and the larger environment, in what could be seen as a dialectical return to a pre-industrial form of education. I would suggest, however, that the phenomenon of *skholé*, per archetype, represents a virtual form of intergenerational dialogue that is present *in potentia* wherever children and youth are understood as inhabitants of an evolutionary frontier, which is to say wherever neoteny is understood as a space charged with the possibilities of psychocultural reconstruction—wherever, that is, the new sensibility is recognized as grounded in that "well of being" (Bachelard 1971) we call childhood.

I would also suggest that—beyond the obvious fact that the way we see children is determinative of the form of education we practice with them—there are at least three regulative concepts at play in all educational theory and practice, which I have identified as order, authority and agency (Kennedy 2017, 2018). Not only are the beliefs and assumptions informing these three concepts fundamental to how we understand anarchist theory and practice generally—take, for example Proudhon's dictum, quoted above—"liberty is not the daughter but the mother of order"—but they also are continually put to the test in any collective, particularly in intentional communities such as *skholé*, where procedural transparency is fundamental to an emancipatory rupture of the "so-called natural, unequal order." As an adult-child collective rooted and grounded in the principle of dialogue, *skholé* is a social assemblage which, in its very structure, functions as a goad toward reconstruction of these three concepts—a goad whose point is sharpened by the fact that children and youth are major protagonists in the process. After all, children have served for centuries as proof texts for authoritarian narratives justifying heteronomy, hierarchy, domination, subjection, infantilization, and disempowerment, all of them informed by beliefs, whether vague or pointed, organized around a dystopian reading of the binary constructs order/chaos, authority/rebellion, and agency/license. It is through the rupture and ongoing reformulation of these binaries that new social forms will emerge, and *skholé* represents one theater of operations in the grand scheme of this struggle.

The tension between authoritarian and libertarian narratives appears to be irresolvable. However, anarchist theory and practice, and anarchist educational configurations in particular, may be seen as prefigurations of a form of life that is in fact already among us, albeit just beyond us—a "not yet," a form of becoming. As such, the anarchist educator lives in a sort of suspended time, in weak messianic preoccupation, in the deep intuition that "the history of human reason has not yet reached its culmination, much less its end" (Bookchin 2005, 369), even as we glimpse an (im)possible future in each child's face.

The next chapter is the first of two that take closer approaches to the structure and function of community of philosophical inquiry, which is understood here as the curricular baseline of *skholé*, the dialogical discourse that, as we have seen, acts as a model for three of its dimensions: it grounds the approach to the study of the academic disciplines through the philosophical exploration of the concepts that underlie them; it functions as a site for communal philosophical dialogue tout court; and it acts as a model for the deliberative democratic process by which the school is governed.

Chapter nine explores the phenomenon of CPI under the overarching concept of play understood, as Lev Vygotsky (1978) put it, as a "field of meaning" in which a "new relation between thought and reality" is made possible, and which James Hans (1981) speaks of as an "altered epistemological framework" (22–23) that explores the relation between outward and inward, reason and sense, freedom and necessity. It reviews the ideas of some major play theorists from various fields of study and practice—philosophy, cultural anthropology, evolutionary psychology, cognitive psychology, psychoanalysis, and education—and identifies the epistemological, ontological, and axiological judgments they share in their analyses of the phenomenon of play. It identifies five psychodynamic dimensions in which the Socratic play of "following the Argument where it leads" can be identified: the "play space," the "time of play," "the rules of the game," "the stakes in play," and "play and power." Finally, it suggests that there is a historical relationship between the reappropriation of Socratic dialogue in CPI and the cultural reconstruction of "child" in postmodern philosophy, with special attention to the notion of "becoming-child" as emblematic of an emergent post-human style of subjectivity. As such, the next chapter deepens the analysis of the educational model represented by *skholé* as play-based in its most fundamental, universal sense.

Chapter Nine

Community of Philosophical Inquiry and the Play of the World

In questioning the structure and dynamics of communal, collaborative philosophical inquiry (CPI) in the classroom and their implications for philosophical pedagogy, it might be good to begin by thinking more comprehensively about the phenomenon of play, and its ontological and epistemological status. Erik Erikson (1963) called play the "royal road to understanding" on the way to "the ego's efforts at synthesis" (209), an "intermediate reality between fantasy and actuality" (212). Lev Vygotsky (1978) characterized play as a "field of meaning" in which a "new relation between thought and reality" is made possible, and James Hans (1981) speaks of an "altered epistemological framework" (22–23) that explores the relation between outward and inward, reason and sense, freedom and necessity. Can we say this about the nature of community of philosophical inquiry, whether among children or adults? Is CPI—as a logical, cognitive, discursive, affective, and linguistic structure and process—inherently playful? When we experience what we consider to be an exemplary session, do we feel that we are "at play"? And if so, can the field of meaning that is play be entered at will, and manufactured as curriculum and pedagogical method? Are there different types or levels of play, and can we make qualitative judgments about their value for philosophical inquiry? What is play?

The significance of CPI as a pedagogical innovation is difficult to overestimate. Broadly speaking, it could be said to represent the transition (or transformation) of philosophical practice from a monological to a dialogical one. Its form and function is typically associated with Socrates's practice, and apart from the aporias, ambiguities, and ironies that permeate the relationship between his ideas and those of his amanuensis (or fictionalizer) Plato, it signals a fundamental shift from philosophy understood as an aristocratic, prophetic, spiritual, inspired, cataphatic activity to a communal, democratic, deliberative, secular, and apophatic one, and as such an enduring connection between philosophical practice and the practice of democracy. More than two millennia later, the Socratic method is practiced in a variety of styles, whether in the classical form of law school pedagogy, in Leonard Nelson's more scripted protocols (Chesters 2012), in Ekkehard Martens Five-Finger Model (Marsal 2014), or in the manner articulated by Matthew Lipman (1993) and Ann Sharp, founders of Philosophy for Children, who, it could be argued, have captured its dialogical, emergent, autotelic properties—and as such its playful qualities—most compellingly. Communal philosophical inquiry on this model introduces a shift in our understanding of: (1) the philosophy teacher's role to interlocutor, coach, model, and fellow participant, as opposed to encyclopedist and keeper of a given tradition; (2) to philosophy as a discursive activity based on participants' questions rather than a collection of knowledge claims, and hence the deconstruction of the tradition into the questions and concepts that led to it; which results in (3) the autopoietic emergence of an "Argument" that, if we "follow it where it leads," (the dictum of the Socratic group encounter), promises, however distantly, the reconstruction of that tradition; and finally (4) a form of ethical practice, implicitly emancipatory, in which the question "What shall we then do?" tends to precede rather than follow questions of metaphysics, and which thereby encourages actual democratic practice.

In the genealogy of play as an ontological category that follows, and in its application to the practice of CPI in the classroom, I wish to offer an understanding of the latter as an ideal setting for the autopoietic play of ideas, and the power of this understanding as a concrete framework for philosophical pedagogy. In order to ground this understanding, I will attempt a synthesis of the ideas of some major play theorists and apply their analyses to the phenomenon of communal philosophical dialogue as it unfolds in the classroom. They come from various fields of study and practice—philosophy, cultural anthropology, evolutionary psychology, cognitive psychology, psychoanalysis, phenomenology, and education—and their ideas are deeply interwoven on the philosophical level. There are multiple other emergent subfields of play studies, most notably game theory, anthropology of play and philosophy of sport, which are not reflected here.

Most recently, a three-volume series (Russell, Ryall, and McLean 2018) includes a range of papers that represent multiple perspectives on the relation between play and philosophy, reflecting Deleuzian, post-human, and new materialist philosophies, an account of which is not possible in the space of this chapter. The underlying theory of play that informs all of the perspectives reviewed here may, following Brian Sutton-Smith's (1997) broad taxonomy of the various "rhetorics" of play, be characterized as one aspect of what he calls the "Rhetorics of Fate," the assumption that "the universe [is] at play" (53)—that play is a transcendental state of being, or "flow" and a virtual dimension of the very structure of consciousness.

The Play Space

One image that occurs repeatedly in the literature on play theory is a spatial one. Both Lev Vygotsky (1978) and Hans-Georg Gadamer (1975) use the term *field*—"field of play" or "field of meaning." Friedrich Schiller (1965/1795), who may be characterized as the initiator of play theory, speaks of a *spielraum* or "play space," and Gadamer, in amplifying this idea, goes so far as to characterize this space as a "sacred precinct," a sort of temenos, a "closed world . . . marked out for the movement of the game . . . without transition and mediation over against the world of aims" (1975, 96). D. W. Winnicott (1989), the infant psychoanalyst also deeply influenced by Schiller, speaks of "transitional" psychological space, an "intermediate zone" or "third area," and elsewhere as a "potential space." It is a space, like the space of theatre, of profound aesthetic experience, in which the hard line between fantasy and reality, the subjective and the objective realms, is blurred or ruptured, and things appear in a new light. Schiller identified a transitional divide between the "sensuous" impulse—immediate existential experience, sensation, materiality, necessity, finitude, contingency—and the rational or "formal" impulse, which "strives to set [us] at liberty, to bring harmony into the diversity of [our] manifestation, and to maintain [our] person through every change of circumstance" (66). Their confluence—in art, philosophy, and deep emotional experience—is the space of the aesthetic, where the "play impulse" (*spieltrieb*) "would aim at the extinction of time in time and the reconciliation of becoming with absolute being, of variations with identity" (74). It is, as Winnicott describes it based on his experience with young children, a "third area of human living, one neither inside the individual nor outside in the world of reality." This is echoed by the play therapist Russell Meares (1993), who discovers in his patients' experience "a space in which there is neither inner nor outer, and in which internal reality and external reality coexist" (39).

In the circle of CPI, the stage is set for the emergence of such a *spielraum*, a potential space that is also fundamentally intersubjective and interlocutive—a space in which self and other are felt as inextricable. It is, of course, a performative space, but an involuntary one—a living space in which the "Argument," in the give and take of the dialogue of ideas, writes itself; ideas are, so to speak, elicited from us by the triggers and prompts of other ideas. In this discursive space, the signifiers (ideas, judgments, analogies, definitions, etc.), which represent each of us as we speak them, also have a life of their own. We are led by the Argument, we do not lead it; we are directed by the play and not vice versa. As Gadamer (1975) says, "The players are not the subjects of play; instead play . . . reaches presentation through the players" (92), who are triggered by whatever stimulus the teacher or the students have chosen in order to inaugurate the play of ideas.

The Time of Play

The temporality of play is also transitional, in the sense that it is an interruption of chronos or linear, chrono-logical time, and an experience of what Gadamer refers to as "the temporality of the aesthetic," which is "timelessness, . . . a dialectical feature which arises out of temporality and in contrast with it" (108). Play-time is ek-static time—a being-present that has the character of being outside of oneself, of seeing the whole—not from the outside, as from an Archimedean point, but from the inside, through losing oneself in the play—in the case of CPI, the play of concepts. Our being-played results, Gadamer suggests, in seeing the world "in the heightened truth of its being" (121), which invokes the temporality of *kairos*, the experience of time associated with epiphany, manifestation, fulfillment, completion.

The shared space-time of the CPI group is an exercise in simultaneity, and we may characterize the group as a virtual collective subject. As such it has a certain telepathic quality, which Maurice Merleau-Ponty (1964b) referred to as mutual "contagion," or Paul Schilder "the movement of body images into each other" (quoted in Kennedy 1997). This ghostly intimacy of the collective subject is a kairotic epiphany of group consciousness—a virtual consciousness whose language is expressed in the moves and permutations of the Argument, as well as in the interplay of gaze, gesture, and vocalization (prosody). The group is one polymorphic body whose various parts are dancing with each other, however clumsily or indecisively. Here, in *kairos*, we approach Gadamer's characterization of play as "transformation into structure," in which "all playing is a being played . . . the game tends to master the players" (95), and "the player experiences the game as a reality that surpasses him" (98).

Put differently, when we are playing we experience time as what, as we have seen, Schutz (1973) called an altered "tension of consciousness" that is unhindered by the drive to produce, to acquire, to dominate or submit. So, both Jerome Bruner (1981) and Erikson, in their topographies of play, identify it with "drive reduction"—that is, play is not excessively attached to results, maintaining as it does a loose linkage between means and ends; the means become the ends, and we experience the release from drive that is necessary for problem-solving, creativity, for "thinking again." We are speaking here of a form or style of being in the world, an experience of time that mediates between what Schutz calls "wide awake" consciousness—a world of objectification, use, goal orientation, and strictly linear organization of time—and oneiric (dream) time, which is the time of one's own imagination, a kind of time in which the divided, exclusionary organization of *kronos* between past, present, and future breaks down and we are caught up in the to-and-fro self-renewing movement of the event. As a tension of consciousness, the temporality of play is identified by Heraclitus as yet a third category—*aion*—as in his fragment "Aion is a child playing ['childing'] a board game. The kingdom is the child's." *Aion* is the temporality of existence itself, of Henri Bergson's *la durée* in its flows, cuts, and intensities, and with the time of festival, of revel, of release from the instrumental. Philosophy, like art, unfolds in this zone of indeterminacy—the zone of the "what is? "what if?" "what can?" "what might?" and "what should?" Its association with childhood is significant for Philosophy for Children, a movement whose historical distinction is to have reappropriated the Socratic dialogical circle and transformed it in the context of children themselves.

What is particularly compelling about the phenomenon of fully functional community of philosophical inquiry is that this experience of aionic time is a shared one—a mediation of each individual participant's lived time with the lived time of the others in the virtual space of the dialogic circle. In this form of cooperative play, two forms of existential temporal alienation are—if provisionally and often only fitfully—overcome: (1) The chrono-logical experience of interpersonal disruptive asynchronicity that Levinas (1987) identified as our ontological condition, in which ". . . the time of the other and my time do not occur at the same time; the time of the other disrupts my temporality" (12)—and (2) in Jean-Paul Sartre's terms, the existential experience of chronos as "being-for-itself"—a divided mode of being that can never be wholly identical with itself—can never attain to "being-in-itself," the way rocks and trees and even other animals are. Temporally, this means that I am never completely myself. Of the temporal moments of the for-itself, Sartre (1966) says, ". . . at present it is not what it is, [because I am also my past,] and it is what it is not [because I carry my future with me as a horizon]" (168).

The intra-subjective alienation that is at the heart of the being of *chronos* is overcome in *aion*, which, as Heraclitus tells us, is manifest as "child playing" (or literally "child childing"), in what Gadamer, in his analysis of play, characterizes as the time of celebration, festival, of "self forgetfulness and reconciliation with self," of "ek-stasis" and "absolute presence" (111), in which we are played by something beyond us—in this case, the Argument, which we are committed, with Socrates, to following where it leads. It is also a moment in which the Sartrean "being-for-others"—that condition of intersubjectivity in which, on his (Sartre 1966) account, "the Other is . . . the radical negation of my experience, since he is the one for whom I am not subject but object" (310)—is overcome. In the aionic space and time of communal philosophical play, "the thematic horizon [in this case, the Argument] is not limited by any being-for-itself of subjectivity . . . there are no subjects who are behaving 'playfully' . . . The players are not the subjects of play"; instead, to repeat, "play reaches presentation through the players" (Gadamer 1975, 92). In the "pure self presentation" (94) that is the emergence and development of the Argument in CPI, the ontological conundrum, the onus of mutual objectification represented by my being-for-others and being-for-itself is lifted.

This is obviously an idealized picture, and the success of any particular instance of CPI depends, not just on our shared ability to enter (or rather, to be entered into) aionic time together and to stay there, but also on our sensitivity to the implicit rules or principles that organize the self-structuring, autotelic movement of the conceptual play of the dialogue, and our sensitivity to the Argument that is continually emerging through that play, in what Gadamer calls its "to-and-fro movement . . . which has no goal that would bring it to an end . . . [and] which renews itself

Community of Philosophical Inquiry and the Play of the World | 133

in constant repetition" (93). This sense of space, time, and their implicit rules and principles are, I would argue, present to some degree, not just in the philosophy classroom in which the structured, open-ended, participant-driven dialogue of CPI is practiced; they are latent in our most meaningful classroom experiences, even those superficially governed by a monological model, where a sense of spontaneity and self-organization is allowed free play. And this is particularly true of the philosophy classroom, given that its founding, organizing curriculum is in fact a set of questions as opposed to a set of facts or claims.

The Rules of the Game

The rules of community of philosophical inquiry are variously explicit and tacit, present on several levels and in several domains. An apparent freedom from external rules hides a level on which rules are continually being negotiated. They are specifically play rules to the extent that they match Erikson's description of the experience of children's play as ". . . free movement within prescribed limits . . . a sense of choice and ease and yet also of driving necessity; of a highly personalized and yet also a traditional pattern; of improvisation in all formalization, of surprise in the very reassurance of formality; . . . of some leeway for innovation in what must be repeated over and over again" (1965, 212). The first and perhaps overarching rule is the framework of any scenario that we identify as play. Vygotsky (1978) offers an example in which two sisters decide to "play sisters," thus stepping outside of and re-representing an actual situation in order to explore a normative theory (theory of sisterhood) through playing that situation. The normative "rules" of sisterhood (e.g., everything must be shared with absolute equality, we always take care of each other, and so on) are clarified through their representation in play. Just so, in CPI the concept "fair" for example, is removed from its embeddedness in the interactive world of the everyday and thought again through its playful problematization in the dialogical circle.

This is at least suggestive of the first implicit rule of Gregory Bateson's (1972) definition of play, which is the paradoxical message, accepted by all participants, "This is play." As he unpacks this statement it means, "These actions, in which we now engage, do not denote what would be denoted by those actions [were they not play] which these actions denote." And he offers an example: "The playful nip denotes the bite, but it does not denote what would be denoted by the bite" (180). He also ties this to Alfred Korbyzki's notion of the map-territory relation, where "language bears to the objects which it denotes a relationship comparable to that which a map bears to a territory" (180). In communal dialogical inquiry we are engaged in playfully mapping the territory of the rough, mostly unconscious and often problematic terrain of the interaction between the common, central, and contestable concepts—friendship, justice, happiness, beauty, success, person, animal, god, death—by which we guide and understand our lives, and our lived experience, which both shapes and is shaped by those concepts. We are so engaged playfully—with what Erikson calls a "non-literal attitude" ("the map is not the territory") and which Vygotsky identifies as a form of abstraction (the sisters are developing an abstract concept of sisterhood). Our concepts (maps) of friendship, justice, happiness, beauty, success, person, animal, etc., are not the experience (territory) of friendship, justice, happiness, beauty, success, person, animal, etc. They are "as if" concepts, a "projection," as Bruner (1981) puts it, "of interior life onto the world, . . . through which we interiorize the external world and make it part of ourselves" (77). And as the play therapists Erikson (1963) and Meares (1993) argue, this interplay between map and territory operates in the interest of competence, equilibration, mastery of traumatic experience, and mastery of the map-territory relation in general.

On the discursive level, CPI is governed by the rules of both informal and formal logic, which in a typical session it is the job of the facilitator to identify, model, and invoke. They need not, however, be taught, for they are coded, however crudely, into the semantical rules of grammar. When I say "it is a cat," I am implicitly committing an act of classification. When I say "cats can't talk," I am implicitly committing an act of categorical exclusion. When I say "it's talking, so it can't be a cat," I am performing a syllogism and invoking the law of the excluded middle. When I say "it must be a human pretending to be a cat," I am making a hypothetical inference; and so on. These are the linguistic/logical rules of argumentation that are typically given the most attention in the practice of communal inquiry since we associate them with critical thinking and scientific analysis. This, indeed, is the most common justification offered for the virtues of structured philosophical dialogue. But we also find in CPI—because it is a philosophical play space, a transitional space-time in which the boundary between outward and inward, reason and sense, objective and subjective experience, are blurred and complicated—that the play of ideas takes over, and we are, as James Hans (invoking Gadamer) points out, "being played by the play, . . . being mastered by the activity itself" (1981, 56).

Hans identifies the Socratic position of ignorance—which epitomizes the initial play position of the game of CPI—as a willingness to be appropriated by the play of discourse, which, if we allow it and remain attentive to it, "takes on a life of its own, leading the participants where it will" (70). The implicit rules that we must observe if we follow the Argument where it leads are not just formal rules of argumentation per se. As Dale Cannon and Mark Weinstein (1993) have pointed out, they include emergent habits of informal reasoning—recognizing patterns and structures of ideas, exemplifying, applying abstract principles to concrete situations and contexts, playing with analogies, models and metaphors, and counterfactuals—as well as interpersonal reasoning, which involves the disposition and ability to take various points of view into account, and a respect for the opinions of others; and philosophical reasoning, which involves identifying and exploring assumptions, clarifying basic criteria of judgment, and exploring and clarifying basic concepts (599–600). It also implies the recognition, after Wittgenstein (2009), that concepts are tools rather than entities (para. 569), ways of "finding our way about" within a language/thought world in which the rules of use are circumstance dependent, open to revision, and often non-explicit, and in which our concepts are related by family resemblance (para. 670) as opposed to strict propositional rules, as the Argument undergoes continual reconstruction. The inherent nonlinear, autopoietic character of group dialogue seeks, as water seeks its level, the "complete system," which is continually under deconstruction and reconstruction, propelled forward into continual transformation by disequilibrium (disagreement, emergence of contradiction, search for criteria, new data, identification of an underlying assumption that must then be explored, etc.) and is always building, dissipating, or in some chaotic intermediate stage, goaded forward by the play of difference.

These rules of the game are beyond us: all we can say, with Gadamer, is that the Argument "reaches presentation through us." Or as Hans puts it, ". . . it is not the play of subject and object, but the play which produces subject and object as residues" (1981, 55). This does not, however, mean that we are without a task. Our task is, following Socrates's third great adage—the first two being "assuming the position of ignorance" and "following the Argument where it leads"—is to act maieutically, to play in such a way that we assist at the birth of the Argument. Philosophical maieusis operates through the interpersonal, interactive rules of dialogue:

listening; restating; reformulating; summarizing; clarifying; translating between various cognitive, discursive, and expressive styles and registers; sharing control; and so on. All these behaviors can be grouped under the methodology of "active listening" (Rogers and Farson 2015), and as such they emphasize the extent to which the practice of communal philosophical dialogue is intrinsically a therapeutic one, in keeping with the ancient notion of philosophy as "care of the self," taking the term *care* in its most inclusive sense. As such, CPI is a form of conceptual play therapy. To reclaim this ancient notion of philosophizing for the classroom is not to reformulate the inherent goal of philosophy pedagogy, but to return to it.

The Stakes in Play

Philosophical play is "serious" to the extent that it "begins with the putting-in-question" of our own deeply held beliefs and assumptions (Hans 1981, 8). Every form of play embodies its own risks in that it is dedicated to testing the limits of its own domain, whether it be of body, mind, or emotions. The fact that play transpires in the realm of the map rather than the territory does not sever their connection, but in fact challenges it, vivifies it, and probes the boundary between the two; the playful nip and the bite are never far from each other. Hans argues that "play at all levels is characterized by rupture" (1981, 43), a rupture that is perhaps exactly analogous to the cognitive disequilibrium that results when, in Jean Piaget's (1981) account of human learning, our cognitive schemata are confronted with information (elements of the territory) that doesn't fit their classificatory structure. According to Piaget, this moment of disequilibrium puts into play an exploratory search dedicated to the reorganization of our schemata such that they can assimilate the new information (see Bjorklund 1995). Experience in the world is an ongoing process of equilibration—of going out of and coming into balance in the relation between map and territory. In the "as if" world of communal philosophical inquiry, this process is, to be sure, "buffered from its consequences" (Erikson 1963) by the fact that we are talking about rather than directly experiencing, for example, justice or friendship. However, inquiry dedicated to the map has its own vertiginous quality. There in the dialogical circle, "justice" and "friendship" are grappled with within the limitations imposed by language and logic. We experience the inability to say exactly what we "mean," and the contradictions that we discover in our thinking force us into self-reflection, which we are often inclined to resist. We discover that indeed the map is not the territory, but that their relation is ineluctably complicated, and we are returned from the former to the latter—the everyday world of relation—with a metacognitive space in our heads where there once was a wall, or nothing.

The risk is also (and perhaps more so) social, given the intrinsically interactive, intersubjective, and communicative nature of group philosophical dialogue. Hans associates the risk in undertaking Socratic dialogue with the "willingness to be appropriated by the play of discourse" and identifies the interruption with the ". . . obligation to put [one's] cherished beliefs on the line, to test his beliefs in the play itself, which can only be done if one is assured that the other participants are doing the same thing. Calling one's beliefs into question, after all, is a fundamental way of subjecting oneself to great risk, for if those beliefs fall, so does one's self-conception. Everyone must be willing to assume the same risk, or the play cannot proceed" (1981, 70–71). Hans goes on to suggest that it is in giving oneself to the play of the discourse—allowing it to unfold through oneself, being committed to not blocking it—that the real, or deeper challenge lies; for in refusing the inquiry, "the continual redefinition of man [sic] through the play of discourse," which is at the heart of the game of Socratic inquiry, is blocked. Outside the "sacred precinct" of the Socratic circle, the conceptual work we have done with the map affects our experience of the territory—the world of action and interaction, truth and consequence. As Hans puts it, ". . . whereas its [play's] rules are mastered in a secure setting, they are meant to apply to situations in which the setting is not secure, when one is at stake . . ." (72). And while we accept his broad claim that play is an ontological category, a fundamental modality of the world, whether material, social, or psychological, we also understand the world, after Dewey's pragmatic logic, as a field of inquiry within which we experience the ongoing deconstruction and reconstruction of the beliefs and theories that we live by and through. Dewey put it succinctly: "Inquiry is the controlled or directed transformation of an indeterminate situation into one that is so determinate in its constituent distinctions and relations as to convert the elements of the original situation into a unified whole" (Dewey 1938b, 104–5). So understood, the inquiry circle takes on a particularly compelling quality, promising as it does the growth of concrete reasonableness through linguistic and logical exploratory play. And again I would emphasize that this sense of adventure and heightened meaning—of *kairos*—is inherent in the practice of philosophizing in general, even when it is organized as a monological pedagogy; for the common, central, and contestable concepts that make up the warp and weft of the discipline, when encountered in good faith, immediately resolve themselves into questions, and as such trigger the play of inquiry. What is distinctive about CPI as a pedagogy is that it organizes the classroom to allow for and encourage this play.

Play and Power

The radical intersubjectivity of the field of meaning of community of inquiry makes of it a space inextricably associated with the play of power, and therefore with politics on a most fundamental level. An archeology of power reveals it as, in Hans's words, "flows of energy and of the markings that provide the direction for the flows" (74). The flows of energy are expressions of the play of differences. In the inquiry circle, as in any social circle, the stage is set for a struggle for dominance, and on one level, a playing out of the natural human drive toward inequality. Indeed, most competitive forms of play are intentionally constructed as ritual struggles for dominance—as agon, whether between individuals or groups. But in CPI, which has ancient roots in the *Boule* or representative citizens council, in which Socrates served, as well as in the group dialogues he convened in multiple venues all over late-fifth-century Athens, we recognize an original form of democratic discourse—of a struggle for equality.

Another genealogical element of communal dialogue is found in C. S. Peirce's (1966) notion of a "community of inquirers," which is associated as much with scientific as with philosophical inquiry, and which is operationalized by Jurgen Habermas (McCarthy 1978) in the notion of an "ideal speech situation"—a situation, that is, of complete equality in the right and freedom to speak. This, in turn, is influenced by dialogue theory (Buber 1948; Silverman 1986; Bohm 1996; Rogers and Farson 2015; Hermans and Hermans-Konopka 2010), which assumes a form of self-imposed discipline in speech, and an emphasis on careful listening, restatement, and commitment to respectful address. As such, CPI may be understood as a primary building block of participatory democracy, a form of discourse that inherently rejects any authority based on social status, and in which the only authority that is recognized is the authority of the Argument itself. In fact, Hans argues that this quality is intrinsic to the nature of play: "Play itself is not formulated according to a master/slave dialectic . . . nor does domination have anything to do with it. On the contrary, play requires foregoing any attitude that centers on domination. It may be a demonstration of skill or excellence, but their goal is never specifically to dominate the players involved" (1981, 52). The upshot of this is that CPI, precisely as a form of play, is inherently democratic. So understood, it links/reaches back to the rise of political democracy in fifth-century Athens, and forward to the promise of direct, "deep" democracy announced in the emergence of anarcho-socialist theory and practice in the nineteenth- and twentieth-century West. For participants in a successfully functioning dialogical community, perhaps the most significant and vivid lesson is in the experience of the "disappearance" of the facilitator as the group assumes his or her role. Group members increasingly take on facilitation moves and responsibilities—speaking up if someone is dominating the conversation, asking for summarization, calling for the judgment of the group on whether to pursue a particular line of argument, attempting to locate the Argument, and so on. This in itself is a profound lesson in the noncoercive and nondominating uses of power—of power dedicated to the thriving of the whole rather than winning personal status or self-gratification. As such CPI is a "school for democracy" in the most direct sense of that term, and emblematic of the connection between philosophical dialogue and healthy democracy that is the gift of Socrates and of Periclean Athens to Western history. Issues of power abound in the classroom, whether in the kindergarten or the university, and the philosophical issues associated with them are among the most important and immediate in the realm of teacher-student relations—especially given power's institutionalization in hierarchical, quantified evaluation procedures. The shift from a monological to a dialogical and polyphonic discourse, especially in philosophy classes, announces a repositioning of the teacher as primus inter pares, and the curriculum as a field of playful inquiry as opposed to a reproductive apparatus for any given historical canon or school of philosophy.

Can CPI not be play? Of course. The very experience of the expression and mediation of difference that is at the core of this discourse as a form of play also represents the possibility of chaos or stagnation and even repudiation. The attempt to suppress the indeterminacy that this difference represents amounts to a suppression of the game itself. The element of risk that is at the heart of play cannot be foreclosed without foreclosing it altogether. And when we consider CPI as a game played with and among children, whose level of curiosity and explorative impulses tends—no doubt for evolutionary reasons—to be higher than adults, the situation becomes more complicated. As Dewey pointed out, the questions that will make for optimal educational experience are the questions put by the students themselves. No matter how universal we consider certain questions, or questions that we feel ought to be important to students—"What is friendship?" or "What is justice," for example—if a question doesn't represent some kind of problem for the person asking it, then it is not as liable to trigger the play of dialogical inquiry.

Children in conventional schools have typically been conditioned by adult commonsense discourses from an early age to understand every question as having an answer. They are taught by the hidden curriculum or "habitus" of the everyday to ignore the questions that don't as a waste of time. I once facilitated a session with third graders on the phenomenon of thinking ("What is thinking?"), and after thirty minutes of interesting dialogue following the concept through multiple permutations, one of the students asked me, "Now tell us teacher, what is the answer?" My answer ("I don't know") was received with nods, as if they already understood that the question was rhetorical, or even comic, and marking a moment of epistemic realization. But that was just one moment in a process that represents the great risk and opportunity of community of philosophical inquiry—perhaps the one that led Plato to condemn doing philosophy with the young as inherently corruptive, because the next stage tends to be one in which we decide that there is in fact no answer, and that therefore any one answer is as valuable as the next. To move beyond the epistemological relativism that easily moors students in indifference and even a sort of intellectual nihilism is only possible when we are in the play state (i.e., when we are "the subjects of play") when the answer is, as Gadamer argues, "reaching presentation through us." When we realize this, we no longer believe that there is no answer, but rather that the answer will, as Charles Sanders Peirce argued, be determined by the community of inquirers "in the long run." As such, the "answer" is represented by the infinitely receding horizon of our collaborative inquiry, and acts as a lure and a vague promise.

Can the play of communal philosophical dialogue be planned? I would argue no—the stage can only be set for the play. It depends upon the characters involved, and the particular qualities of the whole—the "chemistry" (which may in fact be an exact analogy in this case) of the group—as to whether and how each member gives him or herself (or does not) to the process. Since shared agency, democratic process, and dialogical communication are fundamental principles of the game, any success will reflect the fact that no "one"—facilitator or student(s)—is in charge of posing the question, the emergence of positions, and the logical and metalogical moves that act to deconstruct and reconstruct, in a recursive process of novelty and repetition, the Argument. The autopoiesis of the Argument proceeds through the play of difference in the context of the same, or as Hans puts it, "a familiar structure that allows one to play with the unfamiliar" (1981, 28). And in that CPI is implicitly understood as an ongoing diachronic process, that autopoietic movement will shift, transform, switch, detour, return from session to session.

Given the close connection between play and childhood, it is no accident that the historical reconstruction of the Socratic inquiry circle in the recent development of theory and practice of CPI is directly associated with the formulation and development of the Philosophy for Children program in the 1970s. As Walter Kohan (2017) has argued, Socrates took "a childlike position in relation to knowledge . . . for Socrates the truest relationship to knowledge—knowing nothing and not believing he knows—is childlike, playful," and in conflict with Plato's view that philosophical play was "not serious enough for the political challenges of the polis," that it was "too close to childhood, too open to play, to not knowing, to questioning, to not teaching" (35).

I would take it one step further and suggest that there is a historical relationship between the legitimation of philosophical play among children and the cultural reconstruction of "child"—in the modern West anyway—as agentic as opposed to "innocent," "evil," "animalic," "adult-in-training," or "little adult." The agentic child, on Reesa Sorin and Greta Galloway's (2006) account, is understood by the adult as co-constructor, as dialogical interlocutor, as epistemologically interesting, in that he/she embodies a "way of knowing"; and above all as playful in the Heraclitean sense of *pais paidon*. As we have seen in chapter one, Heraclitus is among the first (along with Lao Tzu) to understand childhood as emblematic of a prophetic condition—as, in Schiller, a "representations of our highest fulfillment in the ideal," of "what we were and should once again become." This prophetic understanding of "child" is exemplified in postmodern philosophy most vividly in Deleuze and Guattari's notion of "becoming child" whereby childhood is understood "not only as a period of life but as a specific strength, force or intensity that inhabits a qualitative life at any given chronologic time" (Kohan 2012, 172). In this formulation, childhood is freed from any specific moment of the life cycle and understood as a zone, a region of the psyche, a way of being in time (aionically) a form of intentionality or attention, a field of intensities and flows, affective and noetic. Becoming child means a process of continually becoming other, de- and reterritorializing along "lines of flight" of becoming, of escaping the grasp of the illusion of sovereign subjectivity. So understood, "child" is emblematic of an emergent posthuman style of subjectivity, more attuned to the play of the world itself, and an exemplification of Nietzsche's (1999) "child" of his "three metamorphoses" or stages/states of human development, here understood as a creator of new values, and as such a central actor in human evolutionary possibilities. "Innocence" he proclaims, "is the child and forgetfulness, a new beginning, a game, a self-rolling wheel, a first movement, a holy Yes" (14).

To identify Nietzsche's and Deleuze and Guattari's "child" with the actual children with whom we enter the play space in the practice of philosophy with children is perhaps presumptuous and even a form of folly, in that the "process of desire" that is becoming-other for Deleuze and Guattari is not ultimately age-related, and both children and adults experience other such processes. As they argue, "A kind of order or apparent progression can be established for the segments of becoming in which we find ourselves: becoming-woman, becoming-child; becoming-animal, -vegetable, or -mineral; becomings-molecular of all kinds, becomings-particles. Fibers lead us from one to the other, transform from one into the other, as they pass through doors and across thresholds . . ." (1987, 272). As such, whatever their age or experience, becoming-child is a hidden imperative for anyone entering the "closed world . . . marked out for the movement of the game" of communal philosophical dialogue.

In this chapter, I have identified five characteristics of play when understood as an ontological phenomenon and applied those characteristics to the dynamics of the event of community of philosophical inquiry, in which philosophical concepts are explored in a communal dialogical setting. So understood, CPI appears as an autopoietic and autotelic discourse phenomenon, in which the structure of the Argument—that is, the organization and evaluation of the philosophical concepts under discussion—grows through a combination of spontaneous, dialogically triggered both substantive and procedural "moves," such as calling for a definition, offering an example or counterexample, making an analogy, summarizing and restating, and so on. On this account, participants' understanding of philosophical issues and arguments is deepened and enhanced through personal encounter with those issues in the context of the encounter between multiple points of view, and through the internalization of argumentation moves as they both emerge spontaneously in the dialogue and are modelled by the facilitator and other members of the group. Finally, I suggest that the dialogical group play of CPI is an inherently childlike discourse, with connections both to Socrates's childlike position in relation to knowledge, and to the postmodern project of becoming-child.

In chapter eleven, I explore another dimension of community of philosophical inquiry, which has less to do with the autotelic character of the Argument, energized and driven forward by the play-drive, and more to do with its directionality and its characteristic patterns of movement. Haunted as we are by the fantasy that the Argument builds and self-organizes towards a horizon of univocal "truth," which, on Peirce's account, is "what the unlimited community of inquirers will discover to be the case in the long run" (Raposa 1989, 154); yet we find that horizon to be an infinitely receding one, and the movement of the Argument, given that it builds through dialogue, to be rhizomatic and polyphonic rather than arboreal and monological, and as such, moved forward through the interplay of differences toward a "long run" infinitely deferred. However, before exploring CPI and the rhizome, I offer a second intermezzo in an example of a philosophical novel for children that attempts to expand Lipman's model, and move it into the realm of myth, fantasy, symbol, and adventure, thereby opening another space for conceptual discovery, interplay, and invention.

Chapter Ten

Intermezzo Two

Dreamers

As we have seen, Matthew Lipman's primary pedagogical tool for drawing children into philosophical dialogue was the novel, and a form of the novel designed to both model philosophical dialogue by presenting characters so engaged, and to plant the narrative text with philosophical concepts. The latter appear, not as ordered expressions of philosophical systems or schools of thought, but as questions arising from the characters' lived experience and addressed to each other as much as to themselves. Each character tends to exemplify a certain characteristic philosophical style or implicit persuasion or tendency. In its basic pedagogical form, which became known as "plain vanilla" for its simplicity, Lipman and his colleague Ann Sharp (1987) constructed a methodology whereby a communal reading of a section of a philosophical novel is followed by the generation of questions, which are then organized by the group on the basis of their philosophical potential, and one question is decided upon, either by consensus or by vote, as a starting point for discussion. The facilitator, who seeks to remain "procedurally strong and philosophically self-effacing" throughout, models dialogical behavior—restating, summarizing, asking for clarification, identifying alternative positions, seeking to maintain equal participation, etc., with the overall Socratic goal of "following the argument where it leads." In the transition into the questioning that it has provoked, the novel drops out of the picture; besides acting as a model for philosophical dialogue, it is not understood as the primary object of the conversation. And finally, each novel is accompanied by a "manual" or guide, which provides resources focused on the concepts found in the narrative. It functions as a resource for the facilitator and the group in the form of short introductions to each concept, discussion plans, exercises, and thought experiments. As such, it plays an educational role for the facilitator, who may or may not use one or more of the abundant discussion plans found there over the course of the conversation.

The novel briefly excerpted here, *Dreamers* (Kennedy 2023), is a philosophical adventure novel for ages twelve and beyond, told through the eyes of four preadolescent children of varying ethnic and racial backgrounds living in a small town in the American Southwest—Kio, Neda, Cynda and Anoke—who embark together on a school inquiry project centered on the phenomenon of dreaming. Not only do they record and share their dreams with each other, but they also inquire together into the role and status of dreaming in cultures past and present, the interpretation of dreams, the scientific analysis of dreaming, and the role of dreams in mythology and religion. They conduct this inquiry in the context of a series of extended sojourns into the wilderness mountain range that rises directly behind their school, where they meet and become involved with Ora, a deaf runaway Hopi girl their age, whose camp they visit, and whose connection with the natural and animal world approaches the mythological. The drama of her fugitive existence unfolds amid a rising tide of right-wing extremism in local and national politics, marked by the existence of an armed camp of white nationalists also hidden away in the same mountain range.

The events of the novel are interspersed with discussions among the four friends revolving not just around the metaphysical terrain of their own dreams, but also around concepts in philosophy of nature, particularly whether all of nature can be considered alive, and if so in what way; as well as issues of awareness and subjectivity—whether for example plants can be said to feel and to communicate, and if so how. The ideas they broach in their communal dialogues evoke the perennial re-articulation of vitalism, hylozoism, and panpsychism in the philosophical tradition, and the queering of the distinction between the organic and the inorganic, the human and the nonhuman implicit in a post-human, relational ontology. Many other common, central, and contestable (that is, philosophical) concepts appear in the narrative as well, whether directly in the dialogue between the four young protagonists, with their parents, or with Ora.

The online text of *Dreamers* (https://sites.google.com/view/dreamers-david-kennedy/home) is woven seamlessly together with an interactive guide. In chapter one, for example, the hyperlinked word *animal* when clicked, leads to a page in the guide (https://sites.google.com/view/dreamers-david-kennedy/home/animals) that offers a handful of short quotes from the philosophical canon on the concept, several discussion plans, and a thought experiment; and one may find some graphic or literary stimuli—whether a photograph or a poem. Another way to access the concepts that are touched upon in *Dreamers* is the philosophical index, where they are listed in alphabetical order, and in some cases broken down into subcategories or cross-referenced with other concepts. This allows for different approaches to the philosophical material in the novel and different strategies for going about "teaching" it. The facilitator (or a participant) may at some point suggest that the group take up an exercise, discussion plan, or thought experiment that seems relevant to the topic, but otherwise the guide does not enter the picture.

At one end of a spectrum of pedagogical intervention—the "plain vanilla" end—the facilitator simply convenes a chosen reading, records the questions that arise from it, and acts to restate, summarize, refer positions to each other, and so on. In the middle of the spectrum, the facilitator has identified one or several discussion plans in the guide that she may (or may not) introduce during the session at "just the right moment." And finally at the other end of the spectrum, the facilitator actually starts off with a discussion plan, thought experiment or graphic stimulus before reading the text and generating questions. And everywhere between there are myriad combinations of text and guide materials possible, limited only by the creativity of the facilitator and the group members.

As such, in its digital form, *Dreamers* is a four-dimensional literary and philosophical assemblage that includes (1) the novel itself; (2) an index of the philosophical concepts found in the novel, hyperlinked to where they appear in the novel; (3) guide containing a series of quotations, discussion plans, thought experiments, poetry, photographs, drawings, and related books and films for each concept identified; and (4) a reader or group of readers interested in engaging in philosophical dialogue around those or other concepts. As an example of how the four dimensions interact, we read an episode in the novel that is focused on the concept *alive* or *living*. We click on *alive* in the index, and it leads us to a section in the guide on *alive, living*. We look it over, and perhaps take up one or more of the discussion plans or thought experiments, or we generate our own questions, which then become our own discussion plan. As such, the guide is interactive with the novel, and capable of being used either in relation to it or not. We might choose a theme or concept from the index without consulting the novel, which will also take us to the guide. And finally, the online guide is emergent, ongoing, and interactive: readers are encouraged to offer discussion plans, quotes, thought experiments, images, poetry, songs, which are submitted to a webmaster for evaluation and inclusion in the guide.

An excerpt from *Dreamers* follows:

Anoke

On Saturday we were up on Little Bear Ridge again. We took Kio's dog Oliver with us this time because it was the weekend, and we were leaving from town. Oliver is a Red Setter and, like Kio says, very smart but more than slightly hyper; his eyes are wild, and he always looks surprised and interested in you're not sure what. Kio kept him on a leash—which he hated—until we walked him just out of town, and when he unhooked him he disappeared like he was shot out of a canon, then would show up every few minutes, panting, his tongue hanging out of his mouth, his legs and belly all wet, wild-eyed, smiling at everyone, running alongside the bikes, then take off again.

We left our bikes in the stand outside Harbor House like we always do and went up the same way—the only way we knew then—along the creek. It was hot and sunny and dry, and there was the beautiful smell of cedar and pinon pine trees, faint but everywhere, like incense. There were pinyon jays calling—sometimes you would see the deep blue flash of them bursting from one branch to another—and some crows flew over us, cawing; they were checking us out and signaling each other about it. There was the sudden sound of insects buzzing in the sun-hot air, like dive bombers. We were meaning to go to the cave, but when we came to the trail leading north, further into the foothills, Cynda, who was leading us single file, stopped and turned around. "Oliver's gone up that way," she said, pointing to the right. "Shall we follow him?" I said "Why not? We've been there before." We had, but only a few hundred feet, because it was getting dark that time.

So, we turned north toward the mountain. The forest got thicker and the light changed—more like a big church. There started to be very tall pine trees, totally straight and really big around, and a new kind of stillness. The path rose gradually. We heard a hollow knock-knocking on a tree: maybe 20 feet above us was a woodpecker, brilliant black and red and white slashes and splashes of color, like a pirate all dressed up for war or a costume party, its head bobbing as it pecked at a huge ponderosa like a machine. It didn't even seem to notice us. We heard Oliver barking—more like a yelping—at something up ahead. "Watch out for rattlers," Kio said. Now the path was wider, and two people could walk next to each other. Kio and I walked in front. Neda and Cynda were talking in low voices behind us.

Sometimes it feels like everything is slowing down, even though it looks the same on the outside. Then everything starts to feel like it's alive. The trees, the plants and bushes with leaves and branches, the little solitary flowers and the bright red berries—it feels like they are breathing too, and they are flesh like our flesh, not so different as all that. And maybe that they are aware of us the same way we are aware of them. Not like seeing us with eyes or anything, but in other ways, like we're in the same energy space, and we are affecting each other. It only happens with me once in a while, like it did this time on that path. Usually, it doesn't last very long because I start thinking about it and my brain is going so much faster than everything else that I can't feel it any more, because everything else is going much slower. But when it's happening even the stones are alive, shining and shimmering in their hardness, and the dirt like fur. And animals—the jays and crows and squirrels and insects, everything that moves around like us, that goes faster—they are just like us, going places with plans and directions and problems to solve and things they have to get done. And Oliver—well he basically is a person just like us because he's been around humans so long.

I tried to describe it one time—we were at the cave—and Neda said, "It sounds like a dream."

"But maybe it's real," Cynda said. "I mean maybe that's more real."

"How can something be more real?" Kio said. "Either it's real or it's not. Things can't be more or less real."

"But plants," Neda said. "The thing about plants is that they can't move. They're rooted to the spot."

"Yeah," Kio said. "Plugged into their food source. They're like people on life-support in the hospital. I don't see how they could think or even feel anything."

"No wait," Neda said. "It's not that they can't move, it's that they don't need to move. Besides, they move by throwing seeds for other plants like them to grow. And they need water, and light, and minerals and stuff from the dirt. And if you need stuff, you must want stuff. That's energy."

"But how is that moving—throwing seeds for new plants?" Kio said.

"Well, it's not the one plant moving but it's the species moving. Like us—we're seeds thrown by our parents to make more creatures like us."

"Absolutely," Cynda said. "I absolutely think that plants have desire, because they need stuff. They have to solve problems just like us."

"But," Kio said, "you desire something that's not there—that's why you desire it. And plants have everything right there where they're rooted. They don't have to reach out for anything, the way animals do. They are completely a part of everything around them. They can't tell the difference between themselves and everything else. They don't feel anything because they don't need to feel anything."

"No," Neda said, "I don't agree! Plants are in an environment just like us. They have to survive just like us. I'll bet they know very well what other kinds of plants are around them, and how to fight a predator, and what plants they have to compete with, and all that."

Kio kind of snorted. "And how do they know all that, and do all that?"

"Chemicals," she answered. "Chemical signals. Smells that say 'come here' or 'go away.'"

"You think a plant doesn't feel it when you touch it?" I said.

There were little patches of moss—fuzzy turquoise green—on the flat rock where we sat facing the huge sky. I reached next to me and stroked a patch lightly with my index finger, like stroking a little animal. It felt soft and wiry at the same time, and it kind of tickled my finger. "You don't think it feels this?" I said.

"Of course, it does," Neda said. "It's alive isn't it? Everything that's alive has an inside! Everything wants to live, to keep on existing doesn't it? Even rocks." She reached out and stroked and patted the reddish rock in front of her with the palm of her hand. "I say this world is one big animal!" We all laughed, and even though Neda really meant it, she laughed too.

It was Oliver barking again up ahead that broke into my dreamy state, and almost exactly at the same time a big wide-antlered mule deer burst into view ahead of us, with Oliver right behind it yelping. It seemed silly and even stupid—a little animal like that chasing such a big one; he could have turned around and smashed him with his big hooves or speared him with his antlers, but I guess he didn't think of that. He was gone almost as soon as he appeared, and Kio shouting at Oliver to stop and Oliver paying no attention at all and disappearing as well into the brush. "Mean old dog!" Cynda said, and then we were surprised a second time by the path suddenly flattening out and opening up onto a wide mountain meadow covered with tall yellow-green grass and wildflowers; and a third time when a big skinny tall-eared jackrabbit exploded into the air right in front of us and took off like a bullet across the field in giant leaps—I swear, each one was about 20 feet! Then here comes Oliver running back, sniffing the ground, and before he could take off again Kio grabbed him by the collar and clicked his leash on him. "Mean old dog!" he said, and Oliver looked up at him, panting and smiling. He had no idea at all, or if he did he didn't really care.

Chapter Eleven

Rhizomatic Curriculum Development in Community of Philosophical Inquiry

The Concept of Rhizome

In its broadest sense, and offered here as an educational master-discourse, community of philosophical inquiry (CPI) may be defined as a form of deliberative dialogue dedicated to the ongoing reconstruction of the concepts that constitute our systems of belief. Those beliefs—about the concept "life" for example—inform and interact with not just our daily practices, behaviors, and reactions, but also with our approach to the disciplines of study. As such, the collective assemblages of concepts that make up our belief systems underlie the school curriculum. How we understand them and their relationships influence how we approach anthropology, history, language, mathematics, art, economics, and so on.

These assemblages are, to be sure, embedded within the larger terrains of a set of material conditions, a set of class markers, the institution of the school, religious traditions, ideologies, and current conditions in the politics of knowledge. The concepts, for example, that are considered central and common in historical inquiry in the nineteenth-century European academy and the twenty-first-century Latin American academy might turn out to be quite different. Each discipline is in a way an implicit genealogy of concepts.

How I understand the concept of "class," for example, is influenced by my "class," the group I identify with in contradistinction from that "other" group or groups, what my religious discourse says or doesn't say about different groups or types of people, and so on, and all kinds of subtle markers that influence me deeply but of which I am to a greater or less degree unconscious. It will also be connected with how I classify and categorize the world of humans using other criteria (intelligence, kindness, sensuality, care, etc.), and the plant world as well, and the world of art, and my everyday experience on the street. "Class," in other words, here opens up the prior concept of "classify," which raises issues of categorization and questions about natural kind, heading right in the direction of ontology. That is, once I allow the concept to spread across whatever semantic fields it touches on—the concept of someone having "class," for example, the question whether every classificatory scheme is culturally and historically constructed, the question of individual and general classes, and so forth—then the interrogation of the concept that CPI initiates could be said to be operating rhizomatically.

As an educational practice, community of philosophical inquiry offers an exemplary methodology for the interrogation of the beliefs that form tenuous lines between these multiple epistemological terrains. CPI lives to problematize concepts like self, justice, nature, truth, fact, plausibility, animal and human, knowing and believing, number, infinity, axiom, variable, function, and so on. As a form of discourse and as a pedagogy, it makes no pretensions to a hierarchical or foundationalist approach, and as such satisfies both Wittgenstein's (1969) claim that in matters of conceptual belief the "foundation-walls are carried by the whole house" (para. 248), and that "If the true is what is grounded, then the ground is not true, nor yet false" (para. 205). It also satisfies Deleuze and Guattari's (1987) suggestion that concepts are arranged, not hierarchically but rhizomatically, and are guided by principles of "connection and heterogeneity" into "collective assemblages of enunciation," by principles of multiplicity, rupture, deterritorialization, and reterritorialization (7–13, passim). The concept of the rhizome allows us to see that the common and central concepts that in fact are the curriculum in community of philosophical inquiry (and of which there is an indeterminate number, including those we invent), run across and through the disciplines, in various combinations, with various emphases, and with various emergent connections. Thus, they afford multiple entries for emergent philosophical reflection within each academic discipline. We can get to the disciplines—math, science, language, and so on—by reflecting on the concepts, and we can get to the concepts through reflecting on the disciplines.

Apart from reflection on the concepts, the disciplines are like the graveyards of the living dead; but through reflection, all the inert conceptual material—rendered moribund by the reification of the concepts in the form of "information" and by their imprisonment within ideologically locked-down networks of concepts—can come suddenly to life. When allowed to, the concepts are continually both challenging and being challenged by our experience and by the experience of others, and thereby de- and reterritorializing, connecting with other concepts, and reentering experience. When allowed free play, we can actually think of the curriculum as a living thing, an emergent whole in ongoing reconstruction, because the concepts that form its nodes of intensity are in constant proliferation and reconstruction. Exploring them through problematization and interrogation in communal dialogue makes a dimension of academic work visible that is typically thought of as coming after mastery of the discipline, but which I would suggest should always come with the discipline. That is to say, the philosophical dimension, in the form of the interrogation of concepts, should be a primary activity from the very beginning, because that interrogation opens a space that renders the nature of the scholarly and empirical work in the discipline more transparent.

For example, in mathematics, when the concept of proof is allowed rhizomatic play—that is, to migrate out of the purely mathematical semantic field and cross into other regions, where it connects with other concepts (like certainty, belief, persuasion), it loses its disciplinary halo and reveals itself as an aspect of lived experience. Once I have examined the concept of proof as a concept in play in everyday life, I am able to use it more flexibly and multivocally—that is, with more "background" information—in the context of tasks involving actual mathematical proof.

The fact that this form of interrogation through which we allow the concept its lines of flight in CPI is a communal dialogical one cannot be overemphasized. In effect the concept is being shared as it is being problematized, and whatever reterritorialization it experiences will be to some degree a collective experience. The concept is negotiated, not just with the other, but also with the others, with the collective. Not only are philosophical concepts common and central—always in part collectively constructed concepts—but they are also contestable, which becomes immediately apparent the moment they enter a space of dialogue, where point of view is the first truth of open discourse. Once they are recognized as contestable, they are open for critique. The concepts that inform the curriculum (for example the concept "fact"), once their solemn aura of univocity is dispersed, become tools for interrogating the curriculum itself as a knowledge system—for demystifying it, for problematizing it, and for transforming it in the image of their connections and correspondences. In fact it is in this interrogative process that reasoning skills are generated and develop robustly, because it is the discovery of contradiction, ambiguity, and aporia that fuels the drive to make judgments, and judgments are based on inferences, and once I start to become aware of my own inferential process, reasoning is the only clear warrant of the judgments that I have.

The Rhizome and the Epistemology of Communal Philosophical Inquiry

I would like to explore some possibilities of a rhizomatic approach to curriculum development, but before moving there, I want to say a few more things about the figure of the rhizome and the epistemology of communal philosophical inquiry. The metaphor of the rhizomatic as opposed to the arborescent structure of concepts was first introduced by Deleuze and Guattari (1987). A rhizomatic structure—of ideas, of relationships, of social organization, of economic or political organization—emphasizes the lateral over the vertical, resists hierarchical and nesting classification, and thereby challenges traditional boundaries and dichotomies. Can communal philosophical dialogue, when not dominated by some closed-system methodology from above, be understood as a rhizomatic epistemological structure?

Well, for one thing, I think that I notice a dialectical struggle between two impulses—crudely put, the vertical and the lateral—in spontaneous group argumentation, and affective and political (that is, power) organization. The vertical impulse moves to unify through establishing classes and categories, and identifying criteria through which the relationships between all things are illuminated. In vertical organization, above is distinguishable from below, and everything finds its proper place. The lateral impulse, which Levinas (1969), in opposition to "totality," calls "infinity," and that here is called the rhizome, is the impulse of difference, multiplicity, the plural. It makes distinctions that are not assimilable by a unity that includes them both; rather, it holds those distinctions in loose and provisional assemblages. Rather than arrange an idea above or below another, or in a relationship of exclusion or inclusion, the horizontal or rhizomatic impulse typically offers the counterexample that negates the all-statement status of the generalization, moves sideways or into another semantic field altogether, and sets up asymmetrical but related connections with the concept from which it broke away. This appears to be directly contradictory to the metaphor that I have found myself using in the past of the "barn-raising"—that is, of constructing a building—because a building requires things that hold each other up and that rest on a foundation. The rhizomatic metaphor has no obvious center or ground, no one fulcrum of support or main root.

Even if we console ourselves with Wittgenstein's (1969) suggestion, already quoted above, that "the foundation walls are carried by the whole house," the conflict between the two principles of organization appears irreconcilable. One is based on criteria that include other criteria, all of them superseded by yet another, higher criterion of "reasonableness" or "likelihood"; the other is based on Deleuze and Guattari's principle of the rhizome. One aspires to order, control, and clear boundaries through the imposition of a binary logic of hierarchical, nesting classes, with clear lines of inclusion and exclusion; the other insists on unpredictable, emergent "assemblages" and a non-hierarchical, a-centered field of knowledge, on the principle of multiplicity as opposed to the principle of unity, and for open-ended creation of new ideas as opposed to the reproduction or repetition of established patterns.

However, in the actual functioning of CPI, both principles can be seen to be operating, playing together, sometimes like a cat chasing its tail, and sometimes in a dialectical struggle. For example, the argument quite often proceeds by someone making a proposition or generalization, an "all statement" direct or implied, which—in the spontaneous emergence of dialogical argumentation—triggers a counterexample, which moves the group (or the personified Argument) to work to reconstruct the concept so that it can assimilate the counterexample. This results in a new generalization, and this movement from general to specific and back to general again contributes to a condition of "connection and heterogeneity," in which the concept divides but its elements remain connected, thus creating a new structure.

By way of a modest example, in a discussion about the question "what is thinking?" a group of ten-to-eleven-year-old children, in pursuing the goal of an overarching definition of thinking that would apply to all instances of the concept, actually generated five or six categories—for example "unconscious" or autonomic thinking, mathematical thinking, the thinking that occurs when listening to someone else, dream thinking, and self-talk (Kennedy, 2001). Each of the group's attempts to find a criterion that would cover all instances generated more, in Deleuze and Guattari's terms, "connected and heterogenous" criteria. When the conversation was called to a halt, the group had a multiplicity of kinds without an unambiguous larger class to fit them neatly into, a set of instances subsumed under a larger question that appeared unanswerable, or a matter of opinion, or a matter terminology. The question was, "Is all brain activity thinking?" If one answered that in the negative, then where was one to make the cut between thinking and not-thinking? It soon became clear that no one was willing to try to make it fall between conscious and unconscious thinking, and if one tried to put it between judgment and non-judgment, it became difficult to find instances of the latter, even in autonomic or reflexive instances like breathing or digesting.

What is significant is that this failure relative to the original mandate to "define" thinking—to answer the question put to the group—was in fact not considered a failure, but an opportunity for the development of a rhizomatic field of concepts and instances, which, had the group continued its inquiry another day or days, might well have taken an arboreal turn through the adding of instances or the refinement of categories; but there would always be one instance that would undermine the hegemonic impulse of arboreal reason. The horizontal, rhizomatic impulse is the direction of motion and the ultimate victor by attrition in any protracted interplay with the vertical, static arboreal, because one is emergent, and the other attempts to close and solidify boundaries. Clarity, intuition, new meanings emerge through their dialectical tension. When the group had finished, it was satisfied with a new, more inclusive, and more sophisticated idea of the phenomenon of thinking but was also freed, so to speak, from the "big question" of what it "is." Freedom from the big question does not mean it disappears, but that we work with it more flexibly, more ironically, more playfully, and therefore with more practical intelligence, more sensitivity to context, and more sense of the multiple ways in which it can be answered.

We may assume or at least hypothesize that the rhizomatic/arboreal argumentation patterns I have just described—the core dialectical tension between horizontal and vertical—operate isomorphically or analogically in the realms of desire and power in group process. Group affect, expressivity, influence, and involuntary relationships of authority or even of domination may be theorized the same way. The rhizomatic impulse is individualistic, egalitarian, multiple, ambiguous, hybrid, ironic, emergent, opportunistic, anarchistic, and communitarian; the arboreal impulse is linear, binary, ordering, centralizing, convergent, inclusive, totalizing. This is particularly meaningful in terms of power, for the rhizomatic—or perhaps the dialectic of the arboreal and the rhizomatic—represents that species-impulse, which Tocqueville (2002) identified nearly two hundred years ago simply as "democracy," which he characterized as "the most continuous, ancient, and permanent tendency known to history"—an "irresistible" movement, ". . . advancing century by century over every obstacle and even now going forward amid the ruins it has itself created" (15). Community of philosophical inquiry represents a form of classroom discourse that realizes and operationalizes a profound educational reconstruction in the interest of a truly democratic citizenry. As a normative speech situation (for which see Habermas 1984), an epistemological structure of assumptions, and a pedagogy that is loyal to both, it acts to produce what, as we have seen, Dewey (1916) called "social democracy"—a set of personal and cultural habits of joint communicative action that he considered the necessary basis for authentic political democracy.

Rhizomatic Curriculum Development

Finally, I would offer three possible models for organizing inquiry into the common, central, and contestable concepts within the school disciplines—a single-discipline, an inter-disciplinary, and a whole-curriculum approach. Each of these corresponds to a more general organization model for curriculum planning, whether within a single classroom, between classrooms, or including the whole school. Each can function more or less emergently, more or less rhizomatically, and more or less democratically.

A single-discipline approach will identify a group of concepts in, say, science, and through a process of shared questioning and their own deliberative dialogue, teachers and students will develop a series of exercises, discussion plans, and activities. Those concepts may be keyed to the science textbook currently in use, such that the concept "organism," for example, is explored through communal philosophical inquiry in the chapter in which it is produced and defined. This is in fact an invaluable strategy for demythologizing official texts and encouraging students and teachers to enter into dialogue with their epistemological assumptions, rather than accept them as given. As an expository text, the textbook presents its assumptions as final and authoritative—that is, it denies they are assumptions, and states them as necessary axioms for learning. It assumes, in a linear and hierarchical fashion, that the grasping the "basics"—in this case a previously determined understanding of the concept—is necessary to constructing further knowledge. To understand the concept as contestable introduces an element of de- and reconstruction into the learning situation and promises the development of new meanings. When a window for problematization of concepts through philosophical dialogue is opened, the textbook loses its status as bearer of hegemonic, officially sanctioned knowledge, and takes on a narrative status with which one can enter into dialogue. It is understood as a voice, a speaker, an interlocutor, as conditioned as any other text by ideology, historical placement, and material conditions. Because it keeps the grounding axioms of the discipline in open view, staying aware of their historical character, this form of reading is fundamental to the development of critical literacy.

The second model extends the identification of concepts across disciplines, and thus connects the elements of the curriculum as whole through an emergent network of contestable concepts. The concept "measurement," for example, can be problematized in multiple school subjects—whether science, mathematics, history, psychology, anthropology, economics, art, or music, and in fact allows the extension of student inquiry into the ruling and guiding assumptions of the process of schooling itself. This model would entail teachers and students keying the concept to the texts in the various disciplines, and thereby creating an interweaving network of inquiry, which would encourage teachers to understand the school curriculum as a whole, and to collaborate in the organization of their material, as well as identifying readings and assigning writings that connect disciplines, and even sharing classroom time and space.

A third model would open the generation of common, central, and contestable concepts to the whole school. The use of a "central subject," either grade-wide or school-wide, is one precursor of this, but the generation of emergent philosophical themes that become the deliberative objects of the entire community—concepts like "justice," "change," "technology," "violence," or "nature"—goes beyond this in scope and participation. A concept like "justice" can be woven through different content areas in the classroom, become the subject of whole- or part-school meetings and dialogue groups, and culminate in school-wide action groups—whether concerned, for example, with "justice" within the school community, within the larger community in which the school is set, or somewhere else on the planet. In this stage of collaborative inquiry, philosophy returns to its own disciplinary boundaries in the sense that it is no longer bound by one content area or another, but it also responds to actual immediate instances where the concept is in play, and results in real democratic action. In fact, it is not just in collaborative deliberation that any philosophical concept undergoes reconstruction, but in lived experience and the politics of relation. Here the school functions as the embryonic community in which habits, not just of deliberation, but also of neighborhood, community, and planetary activism are forged. In this school-wide model, philosophy, after dispersing itself among the disciplines, returns to the agora, which is its rightful place in authentic democratic community, and deliberative communal dialogue functions as the emergent compass, the tutor, and the normative horizon of that collective called "school."

In the next, final chapter I seek to narrow down the discussion of the genesis of the new sensibility and democratic social character, and to focus on the dialectical journey of human subjectivity as understood in dialogical self theory (DST), which starts from the premise that self is multiple, polyphonic, and, in healthy circumstances, engaged over the course of the life cycle in an ongoing dialectical process of transformative reconstruction. The implicit (albeit never quite realized) telos of this process is an ideal of integrity understood as integration or in Jungian terms "individuation," characterized in DST discourse as a subject whose various I-positions are in dialogue with each other rather than opposition, mutual occlusion, or subordination. I identify two broad characteristics of self-systems—authoritarian and democratic, one "closed" and one "open." As a closed system, the authoritarian subject resists dialogue and stochastic emergence, and as such risks stagnation. The democratic or open system is oriented to the integration of I-positions as distinct but interlocutive voices in continual conversation. The self is co-constructed with actual others, whether the introjected voices of significant others or actual, breathing others. And just as the self cannot develop without dialogue between its I-positions, the social, economic, and political world cannot develop towards *shalom* and universal justice (*dikaiosune*) without dialogue between actual others, which is essential to the communicative socio-cultural practice that we call democracy. Finally, I identify the historical emergence of the dialogical self and the democratic ideal with education, which is here understood in it most basic, archetypal identity as, following Dewey, a field of dialogical encounter between childhood "impulse" and adult "habit." Such an intentional community has the capacity to function as a unique holding environment, an embryonic society dedicated to the emergence of new forms of life, a place set apart for acquiring the habits of both democratic selfhood and democratic polity.

Chapter Twelve

Dialogue and Dialectic in the Politics of the Self

To become human is an art.

—Novalis, *Pollen and Fragments*

I Am an Other

"Je est un autre . . . C'est faux de dire 'je pense,' on devrait dire 'on me pense.'" ("I is an other. It is false to say, 'I think.' One should say, 'someone thinks me'" (Rimbaud 2004 27). The problem of the one and the many. The I that is me and the we that is I. In the face of this ambiguity, I start with the concept (which is nothing more or less than a concept) of the multiple self, made up, after Hubert Hermans's formulation, of various "I-positions" in conversation with each other (Hermans 2018; Hermans and Hermans-Konopka 2010). On dialogical self theory's (DST) account, I am a community—a society even—of I-positions, however fraught that community's internal relations may be; and the boundary between that inner society and the "outer" society of which I am a part and that is a part of me is hard to be sure of, sometimes hard to find. Maybe the boundary could be thought of as an inherently intersectional, interactional, transitional zone where subject and object, self and other, ego and alter, real and imaginary, self and world, are entangled.

I am an indeterminate—or never completely determined—number of characters in search of an author. Some talk loudly, some are barely audible, some are offstage. Some are conscious, some are preconscious.

Some are occupational: employee, employer, professional, ruler, subordinate, parent, spouse, proprietor, competitor. Some are socio-historical and positional: class member, culture member, privileged one, subaltern, patrician, insurgent, anarchist, reactionary. The system of interlocutors that they comprise is underlain and informed, suffused, framed, moderated by those symbolic personae that C. G. Jung (1969) called "archetypes of the collective unconscious": child, hero, fool, trickster, lover, hermit, androgyne, wanderer, wounded healer. These emergent unconscious contents, expressed in mythologies worldwide and central to Jungian therapy, are not exactly I-positions but rather archetypal personae, feeling tonalities, affective styles, implicit narratives, perceptual modalities that, when they emerge, suffuse the self-system. For example, the child archetype, expressed in numerous mythologies as the divine child, embodies the abandoned foundling, often threatened by extraordinary malevolent dangers from which it is protected by the forces of nature and the gods; at once an orphan and the cherished androgynous child of the gods living in "primal solitude" but never lonely. On Jung's account, its appearance in dreams heralds future integration, an incipient psychic wholeness, and mediates between the unconscious and the conscious mind, signaling a "shifting of the center of personality from the ego to the [whole] self" (Jung and Kerenyi 1969, 100). The archetypes cannot be summoned at will. They appear like weather at certain moments in the process of the unification of conscious and unconscious contents of the psyche, and the attempt to appropriate them as conscious I-positions only leads to distortion and self-deception.

Some I-positions are ephemeral, episodic, called forth by context or circumstance then retreating into another, less conscious layer of the psyche. Some, on the other hand, are loud superego positions—always active, vying for dominance among the other I-positions: they presume (naively) to be the organizing principle, e.g., "the head of this household," or the "winner" (although always haunted by the "loser"). As such, if you're not with them you're against them: the authoritarian personality within. They tend to be the positions associated with social and professional roles: deeply ambitious one, intellectual, moralist, performer, competitor. And some, finally, are potential black holes: sexual fantast, narcissist, deeply angry one, predator, sadist, masochist, outcast, abject, addict, victim. These are alienated positions that tend to threaten the whole structure, the gateways to psychosis "demons." They are associated with Jung's "shadow," the dark abject psychic materials that we project onto others in order to avoid confronting in ourselves (Jung 2001/1912).

Some I-positions are not even "in" me if it weren't for the fact that they speak in me, in that boundary-zone between inside and out, through the Freudian dynamics of introjection. These are referred to in DST language as "external" I-positions. They are real people—my father, my brother, sister, lover, spouse, partner, friend, even my enemy or detractor. Their voices sometimes speak the loudest—testimony, again, to the fluidity, frangibility, indeterminacy, ambiguity, mutability, liminality of self-world and self-other boundaries. Even the boundary between living and dead becomes ambiguous here: my father, dead these many years, speaks to me, if only implicitly, in a whisper, a nod, a frown, a pointed memory.

The Internal Politics of Self

I myself am a first illustration of the problem of the one and the many. Each of us is a singular concatenation and entanglement of I-positions—a singularity, the "single one"—but only as seen from the outside, by others; inside, I am never fully explicitly me. I'm an "emergent": a virtual being becoming-actual but never fully (Bluemink 2020). Maybe this was what Paolo Freire was talking about when he described the human ontological condition as one of permanent "unfinishedness" (2005, 84); or Deleuze and Guattari (1987) with their notion of "becoming"—becoming child, becoming girl, becoming animal, becoming human . . . becoming me. And how does one deal with the volatility of I-positions continually moving from background to foreground to background to middle ground to foreground to background, conversing and negotiating? That movement has all the characteristics of complex or stochastic systems: change in one part changes the whole; the system operates somewhere between chaos and stagnation, in constant transformation triggered by the influence of "attractors"—"a state or behavior toward which a dynamic system tends to evolve, represented as a point or orbit in the system's phase space" (*Attractor* 2023)—which in DST language may be associated with the emergence of "metapositions"—ways of, heuristics for understanding and grasping all my I-positions as elements of one meaningful system. We may also associate the metaposition with Sigmund Freud's "ego"—the function that works to keep all my I-positions on one page, so to speak.

Stochastic systems, we are told, are emergent, nonlinear, "barely predictable," and characterized by "noise"—ambiguity, ambivalence, bias, variability, error. As "attractors" in such a system, metapositions emerge and dissipate and reemerge. However, at the risk of oversimplification, we may identify two broad metapositional styles, both of them influenced by culture, temperament, ideological formation, experience, and education. The authoritarian self-system gravitates towards system stagnation, the lockdown of I-positions under one ruler—an unruly dictatorship. Hermans's calls this "over-positioning," and Deleuze and Guattari "over-coding." On a social and political level, the authoritarian metaposition is dangerous to us all, not least to the one who is prone to it; as Nicolas Berdyaev, referring to Stalinism, pointed out, "chaos can wear the appearance of absolute order" (Berdyaev 1935, 18).

When self is shaped, either by familial or socio-cultural models or both, into a strict hierarchal system of domination, dialogue between I-positions becomes fraught, and even taboo. Consider Plato's "tripartite soul" composed of reason (*logos*), spirit (*thumos*) and appetite (*epithume*) (Plato 1941, 129–38, iv.434D–441C)). The first must dominate the second in the interest of dominating the third. There is a permanent tension and the possibility of revolt, whether by the common folk (appetite) or the army/police (spirit). Plato's "just" or "righteous" man (*sic*) knows how to balance them, but never such that the hierarchy is disturbed in its basic relations of power. The index of the historical reach of this patriarchal model is the extent to which, as historical mythographer Georges Dumézil (1970) argued, it characterized the basic social and political model of the most warlike Indo-European societies of the ancient world and, arguably, the West until the American and French revolutions: the nobles (reason) dominate the peasants and workers (appetitive) through its police and military (spirit, enthusiasm). On the individual psychological level, we could call Plato's (and Descartes's) reason-as-pure-rationality the "over-positioned" or "over-coded" metaposition that functions by repression and denial, and which promotes a permanent internal atmosphere of equivocation and conflict. In the nomenclature of Freud's psychic economy, we may identify the authoritarian metaposition with a hyperactive "superego," the passionate demanding proud moralistic "ought," which seeks compulsively, neurotically, to act as the master or regulator of the system.

On the other end of the spectrum of relations between I-positions in the community of the self, and in contrast to the authoritarian metaposition, we have what might be called the democratic or dialogical metapositional style. The democratic self-system takes Freud's most crucial observation about modern humanity—that, as rational as it may be, "the ego is not master in its own house"—seriously (Freud 1917). As such, to understand the self as potentially dialogical and democratic seems to imply a loss in the capacity of any given metaposition to unify the different I-positions in any final way—a radical decentering. Without a unifier, the self becomes contested ground among I-positions. The danger at this end of the spectrum is associated with pathologically open systems: whereas closed, authoritarian systems are liable to stagnation, entropy, and implosion, open systems run the risk of chaos and dissolution. This hints at dissociative identity disorder, which I will call the fugal personality: there is a loss of that metapositional optic that manages, in however shifting a light, to see all my I-positions, whether visible to me or more vaguely felt, as parts of one system.

The fugal personality is always waking up in another town (position), not quite conscious of how he got there. His disunity is dangerous for himself and his intimate others, although, like an artist, he or she may well be doing it as a sort of existential evolutionary experiment—witness Dada and Surrealism. Rimbaud, for example said, "The poet makes himself a seer through a long, immense and reasoned derangement of all the senses" (Nicholl 1999, 26). In both cases—the stagnant and the chaotic—there is a disturbance of the metaposition—either an internal tyrant (authoritarian) or dissipating (fugal). However, in a healthy open system, it is just this internal decentering and commitment to ongoing self-reconstruction—triggered by the ego's recognition that it is not master in its own house—that characterizes the dialogical self; and as I shall argue below, it is just the internal democratization of the self that makes possible and is made possible by—is both supported and demanded by—social and political dialogue and democratization. This chiasmic relation between the personal and the political is the hope of humanity's path forward; both the dialogical self and the ideal democratic polis operate as open, self-organizing systems.

In the dialogical-democratic model of the self, the ever-emergent metaposition is not superegoic tyrant or pathological absentee, but facilitator, reconciler of I-positions: the one who gets them recognizing each other and talking, adapting, maneuvering, compromising, repositioning with each other in mind. In providing an emergent narrative of self through time and changes (on the edge of chaos), the facilitator metaposition makes of the ego's loss of mastery a virtue rather than a handicap. There is no master in deep democracy, whether internal or external, except the group, including the group "inside" each individual. This demands greater self-discipline than the authoritarian metaposition (although the authoritarian might claim the opposite), and a greater willingness to deal with otherness—the otherness within the self as well as in the world "outside." It represents a rebuke both to the Platonic notion of self-mastery and to the autocratic imagination, and an affirmation of democracy as an evolutionary necessity, dedicated to renouncing the master-slave syndrome and the psychological engines of domination and exploitation. We must rethink the facilitator metaposition as both overseeing and participating in the continuous conversation between I-positions, and dealing as a therapist with the pathogenic, over-positioned I-positions—self-condemning, punitive voices as well as narcissistic follies.

Telos/Horizon/Dialectic

The self as being-in-time, as being-towards-death, as becoming-self, as becoming-whole, as becoming-actual, as a grand narrative under endless revision, as characters in search of an author. In a situation of health (Old English hælþ "wholeness, a being whole, sound, or well"), the psyche's autopoietic movement is towards an ideal state of coordination of I-positions, and coordination of perspectives with actual others: the intersection of internal and external community and the reconciliation of conscious and unconscious elements of self. This ideal state has been named *Self* (Jung's term for the integration of conscious and unconscious), individuation, self-actualization, self-realization, wholeness, *shalom*, righteousness (*dikaiosune*), integrity. In this figure, the paradisiacal or infantile openness to the world that was lost in growing up is projected forward as a goal of the life cycle: to experience oneself as a whole—a recovery of infantile narcissism. As N. O. Brown put it, the "human" is "that species of animal who has the historical project of recovering [his or her] own childhood" (Brown 1959, 84). The paradox lies in the fact that to reach it would mean entropy, stasis—system death. In fact there appears to be no actual, finally integrated "I"—only virtual, metastable, becoming-actual "me." There is no final overcoming of the internal contradictions that in fact drive selving, which is an unending process, dedicated to an infinitely receding horizon. The integration of conscious and unconscious, mind and body, ego, superego, and id—a "new mind," "one voice," the golden body—infinitely deferred. Final reconciliation with the other and with one's own otherness (which is the same thing): infinitely deferred. Being as becoming-other in the service of becoming-self.

I am a complex of elements whose unity is inseparable from the tensions among them. My personal existence is a dialectical structure of contradictions, a working pattern dedicated to seeking unity among opposites, to working through, a search for a "third thing." Here dialectic is understood as a process of continual reconstruction: chaos becoming order just beyond my understanding/grasp. To speak through and across boundaries. To allow contradiction in order to overcome contradiction, albeit every resolution of a contradiction presents us with a situation in which new, unpredictable contradictions will emerge soon enough, which, if I am to be happy—*eudaimonia*—I must learn to welcome as opportunities for becoming-self, which in the end means relinquishment and reconciliation. Self-renunciation as the final act of self-actualization.

At the various levels of awareness that characterize self, the ego, albeit no longer master in the house, presides over the multiplicity of I-positions in their various connections with each other, whether mutually supportive, antagonistic, or indifferent. The "good" boy or girl, the rebel, the addict, the shy one, the egotist, the compassionate one, the competitive one, the jealous one, the generous one, the frank one, the secretive one, the quick one, the slow one, the dependent one, the independent one, the brilliant one. All are timeless: they have no clear beginning in me except in dramatic cases of trauma or positive breakthrough experience of some kind. They are deeply shot through with the experience of other people, and entangled with those external I-positions that are in fact also embodied others—who are physically outside us but psychologically inside us, living or dead, individual or generalized: my lover, my father, my mother, my brother or sister, my child, my friend, my enemy, my double ("semblable"), my competitor, benefactor, boss, subordinate, or nemesis. These external I-positions do not so much speak within us as watch within us. My internalized father watches the bad or the good boy, my mother watches the creative one, my partner watches the relational me.

Typically—unless unrepentantly channeling Walt Whitman (1851) ("Do I contradict myself? Then I contradict myself. I am large. I contain multitudes," in Song 51)—one feels the intrinsic need to harmonize the multiplicity of I-positions. One feels the need for a stable metaposition (although Whitman's may be just that), a narrative that allows them all to speak, to influence each other; in fact, to change, to transform, to reconstruct each other. But the ego is not master in its own house, and dialectical reconstruction is driven by contradictions. Pathology—both social and individual—haunts the scene. Often there is an I-position that seeks to dominate, a hegemonic impulse that reflects the need for security, often closely connected with an external I-position—my father, or some other internalized authority figure. And if my I-positions, because their differences are too contradictory (e.g., chaste and hypersexual, hedonist and acetic, pacifist and patriot, extrovert and introvert) are mutually occluded, self-contained, compartmentalized, out of touch with each other—it is here that the dialogical self shades into dissociative identity disorder.

In fact, one could speculate that the latter, formerly labeled as "multiple personality disorder," represents a historical forerunner of DST: as, we might say, a first, conflicted stage in the deconstruction of the Cartesian punctual self in late modernism, which is later, in postmodernism, de-pathologized and normalized in the sublation of the dialogical self. As such, the victims of dissociative identity disorder might be seen as involuntary psycho-historical prophets, evolutionary precursors, failed but crucial experiments in the politics of internal multiplicity. The form of selving that would make them healthy calls for initiating dialogue between the occluded I-positions, which is the mission of DST practice. It is this opening of dialogue between antagonistic positions that holds promise for their mutual reconstruction, leading to a more open system—a more democratic system, in that it allows all positions a voice.

As such, the implicit ideal of DST is integrity—the integration of I-positions as distinct but mutually supportive voices—although that ideal is always held in the face of the paradox of development: integrity is only realized by undergoing contradiction, interruption, difference, deconstruction. The dialectic of selving is in keeping with the psychoanalytic theory of healthy regression—*reculer pour mieux sauter*—and the developmental doctrine, championed by Heinz Werner (1957) that integration proceeds through differentiation and reconstruction, is in fact always re-integration on another level. The situation is further complicated by the fact that I-positions are relatively autonomous—they have a life of their own, and are fueled and animated by psychological archetypes (child, hero, trickster, etc.)—autonomous complexes whose roots are just beyond conscious reach,

Is final integration ever possible? Maybe there are moments of a different kind of time—*aion, kairos, ekstasis*—exemplary, premonitory, prophetic moments "on the mountaintop"; moments when the ceaseless flow of difference and repetition—of disruption, self-interrogation, positioning and repositioning and counter-positioning—expands into the present moment, which is now, and new configurations of self open up: moments in which we experience simultaneously the unity and the multiplicity of the self. But there is no dwelling—even in tents—on the mountaintop.

Dialogue and Dialectic

The dialectic of selving is moved by the engine of dialogue. It works *dia* (through) the *logos* (the word, narrative, discourse). Whereas the dialectic represents an inexorable demand—an autopoietic *conatus* or *nisus*, an intrinsic drive for transformation ("I must change my life")—dialogue implies a conscious choice to encounter otherness, to confront the contradictions within the self, both internal and extended to include actual others, in a discursive zone of mutual both acknowledgment and interrogation.

Dialogue is not a search for fusion; the dialectic is always there as ineluctable difference, demanding resolution, the third thing, the sublation, the reconciliation. Dialogue is boundary-work; a purposive opening onto both the other before me and the other within me. Dialogue talks across the fence for the purpose of dismantling it, although (again, paradoxically) to do so completely would be fusion, and hence entropic. Dialogue is inseparable from the willingness to be changed through encounter with another perspective, by stepping into that space between self and other—Martin Buber's "between" (Buber 1965; Buber 1948; Silverman 1986)—and to "self-correct," to undergo reconstruction. Inwardly, multiple I-positions speak to each other, get to know each other's voices and narratives, accept each other, see each other in themselves, themselves in each other, seeking freedom to be at home with themselves in their otherness. The goal is mutual reconstruction, a third thing. As such, dialogue is inherently creative and transformative; the healthy self is an open system on the edge of chaos, walking a fine line, continually transforming, reconfiguring the relations between identity and difference.

The reconciliation and integration of my I-positions goes hand in hand, succeeds or fails, in its capacity to relate dialogically with others. This relationality is not just a socio-culturally induced habit ("nurture") but the expression of an ontological imperative ("nature"). As Emmanuel Levinas, expanding on Buber, put it, "The I in its relation with the Thou is further related to itself by means of the Thou, i.e., it is related to the Thou as to someone who in turn relates itself to the I, as though it had come into delicate contact with itself through the skin of the Thou. It thus returns to itself by means of the Thou" (1991, 142). This return to itself, if it is made possible "by means of the thou," means that selving is always that working out of I-positions that involves interactions with living breathing others. The most obvious and direct example of this process is the internalized position of an intimate other, the spouse or "partner" for example, who is both outside me, and is an internalized I-position who carries something like a superego function: she or he is that other self who is also myself, and who implicitly observes, judges, idealizes, accepts, encourages, or criticizes me, both as a flesh and blood singularity in our actual ongoing relationship and as a voice within me. If there is conflict or contradiction between my I-positions, my intimate partner is implicated both as a living breathing person and as an external I-position. I am driven dialectically to resolve this contradiction, spurred on by the *nisus*—the search for integrity. This is demanded of me by my I-position of parrhesiastes, the one who practices *parrhesia*, who speaks the truth openly, the one who must have nothing to hide, for whom transparency is the only valid token of ongoing integration (Foucault 2019).

The situation is further complicated to the extent that my partner as an external I-position is not the same "person" as my flesh and blood partner. The former is virtual and the latter is actual. The former, as an introject, is an amalgam of my own fears and desires, a superego figure; the latter is a living breathing singularity, a veritable Other. We are, as Levinas (1987) remarked of the human condition, marked by radical alterity and unalterable difference—by the "irreducible alterity of the other person" (13), although we are also mirrors for each other and of the same flesh, both essential sameness and incommensurability, a site of mutual contagion and entanglement. As a weak telepathic system, we know things about each other that we don't even know we know, and don't know things that we think we do.

Faced with contradiction within the system, I seek, not to repress its source but to reintegrate it in a third thing, a reconstruction, a re-balancing of internal and external I-positions, a sublation through which it no longer represents a threat or an occlusion—in Hermans (2010) term, a reconstructed "position repertoire." The problematic element in the system, once freed to speak frankly (parrhesia), to enter dialogue with the other I-positions, becomes, for the moment anyway, the system "attractor"—it triggers system reconstruction. The conflict is solved, not through repression but through an alteration in its emotional valence. In being acknowledged, addressed, and listened to, it is no longer a threat to the relationship that needs to be suppressed or compartmentalized, but the site of an exercise in transparency, through which the impulse it represents is acknowledged and thereby takes on a new meaning, one that no longer threatens the self-system and the partnership system, but rather enlarges and enhances them. It is, in other words, sublimated non-repressively; and it is accomplished through opening a dialogue between the positions in play, through which they reposition themselves.

In such a process of facing and working dialogically through contradictions in the self-system, what Hermans has called the "promoter position" assumes a key role. The latter is understood as the internal voice that supports and encourages my search for the ongoing reconstruction of I-positions. It may be an external I-position—a parent, friend, partner, colleague, or teacher—who affirms, implicitly or explicitly, my self-project. The promoter position is epitomized in the educator and the prophet—the one who sees my possibility where I do not, a voice of unconditional encouragement whose role it is to "lead forth" (*educere*). It is also present, however marginalized, in any given culture as what Hermans calls a "we position": a set of values, sometimes codified in a religious faith, but in fact in any familial, social, economic, and political discourse that insists on the emancipatory possibilities of the human project and on the evolutionary possibilities of the human species for realizing universal peace, justice, and mutual aid.

Democracy Internal and External, and a New Sensibility

The self is co-constructed with actual others, whether the introjected voices of significant others or actual, breathing others. And just as the self cannot develop without dialogue between its I-positions, the social, economic, and political world cannot develop towards shalom and universal justice (*dikaiosune*) without dialogue between actual others, which is essential to the communicative socio-cultural practice that we call democracy. As Peter McLaren and Ramin Farahmandpur (2005) point out, "the reinvention of the self must be linked to the remaking of the social, which implies a shared vision . . . of democratic community and an engagement with the language of social change, emancipatory practice, and transformative politics" (44). That shared vision, which is constructed on the notion of concern for the Other as the only universal moral good, implies that any project aimed at reconstructing the self needs to address the broader issue of social reconstruction, and vice versa; McLaren and Farahmandpur's link connects in both directions. As such, the dialectic of selving has political implications. The metaposition in the self that puts my I-positions in a dialogical relation also puts me in a dialogical relation with my social and cultural and political context. A democratized internal self-system intersects with the larger "self" of the culture and acts to change it, to open, orient it—again after McLaren and Farahmandpur, to make space for a "revolutionary citizenship," one that "work[s] toward a new type of democratic governance and redistribution of economic and political power" (157). Given that the dialogical self is located at the intersection of the internal and external psychological environments, the dialectical process of selving, of ongoing reconstruction of the inner, is ineluctably entangled with the ongoing reconstruction of the outer.

We may speculate that the internal conflict of I-positions reflects, analogously or otherwise, some outer conflict between the we-positions (race, ethnicity, gender, sexuality, class, agency) of the culture system, and that the resolution of discord among internal I-positions has the potential to introduce new attitudes, practices, and beliefs in the culture, and vice versa. In the process of cultural and social evolution, those who resolve internal issues with new solutions in the microsphere of the self become potential leaders or prophets of those solutions in the macrosphere of the social, and thus exemplars of what, as we have seen, Dewey (1916) called "social democracy," or the democratic social character, without which, he argued, genuine political democracy is impossible. A good number of the conflicts within the self—and hence within the culture—have to do with gender and sexuality, but others have to do with social justice—issues of economic equality for example, or racial justice, or inter-species relations. The vegan, for example, who has become convinced through internal dialogue that the mass torture and slaughter of animals for food and trophy represents a form of unconscionable genocide, plays a prophetic role, becomes a voice for abolition within the culture. In a genuinely democratic system, there is a chiasmic relation between individual and society: society provides a place for the ongoing reconstruction of the dialogical self, and the dialogical self (that is, the democratic social character or personality) makes possible the openness to social change that political democracy requires in order to survive and flourish.

The democratic personality is, in the terms stated above, an open system in the sense of self-positioning on the edge of chaos, as opposed to closed system of the authoritarian personality, which is afraid of change and positioned on the edge of stagnation. The closed system fears chaos as an existential peril, and its negative epithets—"the far left," or "socialism," or "communism," or "radicalism," or "perversion"—or all five in one breath—signal the fear of the potential rupture and deterritorialization that open systems, characterized as they are by sexual and gender mutability, ethnic multiplicity, and class mobility, represent. Haunted as it is by a sense of moral danger, the authoritarian personality is dedicated to exclusionary politics and control; it resists the stochastic emergence of new solutions by over-positioning, and clings to relations of hierarchy and domination, both within and without. Fearing as it does the shadow of the monstrous in social change, it becomes monstrous itself, as is so often illustrated by the loud public moralist and his dirty secrets.

The democratic personality on the other hand is fueled by an emancipatory impulse, which Paulo Freire characterized as an existential sense of our "unfinishedness" both as individuals and as a species, our desire to "become more," which he describes as the human "ontological vocation" (2005, 84). What drives the dialectic is our sense of what we could be, a token of our positive experience of identity-in-difference and is as much a collective as an individual impulse—a we-position. It represents our felt recognition that we are ontologically entangled with the other and with others, and that this entanglement is to be navigated through dialogue and ongoing reconstruction. It is a utopian impulse, but only in the sense in which Marcuse (1969), as we have seen, uses the word—as "that which is blocked from coming about by the power of established societies." (4). It may be associated with not just the Freirean ontology of the "unfinished" species, but also in Dewey's (1916) more secular, pragmatic notion of social democracy, which, as we have also seen, he describes as ". . . much more than a form of government; it is primarily a mode of associated living, of conjoint communicated experience" (87). The form of subjectivity this suggests is characterized, he says, as realizing both "greater individualization on the one hand, and a broader community of interest on the other." What might seem paradoxical—the more individualized the more identified with the collective—is in fact consistent with the notion of the dialectic of selving explored above: a becoming-porous of the boundaries between self and other, the opening of dialogue between internal and external I-positions; the isomorphism of the politics of the self and the politics of the polis, of microstructure and macrostructure.

Dewey (1916), writing early in the last century, does not, at least directly, associate the historical emergence of social democracy with an ontological vocation or evolutionary drive, but with the material base—"modes of manufacture and commerce, travel, migration and intercommunication"—which implies a gradualist, pragmatic approach to its advent. Marcuse, on the other hand, speaks at that century's midpoint, when the stakes are even higher, marked as they are by the astonishing, mind-numbing human monstrosities of the Holocaust and Hiroshima, and when capitalism has begun to generate contradictions that now, early in a new century, present themselves as existential threats to the whole planet: extreme economic inequalities, permanent war, and rapidly advancing climate change with its three (among many) consequences: worldwide viral epidemics as a result of ecological disruption, exploding global migration, and the return of reactionary politics.

This "perfect storm" of mutual causation mocks a gradualist approach, and triggers what Marcuse called the Great Refusal to participate in the structures of domination, alienation, and mental slavery within which we are interpellated. And the dialectical response to this condition of alienation, the evolutionary advance that it triggers, emerges, as we have seen, in the form of "new sensibility"—the reconstruction of the desiring system marked by "a new experience of nature," by "an instinctual revulsion against the values of the affluent society" and "the appearance of new instinctual needs and values." He announces, as we have seen, a new "libidinal rationality" or "sensual reason" in "the emergence of "a new type of [hu]man, with a vital, biological drive for liberation" (Marcuse 1969, 23, 28, 37; Kennedy 2012b). And to what extent, we may ask, is Marcuse's utopian formulation, this transformation at the level of "instinct" and the unconscious, connected with what I have called the democratic personality—the open, dialogical self-system, which to the extent that the reconstruction of self is isomorphic with social reconstruction, identifies the politics of selving with the politics of the polis?

It has recently been suggested by anthropologist David Graeber and archeologist David Wengrow that the democratic—or on a more generic level, the anarchist—impulse, is a perennial element in the history of the species; that "from the very beginning, or at least as far back as we can trace such things, human beings were self-consciously experimenting with different social possibilities," and that one of those possibilities was and is what we call direct democracy, or anarchism, which Deleuze and Guattari would describe as a "line of flight" that evades the "overcoding" and control of the "plane of organization," the closed system of power and domination, and out of which new social forms can come into the world, "allowing people to imagine that other arrangements are feasible for society as a whole" (Graeber and Wengrow 2021, 107, 117).

Democracy and egalitarianism represent for Graeber and Wengrow an inherent psycho-social form of life that is in our DNA as a species, a permanent possibility. Those who explore that possibility tend to attribute its emergence to changes in the material base in the form of greater general economic equality—changes in Dewey's "modes of manufacture and commerce, travel, migration and intercommunication," or Marcuse's technologically enabled post-scarcity economy that, he argues (1955), represents the possibility of mitigating "surplus repression," and hence enabling the new sensibility. In turn, the new sensibility may also be associated with Wilhelm Reich and Alexander Lowen's bioenergetic theory, which identifies "character armor" as at the instinctual source of the authoritarian personality, and offers the possibility of lifting it through "orgonomic" or somatic therapy (Reich 1946). What dialogical self theory helps us understand is that those social, economic, and political dimensions are mirrored in the internal politics of subjectivity, and that they operate through mutual causation between inner and outer worlds. As I-positions form, reach consciousness, encounter each other, experience harmony or conflict, reposition, reconstruct, and reformulate under the aegis of an emergent metaposition, those ongoing changes alter the way we experience the social and political domain, and the possibilities we see there for agentic change. In an open system, the healthy dialectic of selving manifests in the world as lines of flight, a breaking away from overcoded systems of domination, exclusion, exploitation, and the possibility of a "new experience of nature," "new instinctual needs and values," the "actual felt liberation of the mind and of the body from aggressive and repressive needs," "the emergence of vital, biological drive for liberation"—the new sensibility.

Childhood and Education

If we do believe that the open-system dialogical self and social democracy represent an intrinsic evolutionary drive, a deep tendency of the human heart and a developmental promise of the species, then what form of education, in the broadest sense of that term, acts to nurture it? Can it be fostered in the next generation in an institution such as the school, or is it always only a line of flight, a molecular movement, a deterritorialization from the overcoded molar structure that is state and economy and class, trapped as it is in binary constructs (man-woman, gay-straight, child-adult, black-white, public-private, etc.)? Can education structured as "school" function as a laboratory of the new sensibility? What promise does the phenomenon of neoteny—the extraordinarily long human childhood and development of the big human brain—represent for a dialectics of selving and for socio-cultural reconstruction?

As we have seen, Dewey (1922) suggested that it is in the encounter between adulthood and childhood that the promise of new "habits" lies. In his sense of the word, habits "form our effective desires and furnish us with our working capacities . . . [they] constitute the self," and "in any intelligible sense of the word will, they are will." What he calls "impulse," on the other hand, "brings with itself the possibility but not the assurance of a steady re-organization of habits to meet new elements in new situations." On his account, the promise and the problematic of the encounter of the generations lies in allowing childhood impulse (also referred to as "instinct") to act as a "pivot of readjustment upon which the re-organization of activities turn, agencies of deviation for giving new directions to old habits and changing their quality." The problem with formal education so far is that "an impatient, premature mechanization of impulsive activity after the fixed patterns of adult of thought and affection" has, in the encounter between the generations been "too strong to permit immature impulse to exercise its reorganizing potentialities." The original plasticity or "modifiability" of childhood, which has the "power to remake old habits, to recreate," is neutralized by a closed gerontomorphic system that suppresses lines of flight or detours them into the "black holes" either of "the territory of arrested and encrusted habits," or "the region in which impulse is a law unto itself" (Dewey 1922, 25, 96, 98, 104). As such, the evolutionary possibilities inherent in neural development throughout the long human childhood (Pearce 2002) are forfeited.

This analysis would suggest that it is in the evolution of the adult-child relation, or what DeMause (1975) called "child-rearing modes," that the promise of personal and social reconstruction lies—where the open self-system of the democratic personality can emerge on a universal level. Re-cognizing childhood as an evolutionary frontier and constructing the child-adult encounter that is school in light of that recognition is critical to the emergence of the new sensibility, or, as Dewey (1922, 128) put it, to the emergence and formation of habits that are "more intelligent, than those now current," which is to say a form of "self" or "will" that provides a social space that fosters and encourages the dialogical self and the dialogical polis. Understood as an outpost of an evolutionary frontier, school functions as what Dewey called an "embryonic society"—an intentional intergenerational community dedicated to the new solution, the becoming-human of the species, the dialectical advance, orchestrated in the encounter between child and adult.

Child-self starts as one I-position. The elements have not differentiated; there is no audible internal conversation. Child inhabits a system in which significant others—father, mother, sibling grandparent, teacher, friend—in their capacity as introjects, function as I-positions; that is, internal and external positions are indistinguishable. The actual, not imagined, voice of my father is one of my I-positions, and so with mother, sibling, friend. There is no boundary between inside and outside—or just the rudiments of a boundary, a virtual infrastructure. As mental space opens between positions and I become an other to myself (epitomized in the "mirror stage" [Lacan 2007, 7]), the multiple self-system begins to emerge, but the conversations between I-positions is still heavily dominated by the internal presence/values/voice/judgment of significant others, which are, in the best circumstances, promoter positions, and in the worst, mistrustful, indifferent, or condemnatory. The child awakens to her own internal I-positions like a distant soundtrack that gets closer and closer, until she can make it out.

The self-system has its structural origins in the pre- or unconscious, and it takes its particular character through experience, modified by genetic temperament—activity level, adaptability, rhythmicity, distractibility, intensity of reaction, threshold of responsiveness, etc.—which in turn is modified by experience (Thomas and Chess 1996). Most crucially for the evolutionary possibility represented by the new sensibility, childhood experience literally shapes the proliferating synaptic structures of the brain. Deeply felt, repeated hands-on interactive experience with persons, materials, and ideas—aesthetic experience—results in the concrete development of synaptic structures and makes them permanent through myelinization. Shallow alienating experience leaves unconnected or weakly connected synapses vulnerable to the periodic hormonal "pruning" that takes place throughout childhood. Most importantly for the new sensibility, it is in the growth of connections between the pre-frontal cortex and the lower brain—brain stem, limbic region, and amygdala (Pearce 2002)—between conscious and unconscious—that possibilities lie for

Marcuse's "new experience of nature," "new instinctual needs and values," and the "actual felt liberation of the mind and of the body from aggressive and repressive needs."

It is through shutting down the psychological bases for the ongoing dialectal reconstruction of self that traditional schooling comes to reproduce the closed system of selfhood and the authoritarian personality. If we can imagine a form of schooling that capitalizes on the open relation between impulse and habit—that, in Dewey's (1922) words, "allows impulse its reorganizing power"—we can imagine a form of education that lays the groundwork for the dialogical personality, and therefore the opening of the dialogical polis. A brain-friendly school creates an environment structured for aesthetic experience as well as opportunities for participatory democratic practice in the art of collaborative community governance. In such a setting, the gradually developing and articulating I-positions of the child, the internal society of self, is schooled in dialogue through its actual practice in all areas of school life.

Finally, and what is often overlooked in educational discourse, such an environment is also a school for adults, intrinsically primed and organized as it is as a field of encounter between childhood impulse and adult habit. Such an intentional community is a unique holding environment, an embryonic society dedicated to the emergence of new forms of life. Here the ontological vocation to become more human for which the new sensibility is an ever-present goal is focused through Deleuze and Guattari's "block of childhood," which represents, in persons of whatever age, an affective and noetic space in continual transformation (Deleuze and Guattari 1987, 294). Here "child" represents, not a particular age or stage of life, nor a predetermined category of identity and experience, but the psychological archetype of a form of experience inherently signifying new or original life, which manifests as a symbol of wholeness (Jung and Kerenyi 1969, 97) and which, as we have seen, involves unlocking affect in new combinations and flows. So understood, "child" is emblematic of an emergent post-human (which is, arguably, identical with Freire's "more human") style of subjectivity, an "enlarged self," an ongoing process which, as we have also seen, they name "becoming child." In a form of child-rearing and schooling understood as dialogical, the adult's project of affective enlargement and unification that is becoming child forms an assemblage with the child's project of differentiation, articulation, and putting-in-relation that is "becoming adult." So, we might say that in the dialogical adult-child encounter both are converging from different moments in the life cycle on the new sensibility, the new relationship between the upper and the lower brain, the open self-system.

Boundary Work

In fact, the new sensibility is already everywhere, and always has been in some degree. The "liberation from aggressive and repressive needs" is the implicit preoccupation of a majority of the human population. It is thwarted on one level by the failure of the material base to promote and provide for equal distribution of resources, on the ontological assumption of permanent scarcity, which cheats us out of that psychological space called "free time" (*skholé*)—in which to cultivate that preoccupation. But exigence and inequality on the material plane is not all that thwarts the evolutionary impulse. The new sensibility is neutralized by closed systems of ideological and psychological domination and exploitation that trigger and maintain the darkest impulses of the human animal—hypocrite, demagogue, grifter, sociopath, bully, tyrant, sadist, abuser, torturer, murderer—persons in whom the elements of the self-system have become dangerously polarized and dissociated, to the point of mutual indifference. We must insist that these are aberrations, however pervasive they are—forms of psychopathology at both the individual and the collective level. Nor, it appears, is there one prevention or one cure. At this historical moment, we live with the real possibility that the cumulative effect of our collective psychological and cognitive disorders will lead either to our extinction or to the most profound material degradation as a species, whether through catastrophic climate change, nuclear holocaust, global pandemic, or toxic social and political organization; or alternatively, that they will be brought under control only at the expense of the eradication of the human through automation and control—through our becoming machine—the emergence of a self-system that is closed in the most profound sense.

On the other hand, a historian may suggest that the species has been in this position more than once—whether the collapse of the Bronze Age around 1100 BC, or the tenth-century-AD climate catastrophes, not to speak of millennia of genocidal wars and organized persecution; that, although trillions have died catastrophically, the species has endured and in fact advanced in some measure (Cline 2015; Heinsohn 2021). Or, more optimistically, that we are in fact following our ontological vocation, but much more slowly than we, short-lived creatures that we are, would prefer;

that we approach the new sensibility through, as Deleuze and Guattari put it, the continual emergence of deterritorializing "flows," in lines of flight that escape the overcoding of the dominant "signifying regime," and seek to reterritorialize on a new "plane of consistency." We might understand the emergent recognition of the dialogical self in its deep connection with democracy as such a flow, through which the chiasmic relations between the politics of the self and the politics of the polis establish a plane of consistency that is capable of dealing (eventually) with the dark fears and urges of the human animal's lower brain.

Deleuze said, "Psychology, or rather the only supportable psychology, is a politics because I always have to create human relations with myself. There is not a psychology, but a politics of the self" (Deleuze and Parnet 2007, 155). In fact, we may identify three forms of politics: the internal politics of the self, the politics of everyday life, and the politics of collective governance, or politics per se. All three interlocking entangled realms are about boundary work. The boundaries between I-positions are negotiated within the self. The boundaries of everyday life are set and negotiated in everyday relationships between both acquaintances and strangers within and between groups, among neighbors, in the grocery store, at the office, on the street. In the realm of politics per se, the boundaries are coded, reified, amplified, and subjected to the "binary machine" in the form of parties and ideological positioning.

Boundaries are liminal zones that both separate and connect. Boundaries are always, implicitly or explicitly, under negotiation: always contested, in doubt, played and replayed, redrawn. They are liable to binarization and overcoding—black-white, good-evil, appropriate-inappropriate—but they are also forever susceptible to deterritorializing lines of flight, to new ways of balancing, and of cultivating the edge of chaos. Ultimately, we may hope, the stochastic emergence of new solutions will win out over authoritarian over-positioning and generate literally new brains—brains in which higher cortical structures are capable of moderating the lower (Pearce 2002), thereby opening spaces for dialogue and difference; brains equipped for enhanced internal negotiations within the self system and by extension the social system. This in fact is the promise of the extraordinarily long human childhood, over the course of which the synaptic structures of the human brain are formed and shaped through experience. As such, the human project calls implicitly for "a future form, for a new earth and people that do not yet exist" (Deleuze and Guattari 1996, 107), albeit they are already here among us, and always have been.

Bibliography

Abrams, Howard M. 1971. *Natural Supernaturalism: Tradition and Revolution in Romantic Literature*. New York: W. W. Norton.
Agamben, Giorgio. 1993. *Infancy and History*. London: Verso.
Althusser, Louis. 2008. *On Ideology*. London: Verso.
Arendt, Hannah. 1958. *The Human Condition*. Chicago: University of Chicago Press.
Aries, Philippe. 1962. *Centuries of Childhood*. Translated by Robert Baldick. New York: Knopf.
Aristotle. 1962. *Nichomachean Ethics*. Translated by Martin Ostwald. Indianapolis: Bobbs-Merrill.
Aristotle. 1987. "Eudemian Ethics." In *A New Aristotle Reader*, edited by J. L. Ackrill, 1224a:27–29. Princeton: Princeton University Press.
Attractor. 2023. Accessed November 30, 2023. https://www.dictionary.com/browse/attractor.
Augustine. 1961. *Confessions*. Translated by R.S. Pine-Coffin. Harmondsworth: Penguin Books.
Avrich, Paul. 1974. *An American Anarchist: The Life of Voltairine de Cleyre*. Princeton: Princeton University Press.
Avrich, Paul. 2006. *The Modern School Movement: Anarchism and Education in the United States*. Oakland: AK Press.
Bachelard, Gaston. 1971. *The Poetics of Reverie: Childhood, Language, and the Cosmos*. Translated by Daniel Russell. Boston: Beacon Press.
Badiou, Alain. 2013. *Being and Event*. New York: Bloomsbury.
Bales, Eugene F. 1990. "Memory, Forgetfulness, and the Disclosure of Being in Heidegger and Plotinus." *Philosophy Today* 34, no. 2 (Summer): 142.
Barber, Benjamin. 2004. *Strong Democracy: Participatory Politics for a New Age*. Berkeley: University of California Press.
Bateson, Gregory. 1972. *Steps to an Ecology of Mind*. New York: Ballantine Books
Benjamin, Walter. 1940. *On the Concept of History*. https://www.sfu.ca/~andrewf/books/Concept_History_Benjamin.pdf.
Bennett, Jane. 2001. *The Enchantment of Modern Life: Attachments, Crossings, and Ethics*. Princeton: Princeton University Press.

Bennett, Jane. 2010. *Vibrant Matter: A Political Ecology of Things*. Durham: Duke University Press.

Berdyaev, Nicolas. 1935. *The Fate of Man in the Modern World*. Translated by Donald Lowrie. London: Student Christian Organization. https://content.cosmos.art/media/pages/library/the-fate-of-man-in-the-modern-world/1074845792-1601363890/the-fate-of-man-in-the-modern-world-by-nicolas-berdyaev-z-lib.org.pdf.

Bjorklund, David F. 1995. "Some Assumptions of Piaget's Theory." In *Children's Thinking: Developmental Function and Individual Differences*, 53–65, 2nd ed. Pacific Grove: Brooks/Cole.

Bjorklund, David F. 1997. "The Role of Immaturity in Human Development." *Psychological Bulletin* 122, no. 2: 153–69.

Blake, William. 1966. "The Marriage of Heaven and Hell." In *William Blake: Complete Writings*, 148–58, edited by Geoffrey Keynes. Oxford: Oxford University Press.

Bloch, Ernst. 1995. *The Principle of Hope* (3 volumes). Translated by Neville Plaice, Stephen Plaice, and Paul Knight. Cambridge: MIT Press.

Bluemink, Matt. 2020. "Gilbert Simondon and the Process of Individuation." In *Epoche* 34 (September). https://epochemagazine.org/34/gilbert-simondon-and-the-process-of-individuation/.

Bohm, David 1996. *On Dialogue*. London: Routledge.

Bookchin, Murray. 2005. *The Ecology of Freedom: The Emergence and Dissolution of Hierarchy*. Oakland: AK Press.

Brown, N. O. 1959. *Life against Death: The Psychoanalytic Meaning of History*. Middletown: Wesleyan University Press.

Brown, N. O. 1966. *Love's Body*. Berkeley: University of California Press.

Bruner, Jerome. 1966. *Toward a Theory of Instruction*. Cambridge: Harvard University Press.

Bruner, Jerome. 1981. "Play, Thought, and Language." *Peabody Journal of Education* 60, no. 3: 76–81.

Buber, Martin. 1948. *Between Man and Man*. Translated by Ronald Gregor Smith. New York: Macmillan.

Buber, Martin. 1965. *The Knowledge of Man: A Philosophy of the Interhuman*. Translated by Maurice Friedman and R. G. Smith. New York: Harper.

Cannon, Dale, and Mark Weinstein. 1993. "Reasoning Skills: An Overview" In *Thinking Children and Education*, edited by Matthew Lipman, 598–604. Dubuque, IA: Kendall Hunt.

Carini, Patricia F. 2001. *Starting Strong: A Different Look at Children, Schools, and Standards*. New York: Teachers College Press.

Carini, Patricia F. 2011. *Prospect's Descriptive Process: The Child, the Art of Teaching, the Classroom and School*. Revised ed. North Bennington, VT: The Prospect Archives and Center for Education and Research.

Carini, Patricia F., and Margaret Himley. 2010. *Jenny's Story: Taking the Long View of the Child. Prospect's Philosophy in Action.* New York: Teachers College Press.
Chesters, Sarah Davey. 2012. *The Socratic Classroom: Reflective Thinking through Collaborative Inquiry.* Rotterdam: Sense Publishers.
Cline, Eric. 2015. *1177 BC: The Year Civilization Collapsed.* Revised ed. Princeton: Princeton University Press.
Coole, Diana, and Samantha Frost, eds. 2010. *New Materialisms: Ontology, Agency, and Politics.* Durham: Duke University Press.
Corrington, Robert S. 1992. "Signs of Community." In *Nature and Spirit*, 83–119. New York: Fordham University Press.
Deleuze, Gilles. 2005. *Pure Immanence: Essay on a Life.* Translated by Anne Boyman. New York: Zone Books.
Deleuze, Gilles, and Felix Guattari. 1987. *A Thousand Plateaus: Capitalism and Schizophrenia.* Translated by Brian Massumi. Minneapolis: University of Minnesota Press.
Deleuze, Gilles, and Felix Guattari. 1996. *What Is Philosophy?* New York: Columbia University Press.
Deleuze, Gilles, and Claire Parnet. 2007. *Dialogues.* Revised ed. New York: Columbia University Press.
DeMarzio, Darryl. 2011. "What Happens in Philosophical Texts: Matthew Lipman's Theory and Practice of the Philosophical Text as Model." *childhood & philosophy* 7, no. 13: 29–47.
DeMause, Lloyd. 1975. "The Evolution of Childhood." In *The History of Childhood*, edited by L. DeMause, 1–73. New York: Harper.
Dewey, John. 1916. *Democracy and Education.* New York: Macmillan.
Dewey, John. 1922. *Human Nature and Conduct: An Introduction to Social Psychology.* New York: Henry Holt.
Dewey, John. 1938a. *Experience and Education.* New York: Macmillan.
Dewey, John. 1938b. *Logic: The Theory of Inquiry.* New York: Henry Holt.
Dewey, John. 1959. *Dewey on Education: Selections.* Edited by John Dworkin. New York: Teachers College Press.
Dudley, Edward, and Maxmillian E. Novak, eds. 1972. *The Wild Man Within: An Image in Western Thought from the Renaissance to Romanticism.* Pittsburgh: University of Pittsburgh Press.
Dumézil, Georges. 1970. *The Destiny of the Warrior.* Chicago: University of Chicago Press.
Edwards, Carolyn, Lella Gandini, and George Forman, eds. 1993. *The Hundred Languages of Children: The Reggio Emilia Approach to Early Childhood Education.* New York: Ablex.
Elias, Norbert. 1994. *The Civilizing Process: The History of Manners and State Formation and Civilization.* Translated by Edmund Jephcott. Oxford: Blackwell.

Erikson, Erik H. 1963. "Toys and Reasons." In *Childhood and Society*, 209–46. New York: Norton.
Foucault, Michel. 2019. *Discourse and Truth and Parrēsia*. Edited by Henri-Paul Fruchaud and Daniele Lorenzini. Chicago: University of Chicago Press.
Freire, Paolo. 2005. *Pedagogy of the Oppressed*. Translated by Myra B. Ramos. New York: Continuum.
Freud, Sigmund. 1917. "A Difficulty in the Path of Psycho-Analysis." In *The Standard Edition of the Complete Psychological Works of Sigmund Freud (1917–1919)*, volume 17:135–44, edited by James Strachey. New York: Norton.
Freud, Sigmund. 1957. "Five Lectures on Psychoanalysis." In *The Standard Edition of the Complete Psychological Works of Sigmund Freud (1917–1919)*, volume 11, edited by James Strachey. London: Hogarth Press.
Freud, Sigmund. 2010. *Civilization and Its Discontents*. New York: W. W. Norton.
Fromm, Erich. 1994. "Appendix: Character and the Social Process." In *Escape from Freedom*. New York: Henry Holt.
Fromm, Erich. 2013. *To Have or To Be*. London: Bloomsbury Academic.
Gadamer, Hans Georg. 1975. *Truth and Method*. New York: Crossroad.
Garvey, Catherine. 1977. *Play*. Cambridge: Harvard University Press.
Gill-Peterson, Julian. 2013. "Childhood Blocks: Deleuze and Guattari's Infant Affects." Posted on April 29, 2013: https://juliangillpeterson.wordpress.com/2013/04/29/childhood-blocks-deleuze-and-guattaris-infant-affects/.
Gintis, Herbert. 2011. "Gene–Culture Coevolution and the Nature of Human Sociality." *Philosophical Transactions of the Royal Society of London. Series B, Biological sciences* 366 (1566): 878–88. https://doi.org/10.1098/rstb.2010.0310; https://www.ncbi.nlm.nih.gov/pmc/articles/PMC3048999/.
Golden, Mark. 1990. *Children and Childhood in Classical Athens*. Baltimore: Johns Hopkins University Press.
Gould, Stephen J. 1977. *Ontogeny and Phylogeny*. Cambridge: Harvard University Press.
Graeber, David, and David Wengrow. 2021. *The Dawn of Everything: A New History of Humanity*. New York: Farrar, Straus and Giroux.
Grosz, Elizabeth. 2005. "Bergson, Deleuze and the Becoming of Unbecoming." *Parallax* 11, no. 2: 4–13.
Habermas, Jürgen. 1984. *The Theory of Communicative Action*. Volumes 1 and 2. Boston: Beacon Press.
Hadot, Pierre. 1995. *Philosophy as a Way of Life: Spiritual Exercises from Socrates to Foucault*. Translated by Michael Chase. London: Blackwell.
Hans, James S. 1981. *The Play of the World*. Amherst: University of Massachusetts Press.
Harding, Sandra. 1991. *Whose Science? Whose Knowledge? Thinking from Women's Lives*. Ithaca: Cornell University Press.
Hardt, Michael, and Antonio Negri. 2004. *Multitude: War and Democracy in the Age of Empire*. New York: Penguin Books.

Heidegger, Martin. 2010. *Being and Time*. Translated by Joan Stambaugh. Albany: State University of New York Press.
Heinsohn, Gunnar. 2021. "The Disastrous Tenth Century: Cataclysm and Collapse." *Academia Letters*, article 2958 (August), https://doi.org/10.20935/AL2958, https://www.academia.edu/51145748/the_disastrous_tenth_century_cataclysm_and_collapse.
Heraclitus. 2003. *Fragments*. Translated by B. Haxton. London: Penguin Books.
Herbert, Nick. 1995. *Elemental Mind: Human Consciousness and the New Physics*. New York: Dutton.
Hermans, Hubert. 2018. *Society in the Self: A Theory of Identity in Democracy*. Oxford: Oxford University Press.
Hermans, Hubert, and Agnieszka Hermans-Konopka. 2010. *Dialogical Self Theory*. Cambridge: Cambridge University Press.
Hickey-Moody, Anna. 2013. "Deleuze's Children." *Educational Philosophy and Theory*, 45, no. 3: 272–86.
Himley, Margaret, ed. 2011. *Prospect's Descriptive Processes: The Child, the Art of Teaching, the Classroom and the School*. Revised ed. North Bennington: The Prospect Archives and Center for Education and Research. https://cdi.uvm.edu/sites/default/files/ProspectDescriptiveProcessesRevEd.pdf.
Himley, Margaret, and Patricia F. Carini, eds. 2000. *From Another Angle: Children's Strengths and School Standards. The Prospect Center's Descriptive Review of the Child*. New York: Teachers College Press.
Husserl, Edmund. 1990/1928. *On the Phenomenology of the Consciousness of Internal Time* (1893–1917), 1990 [1928]. Translated by J. B. Brough. Dordrecht: Kluwer.
Iannaccone, Antonio, Giuseppina Marsico, and Luca Tateo. 2013. "Educational Self, a Fruitful Idea?" In *Interplays between Dialogical Learning and Dialogical Self*, edited by Beatrice Ligorio and Margarida César, 219–52. Charlotte: Information Age Publishing.
Johnson, Mark H. 2008. *Brain Development in Childhood: A Literature Review and Synthesis for the Byron Review on the Impact of New Technologies on Children*. Access date November 26, 2023. https://www.lloydminster.info/libdocs/byronreview/annex_i.pdf.
Johnson, Mark H. 2011. *Developmental Cognitive Neuroscience*. 3rd ed. Hoboken: John Wiley & Sons.
Jones, Elizabeth, and Gretchen Reynolds. 1992. *The Play's the Thing: Teacher's Roles in Children's Play*. New York: Teachers College Press.
Jung, C. G. 1969. "Archetypes and the Collective Unconscious." In *The Collected Works of C. G. Jung: Volume 9, Part 1*, translated and edited by R. F. C. Hull et al., 207–54. Princeton: Princeton University Press.
Jung, Carl G. 2001/1912. *The Psychology of the Unconscious*. Mineola: Dover Publications.
Jung, Carl G. 2014. *Psychology and Alchemy*, Translated by Gerhart Adler and R. F. C. Hull, 2nd ed. Princeton: Princeton University Press.

Jung, Carl G., and Karl Kerenyi. 1969. *Essays on a Science of Mythology: The Myth of the Divine Child and the Mysteries of Eleusis*. Princeton: Bollingen Series, Princeton University Press.

Kafka, Franz. 1971. "In the Penal Colony." In *Franz Kafka: The Complete Stories*, 140–67. New York: Schocken Books.

Katz, Lillian G., and Sylvia Chard. 1989. *Engaging Children's Minds: The Project Approach*. Stamford: Ablex Publishing.

Kennedy, David. 1989. "Young Children, Animism, and the Scientific World Picture." *Philosophy Today* 33, no. 4 (Winter): 374–81.

Kennedy, David. 1997. "The Five Communities." *Inquiry: Critical Thinking across the Disciplines* 16, no. 4 (Summer): 66–86.

Kennedy, David. 2001. *Transcript of a Discussion Held at the North American Association of Community of Inquiry Conference*, Montclair State University, June 2001. Manuscript.

Kennedy, David. 2004. "The Role of a Facilitator in a Community of Philosophical Inquiry." *Metaphilosophy* 35, no. 4 (October 2004): 744–65.

Kennedy, David. 2006. *The Well of Being: Childhood, Subjectivity, and Education*. Albany: State University of New York Press.

Kennedy, David. 2012a. *My Name Is Myshkin: A Philosophical Novel for Children*. Munster: LIT Verlag.

Kennedy, David. 2012b. "Marcuse's New Sensibility, Neoteny, and Progressive Schooling: Utopian Prospects." *Civitas Educationis: Education, Politics, and Culture* 1, no. 1 (June): 55–72.

Kennedy, David. 2013a. "'A Widened I': The Dialogical Self in Theory and Practice." *Teachers College Record*, December 6, 2013. http://www.tcrecord.org ID Number: 17347.

Kennedy, David. 2013b. "Epilogue—Becoming Child, Becoming Other: Childhood as Signifier." In *Childhood in the English Renaissance*, edited by Anja Muller, 145–53. Trier: Wissenschaftlicher Verlag Trier.

Kennedy, David. 2017. "La Scuola Nuova." Translated by Stefano Oliverio, *Civitas Educationis: Education, Politics, and Culture* 5, no. 2 (2016): 67–87.

Kennedy, David. 2018. "The New School." *Journal of Philosophy of Education* 20, no. 10 (2018): 2–18.

Kennedy, David. 2023. *Dreamers: A Philosophical Novel for Children*. London: Green Team. And online at: https://sites.google.com/view/dreamers-david-kennedy/home.

Kilpatrick, William H. 1918. "'The Project Method': Child Centeredness in Progressive Education." *Teachers College Record* 19, no. 4: 319–35.

Klein, Melanie. 1980. *The Psychoanalysis of Children*. London: Hogarth Press.

Kohan, Walter O. 2012. "Childhood, Education, and Philosophy: Notes on Deterritorialisation." In *Philosophy for Children in Transition: Problems*

and Prospects, edited by Nancy Vansieleghem and David Kennedy, 170–89. Chichester, UK: Wiley-Blackwell.
Kohan, Walter. 2014. *Childhood, Education, and Philosophy: New Ideas for an Old Relationship*. New York: Routledge.
Kohan, Walter O. 2017. "Childhood, Philosophy, and the Polis: Exclusion and Resistance." In *Philosophy of Childhood Today: Exploring the Boundaries*, edited by David Kennedy and Brock Bahler, 31–38. Lanham, MD: Lexington Books.
Koyre, Alexandre. 1957. *From the Closed World to the Infinite Universe*. Baltimore: Johns Hopkins University Press.
Kristeva, Julia. 1980. *Desire in Language*. New York: Columbia University Press.
Kristeva, Julia. 1987. *The Powers of Horror: An Essay on Abjection*. New York: Columbia University Press.
Kropotkin, Peter. 1902. *Mutual Aid: A Factor in Evolution*. New York: McClure Phillips.
Lacan, Jacques. 2007. "The Mirror Stage." In *Écrits*, Translated by Bruce Fink, 75–81. New York: W. W. Norton.
Lancy, David F. 2008. *The Anthropology of Childhood: Cherubs, Chattel, and Changelings*. Cambridge: Cambridge University Press.
Landauer, Gustav. 2010. *On Revolution and Other Writings: A Political Reader*. Edited and translated by Gabriel Kuhn. Oakland: PM Press.
Lao Tzu. 2006. *Tao Te Ching: A New English Version*. Translated by Stephen Mitchell. New York: Harper.
Levinas, Emmanuel. 1969. *Totality and Infinity*. Translated by Alphonso Lingis. Pittsburgh: Duquesne University Press.
Levinas, Emmanuel. 1987. *Time and the Other*. Translated by Richard A. Cohen. Pittsburgh: Duquesne University Press.
Levinas, Emmanuel. 1991. *Otherwise than Being or Beyond Essence*. Dordrecht: Springer.
Lewis, Tyson. 2015. *On Study: Giorgio Agamben and Educational Potentiality*. London: Routledge.
Lindsay, Cecile, 1992. "Corporality, Ethics, Experimentation: Lyotard in the Eighties." *Philosophy Today* 36, no. 4 (Winter): 389–401.
Lipman, Matthew, ed. 1993. *Thinking Children and Education*. Dubuque, IA: Kendall Hunt.
Lipman, Matthew. 2002. "Where to P4C?" *Thinking: The Journal of Philosophy for Children*, 16, no. 2: 12–13.
Lipman, Matthew. 2003. *Thinking in Education*. 2nd ed. Cambridge: Cambridge University Press.
Lipman, Matthew, Ann M. Sharp, and Frederick O. Oscanyon. 1980. *Philosophy in the Classroom*. 2nd ed. Baltimore: Johns Hopkins University Press.

Lovelock, James. 1979. *Gaia: A New Look at Life on Earth*. Oxford: Oxford University Press.
Lyotard, Jean-François. 1991. *The Inhuman*. Translated by Geoffrey Bennington and Rachel Bowlby. Stanford: Stanford University Press.
Lyotard, Jean-François. 1992. "Mainmise." *Philosophy Today* 36, no. 4 (Winter): 419–27.
Lyotard, Jean-François, and Gilbert Larochelle. 1992. "That Which Resists, After All." *Philosophy Today* 36, no. 4 (Winter): 402–17.
Marchak, Catherine. 1990. "The Joy of Transgression: Bataille and Kristeva." *Philosophy Today* 34, no. 4 (Winter): 354–63.
Marcuse, Herbert. 1955. *Eros and Civilization: A Philosophical Inquiry into Freud*. Boston: Beacon Press.
Marcuse, Herbert. 1969. *An Essay on Liberation*. Boston: Beacon Press.
Marcuse, Herbert. 1972. "Nature and Revolution." In *Counterrevolution and Revolt*, 59–78. Boston: Beacon Press.
Marcuse, Herbert. 1978. *The Aesthetic Dimension: Toward a Critique of Marxist Aesthetics*. Boston: Beacon Press.
Marcuse, Herbert. 2009. "Lecture on Education, Brooklyn College, 1968." In *Marcuse's Challenge to Education*, edited by Douglas Kellner, Tyson Lewis, Clayton Pierce, and K. Daniel Cho, 33–38. Lanham: Rowman & Littlefield.
Marsal, Eva. 2014. "Philosophizing with Children with the Five Finger Model: The Theoretical Approach of Ekkehard Martens." *Analytical Teaching and Philosophical Praxis* 35, no. 1: 39–49.
Marshall, Peter. 2010. *Demanding the Impossible: A History of Anarchism*. Oakland: PM Press.
Martin, Luther, Huck Gutman, and Patrick H. Hutton, eds. 1988. *Technologies of the Self: A Seminar with Michael Foucault*. Amherst: University of Massachusetts Press.
Masschelein, Jan, and Maarten Simons. 2013. *In Defense of the School: A Public Issue*. Translated by Jack McMartin. Leuven: E-ducation, Culture & Society Publishers.
Matthews, Gareth. 1980. *Philosophy and the Young Child*. Cambridge: Harvard University Press.
McCarthy, Thomas. 1978. *The Critical Theory of Jurgen Habermas*. New York: Hutchinson.
McLaren, Peter, and Ramin Farahmandpur. 2005. *Teaching against Global Capitalism and the New Imperialism: A Critical Pedagogy*. Lanham: Rowman & Littlefield.
Meares, Russell. 1993. *The Metaphor of Play: Disruption and Restoration in the Borderline Experience*. Northvale, NJ: Jason Aronson.
Merleau-Ponty, Maurice. 1964a. *Sense and Non-Sense*. Translated by Hubert Dreyfus and Patricia Dreyfus. Evanston: Northwestern University Press.

Merleau-Ponty, Maurice. 1964b. "Méthode en psychologie de l'enfant." *Bulletin de Psychologie* XVIII, 3–6: 137.
Merleau-Ponty, Maurice. 1968. *The Visible and the Invisible*. Translated by Alphonso Lingis. Evanston, IL: Indiana University Press.
Miller, Alice. 1990. *For Your Own Good: The Hidden Cruelties in Child Rearing and the Roots of Violence*. New York: Farrar, Straus and Giroux.
Montagu, Ashley. 1989. *Growing Young*. 2nd ed. New York: Bergin & Garvey.
Nandy, Ashis. 1987. *Traditions, Tyranny and Utopias: Essays in the Politics of Awareness*. New Delhi: Oxford University Press.
Neumann, Erich. 1973a. *Depth Psychology and a New Ethic*. New York: Harper & Row.
Neumann, Erich. 1973b. *The Child: Structure and Dynamics of the Nascent Personality*. New York: Harper & Row.
Nicholl, Charles. 1999. *Somebody Else: Arthur Rimbaud in Africa, 1880–91*. Chicago: University of Chicago Press.
Nietzsche, Friedrich. 1999. *Thus Spake Zarathrustra*. Translated by T. Commons. New York: Dover.
Novalis. 1989. *Pollen and Fragments*. Translated by Arthur Versluis. Grand Rapids, MI: Phanes Press.
Ong, Walter. 1982. *Orality and Literacy: The Technologizing of the Word*. London: Methuen.
Parr, Adrian (Ed). 2010. *The Deleuze Dictionary*. Revised ed. Edinburgh University Press.
Pearce, Joseph C. 2002. *The Biology of Transcendence: A Blueprint of the Human Spirit*. Rochester: Park Street Press.
Peirce, Charles S. 1966. *Selected Writings (Values in a Universe of Chance)*. Edited by Philip P. Wiener. New York: Dover Publications.
Piaget, Jean. 1931. "Children's Philosophies." In *Handbook of Child Psychology*. Edited by Carl Murchison, 377–91. Worcester: Clark University Press.
Piaget, Jean. 1979. *The Child's Conception of the World*. Totowa: Littlefield Adams.
Pierce, Clayton. 2009. "Democratizing Science with Marcuse and Latour." In the Marcuse's *Challenge to Education*, edited by Douglas Kellner, Tyson Lewis, Clayton Pierce, and Daniel Cho, 131–58. Lanham: Rowman & Littlefield.
Plato. 1941. *The Republic of Plato*. Translated by Francis M. Cornford. Oxford: Oxford University Press.
Plato. 1961. "Laws." In *Collected Dialogues*, edited by Edith Hamilton and Huntington Cairns, 1225–513. Princeton: Bollingen.
Raposa, Michael L. 1989. *Peirce's Philosophy of Religion*. Bloomington: Indiana University Press.
Reich, Wilhelm. 1946. *The Mass Psychology of Fascism*. New York: Orgone Institute Press. https://ia800402.us.archive.org/11/items/MassPsychologyOfFascism-WilhelmReich/mass-psychology-reich.pdf.

Ricoeur, Paul. 1973. "The Task of Hermeneutics." *Philosophy Today*, 17 (2/4): 112–28.
Ricoeur, Paul. 1974. *The Conflict of Interpretations*. Evanston: Northwestern University Press.
Ricoeur, Paul. 1981. *Hermeneutics and the Human Sciences*. Edited and translated by John B. Thompson. New York: Cambridge University Press.
Rimbaud, Arthur. 2004. *I Promise to Be Good: The Letters of Arthur Rimbaud*. Edited and translated by Wyatt Mason. New York: Modern Library.
Rogers, Carl R., and R. E. Farson. 2015. *Active Listening*. New York: Martino Publishing.
Rousseau, Jean-Jacques. 1979. *Emile, Or on Education*. Translated by Allan Bloom. New York: Basic Books.
Rugg, Harold, and Ann Shumaker. 1928. *The Child-Centered School*. New York: Littlefield and Adams.
Russell, Wendy, Emily Ryall, and Malcolm McLean, eds. 2018. *The Philosophy of Play as Life*. New York: Routledge.
Sartre, Jean-Paul. 1966. *Being and Nothingness: An Essay on Phenomenological Ontology*. Translated by Hazel Barnes. New York: Washington Square Press.
Schiller, Friedrich. 1966. *Naïve and Sentimental Poetry and On the Sublime*. Translated by Julius A. Elias. New York: Frederick Ungar.
Schiller, Friedrich. 2004. *On the Aesthetic Education of Man*. Translated by Reginald Snell. New York: Dover.
Schutz, Alfred. 1973. "On Multiple Realities." In *Collected Papers Volume 1: On the Problem of Social Reality*, edited by Maurice Natanson, 207–59. The Hague: Martinus Nijhoff.
Sharp, Ann Margaret. 1987. "What Is a Community of Inquiry?" *Journal of Moral Education* 16, no. 1: 37–45.
Sheldrake, Rupert. 2009. *A New Science of Life: The Hypothesis of Formative Causation*. 3rd ed. Los Angeles: J. P. Tarcher.
Silverman, Hugh. 1986. "Hermeneutics and Interrogation." *Research in Phenomenology* 16: 87–94.
Skrbina, David. 2005. *Panpsychism in the West*. Cambridge: MIT Press.
Sorin, Reesa, and Greta Galloway. 2006. "Constructs of Childhood: Constructs of Self." *Children Australia* 31, no. 2: 12–21.
Spock, Benjamin. 1946. *The Common Sense Book of Baby and Child Care*. New York: Duell, Sloan, and Pearce.
Suissa, Judith. 2010. *Anarchism and Education: A Philosophical Perspective*. Oakland: PM Press.
Sutton-Smith, Brian. 1997. *The Ambiguity of Play*. Cambridge: Harvard University Press.
Taylor, Charles. 1989. *Sources of The Self: The Making of the Modern Identity*. Cambridge: Harvard University Press.

Taylor, Charles. 1991. "The Dialogical Self." In *The Interpretive Turn: Philosophy, Science, and Culture*, edited by David Hiley, James Bohman, and Richard Schusterman, 304–14. Ithaca: Cornell University Press.
Thomas, Alexander, and Stella Chess. 1996. *Temperament: Theory and Practice*. New York: Routledge.
Thomas, Dylan. 2010. "Fern Hill." In *Collected Poems*. New York: New Directions.
Tocqueville, Alexis d. 2002[1835–1840]. *Democracy in America*. Translated by G. E. Bevin. London: Penguin Books.
Traherne, Thomas. 1965. *The Poetical Works of Thomas Traherne*. New York: Cooper Square.
Vattimo, Gianni. 1992. *The Transparent Society*. Baltimore: Johns Hopkins University Press.
Vygostky, Lev S. 1978. *Mind in Society: The Development of Higher Psychological Processes*, edited by Michael Cole, Vera John-Steiner, Sylvia Scribner, and Ellen Souberman. Cambridge: Harvard University Press.
Ward, Colin. 1978. *The Child in the City*. New York: Pantheon.
Ward, Colin, and David Goodway. 2003. *Talking Anarchy*. Nottingham: Five Leaves Publications.
Wegerif, Rupert. 2013. "Learning to Think as Becoming Dialogue." In *Interplays between Dialogical Learning and Dialogical Self*, edited by Beatrice Ligorio and Margarida César, 27–51. Charlotte: Information Age Publishing.
Werner, Heinz. 1940. *Comparative Psychology of Mental Development*. New York: International Universities Press.
Werner, Heinz. 1957. "The Concept of Development from a Comparative and Organismic Point of View." In *The Concept of Development*, edited by Dale B. Harris, 125–48. Minneapolis: University of Minnesota Press.
Whitman, Walt. 1851. "Song of Myself, 51." In *Leaves of Grass*. Brooklyn: self-published.
Winnicott, D. W. 1965. *The Maturational Processes and the Facilitating Environment*. New York: International Universities Press.
Winnicott, D. W. 1989. *Playing and Reality*. New York: Routledge.
Wittgenstein, Ludwig. 1969. *On Certainty*. Translated by Denis Paul and G. E. M. Anscombe. New York: Harper & Row.
Wittgenstein, Ludwig. 2009. *Philosophical Investigations*. 4th ed. Translated by G. E. M. Anscombe. London: Wiley-Blackwell.
Wolin, Sheldon. 2010. *Democracy Incorporated: Managed Democracy and the Specter of Inverted Totalitarianism*. Princeton: Princeton University Press.
Wollstonecraft, Mary. 1996/1799. *A Vindication of the Rights of Women*. New York: Dover.

Index

Abandoning (child-rearing mode), 72, 74
active listening, 98, 135–36, 138
activism, 24–25, 37–38, 83, 118–19, 161
adaptation, 67, 115
adult: child as model for, 27–28, 30; co-constructor, as, 141; Enlightenment, and, 14, 66, 72; gerontomorphosis / gerontocracy, 34, 39, 178
adult-child dialogue: about, 3, 18, 20; activism and, 37–38; children, interviews with, 41–46; curriculum and, 32–33, 36–37; impulse and habit, and, 3, 28, 29
adult-child relation: brain development and, 26–27; early form of, 2; inhibition in, 18; philosophy and, 4, 8; *skholé* and, 35–38, 83, 94–95
aesthetic state, 24, 33, 46–47, 60–61, 129, 130
Agamben, Giorgio, 120
aion: about, xii, 55; aion time, 30–31, 53, 63, 81, 120, 132, 170; childhood, and, 55, 58, 59–60, 61–62; play and, 5, 131, 132
aionic time. *See aion*; time
alienation. *See* Great Refusal

Ambivalent (child-rearing mode), 72, 73
anarchism: about, 113, 114–16; democracy, and, 113–14, 176–77; new sensibility and, 116, 117–18; *skholé*, and, 119–21, 122–24; state, and the, 114–15, 117, 118–19, 120; utopia, and, 116–17
animism, 23, 68
Anthropocene, 68
Aphrodite, 56, 57, 63
aporia, 35, 48–49, 75, 156
archetypes: child, 9–10, 30, 59–60, 180–81; dialogical self, 66–67, 69, 163–64, 170; educational, 122, 123–24
Arendt, Hannah, 3, 31, 85
Argument, the: community of philosophical inquiry and, 128, 130, 131, 138–39, 141, 142–43; following, 47, 48, 125, 132, 135
Aries, Philippe, 75
Aristotle, xiii, 7, 11–12, 13, 14, 16, 81
armor. *See* character armor
art, dialogue and, 33, 131
Athens, 2, 79, 83, 114, 119, 138, 139
authority: de-/reconstruction of, 36–37, 80–81, 113–14, 138–39, 158–59; irrational, 34; rational, 83

Barber, Benjamin, 4, 36, 114
Bateson, Gregory, 133–34
becoming, 4, 12, 56, 62, 78–79, 93, 124, 142, 165, 168
becoming child: about, 6, 61–64, 141–42; dialogical schooling and, 77–78, 94–95, 121, 180
becoming other, 23, 53–55, 56, 61, 63, 81, 142
belief systems, 29, 34–35, 36–37, 50, 136–37, 153–54
Benjamin, Walter, 116
Berdyaev, Nicolas, 166
Bergson, Henri, 28, 30, 131
bioenergetic theory, 116, 177
biophilia, 1
Bloch, Ernst, 1, 67, 80
block of childhood, 84, 180
Bookchin, Murray, 6, 65, 67, 68, 116, 118
boundaries, 13, 64, 69, 157–58, 163, 169, 181–82
boundary work, 181–82
brain: development of, 26, 27, 31, 77, 79, 121, 178, 182; emotional-rational systems, 5, 59, 67, 179–80
Brown, N. O., 10, 15, 168
Bruner, Jerome, 18, 19, 131, 134
Buber, Martin, 28, 75, 76, 171

Cannon, Dale, 82, 135
capitalism: anarchism and, 117–18; education under, 71, 114, 120; nature, and, 38–39, 67–68, 176; technocapitalism, 23, 35
Carini, Patricia, xiv, 85–86, 91–93, 94, 95
Cartesian model, 22, 70, 71, 75, 170
Cartier-Bresson, Henri, 10
challenge zone, 65, 77, 78
character armor, 116, 177

child / children: archetype, divine, 9–10, 164; coloniality and, 14–15, 59; deficit and danger, as, 7, 12, 13, 15; experimental being, as, 16, 22, 63; genius, as, 16, 30; interviews with, 41–46; model for adult, as, 27–28, 30; original unity, as, 7, 9, 11, 30; polymorph, as, 14, 30, 31, 61, 76–77; prophet of futurity, as, 9–10, 16, 22, 24–25, 53, 60, 63, 141; Romantic understandings of, 9–10, 15, 30, 31–32, 77, 116; second harmony and, 9–11; wild being, as, 54, 55, 59–60. *See also* adult-child dialogue; adult-child relation; becoming child; child-rearing modes; philosophical novels for children
childhood: about, xi–xii, 62; block of, 84, 180; invention of, 75, 121; philosophy and, 2–4. *See also* philosophies of childhood (POC)
child-rearing modes, xiv, 72–75, 121–22, 178
chronos, 130, 132. *See also kronos*
climate change, 23, 176, 181. *See also* planetary crisis
clock, time of. See *kronos*
Cohen, Richard A., 59
Coleridge, Samuel Taylor, 26
collaborative governance, 18, 21, 36, 79, 82–83, 180, 182
colonialism, 14–15, 34, 59, 95, 118
The Common Sense Book of Baby and Child Care (Spock), 74
communal dialogue, 19–20, 79–80, 95–96, 134, 138, 142, 155
communal inquiry, xiv, 49, 82, 134
community: intentional, 2, 77–78, 79–81, 119–20, 123, 161, 180; natural, 80; state, and, 115

community of interpretation, 79–80
community of philosophical inquiry
  (CPI): about, xi, 3–4, 19, 21,
  33–36, 82–83, 128, 153; Argument,
  and the, 128, 130, 131, 138–39,
  141, 142–43; beliefs, and, 153–54;
  facilitators, 86–87, 89, 90, 94, 134,
  139, 143, 145–46, 167–68; ideal
  speech situation, as, 36, 82, 138;
  language play and, 46–47, 49;
  philosophies of childhood (POC)
  and, 85, 86–87, 87–91, 91–93, 95;
  play, and, 129–30, 130–33, 139–40;
  power relations in, 49–51, 138–39;
  rhizomatic structure for, 156–59,
  159–61; roles in, taking on of,
  47–48, 78, 80, 92, 128, 139, 173;
  rules of the game, 133–36. See also
  philosophical novels for children;
  Philosophy for Children program
constructivist learning theory, 19
Corrington, Robert, 79–80
CPI. See community of philosophical
  inquiry (CPI)
crisis, planetary. See planetary crisis
curriculum: dialogical education
  model, in, 18, 32–33, 36–37, 83–84;
  emergent, 19, 21, 81–82, 92; gap,
  child-, 17, 27; negotiated, 155–56;
  rhizomatic, 81–82, 159–61; village,
  34

dark material. See shadow material
deep play, 3, 59, 81, 120
Deleuze, Gilles: on *aion*, 55, 61; on
  becoming child, 6, 61–62, 76,
  93, 94–95, 141–42, 165; on block
  of childhood, 84, 180; concepts,
  rhizomic structure of, 154, 156,
  157–58; desiring-production, 56; on
  education, 119; language used by,
  61, 69, 119, 176–77, 182; on new
  sensibility, 69, 182; over-coding,
  166, 176–77
DeMarzio, Darryl, 98, 99
DeMause, Lloyd, 65, 72–73, 74,
  121–22, 178
democracy: about, 113; Athenian,
  2, 79, 83, 114, 119, 138, 139;
  dialogical education practice and,
  36–37, 159; participatory, 114, 115,
  138, 180; strong, 4, 36, 114. See
  also social democracy
Democratic Education movement, 36,
  72, 74, 83
democratic social character, 64, 65,
  66–67, 161, 174
Descartes, xiii, 30, 66, 166
Descriptive Review process, 86,
  91–93, 95
desire: impulse, as, 28–29; reason,
  and, 5
deterritorialization: lines of flight, 63,
  69, 118–19, 120, 182; mentions, 60,
  61, 123, 154, 175, 178
Dewey, John: on education as
  reconstruction, 17, 18, 25, 27,
  180; on embryonic community /
  society, 4, 31–32, 36, 78, 179; on
  four instincts, 32–33; on growth,
  94, 122, 140; on impulse and habit,
  21, 28–29, 35, 36, 80, 116, 122,
  161, 178–79; on inquiry, 137; on
  social democracy, xiii, 4, 63–64, 66,
  113–14, 159, 174, 175–76, 177
dialogical education. See activism;
  community of philosophical inquiry
  (CPI); curriculum; democracy;
  philosophies of childhood (POC)
dialogical self theory (DST): about,
  161, 177; challenge zone, 65, 77,
  78; I-positions. See I-positions;

dialogical self theory (DST) *(continued)*
  metapositions, 70, 165–68, 169, 174, 177; positioning, 69; promoter positions, 77, 78, 173, 179
dialogue: about, 171; communal, 19–20, 79–80, 95–96, 134, 138, 142, 155; internal, 166–67, 171, 173–74, 175, 179, 180, 182; I-Thou and I-It, 171–72; monologue, and, 20, 80, 83, 127–28, 133, 138, 139; Socrates on, xii, 2, 3, 95. *See also* adult-child dialogue
dialogue theory, 138
dikaiosune (justice), 4, 81, 160–61, 168, 173
discourse, 20, 58, 71, 82, 125, 135, 137, 138–40. *See also* community of philosophical inquiry (CPI)
disembodied rationality, 22, 30
Dreamers (Kennedy): about, xii, 146–48; excerpt, 148–51
DST. *See* dialogical self theory (DST)
Dumézil, Georges, 166

education: Bildung, and, 71; democratic, 36–37, 72, 74; reproduction, as, 6, 26, 34, 71, 120–21, 157; universal compulsory, 71, 72, 73. *See also* reconstruction; schooling; *skholé*
ego: Freudian, 14, 15, 66, 122, 165, 166; play and, 10–11, 55; repositioning of, 57, 164, 167, 168, 169
Elias, Norbert, 75
embryonic community / society, 4, 36, 37, 78, 79, 161, 179, 180
emergent sensibility. *See* new sensibility
Emile (Rousseau), 60, 75, 121
Empathic (child-rearing mode), xiv, 72, 73–75, 121–22

empathic reaction, 73, 74–75, 121–22
enlarged self, 76, 78, 180
Enlightenment, 14, 66, 72
episteme, 23–24, 27, 33, 34–35
Erikson, Erik, 127, 131, 133, 134
eros. *See* desire
Eros, 13, 16, 66
Eros and Civilization (Marcuse), 22–23
eternity. *See aion*
evolution, 1, 25–26, 32, 34, 114, 121–22. *See also* neoteny
expanded reason, 16, 20, 22, 69
experimental being, child as, 16, 22, 63

facilitators (CPI): disappearance of, 139, 141; metaposition of, 167–68; role of, 86–87, 93, 94, 134, 143, 145, 146–47; training for, 85, 88–91
Farahmandpur, Ramin, 173–74
Father Time. *See* Kronos
first nature, 65, 67–68, 69
Foucault, Michel, 12, 99
Fragment 52 (Heraclitus), xii
free time. *See skholé*
Freire, Paulo, 1, 27, 31, 80, 165, 175, 180
Freud, Sigmund, xiii, 7, 12, 13–14, 15, 56, 60, 122, 165, 166–67
Fromm, Erich, 63–64, 65
fugal personality, 167
futurity. *See* child; prophet of futurity, child as

Gadamer, Hans-Georg, 10, 76, 77, 129, 130–31, 132–33, 140
Galloway, Greta, 141
gap, child-curriculum, 17, 27
Garvey, Catherine, 49
gender, 59, 60, 62, 174, 175
genius, child as, 16, 30

gerontomorphosis / gerontocracy, 34, 39, 178
Gintis, Herbert, 114
globalization, 23, 64, 65
Goodway, David, 118
governance, collaborative, 18, 21, 36, 79, 82–83, 180, 182
Graeber, David, 176–77
Great Refusal, 24, 35, 117, 176
Grosz, Elizabeth, 81
group production. *See* activism
Guattari, Felix: on *aion*, 55, 61; on becoming child, 6, 61–62, 76, 93, 94–95, 141–42, 165; on block of childhood, 84, 180; concepts, rhizomic structure of, 154, 156, 157–58; desiring-production, 56; on education, 119; language used by, 61, 69, 119, 176–77, 182; on new sensibility, 69, 182; over-coding, 166, 176–77

Habermas, Jurgen, 138
habit: about, 28, 178; adult-child dialogue and, 3, 28, 29; dialogical education and, 36; formation of, 80
Hadot, Pierre, 5, 99
Hans, James, 125, 127, 134–35, 136, 137, 138–39, 141
Hardt, Michael, 117
Harmonia, 57
Hegel, G. W. F., 9
Heidegger, Martin, 3
Heraclitus, xii, 5, 9–10, 30, 55, 131, 132, 141
Herbert, Nick, 23
Hermans, Hubert, 64, 65, 69, 77, 78–79, 83, 163, 166, 172–73
hermeneutics, 56, 74, 75–76, 77, 84
Hickey-Moody, Anna, 61
hierarchy: anarchism and, 114–15; dialogical model of education and, 70–72, 80–81, 154, 156–57; dismantling of, 16–17, 18, 61, 66–67, 80–81; tripartite self model, of, 7, 8, 17, 19, 66, 166
holding environment, 78–79, 83, 161, 180
human nature, 8, 24, 66–67, 87–88, 113, 116–17, 118, 119

Iannaccone, Antonio, 78
id, 14, 15, 66, 122, 168
ideal speech situation, CPI as, 36, 82, 138
ideological state apparatus, 2, 71, 79, 81, 120
impulse: about, 28–29, 178; adult-child dialogue and, 3, 28, 29
individuation, 55, 62, 76, 78, 94–95, 114, 118, 161
infans, 59, 61
infans theory, 60
infantia, xiii, 14, 16, 30, 53, 55, 59–61
Infanticidal (child-rearing mode), 72, 74
inquiry: child as model of, 27–28, 30; communal, xiv, 49, 82, 134; scientific, 134, 138. *See also* community of philosophical inquiry (CPI)
instinct. *See* impulse
intelligence, 22, 26, 66
internal dialogue, 166–67, 171, 173–74, 175, 179, 180, 182
International Democratic Education Network, 123
interpersonal reasoning, 82, 135
interviews with children, 41–46
Intrusive (child-rearing mode), 72, 73–74, 75, 122
I-positions: about, 65, 70, 163–65; boundary work, 181–82; child, of the, 76–77, 78, 179; ego and,

I-positions *(continued)*
169–70; external, 77, 165, 169–70, 172–73; integration of, 170–73; internal conflicts of, 174–76; new sensibility and, 69–70; promoter positions, and, 77, 78, 173, 179; shaping of, 166–68, 177, 179–80
irrational, the, 8, 16, 19, 22, 69
irrational authority, 34

Jesus, 9
Jones, Elizabeth, 92
Jung, C. G., 77, 161, 164, 168
justice. See *dikaiosune* (justice)

kairos, 57–58, 61, 81, 120, 130, 131, 137–38
Klein, Melanie, 10
Kohan, Walter, 3, 30, 141
Korbyzki, Alfred, 134
Koyre, Alexandre, 48
Kristeva, Julia, 7, 16
kronos, xii, 43, 56–57, 58, 59, 60, 63, 81, 120
Kronos, 55, 56, 57, 63
Kropotkin, Peter, 67, 118

Landauer, Gustav, 117
language play, 46–47, 49
Lao Tzu, 9, 53, 141
Leonardo, 10
Levinas, Emmanuel, 55, 59, 132, 156, 171, 172
Lewis, Tyson, 120
libidinal reason, 68, 176
Lipman, Matthew: philosophical novels for children, 30, 97–99, 145; Philosophy of Children program, xii, 31, 95, 96
listening. See active listening
Lochner, Stefan, 10
Lovelock, James, 23

Lowen, Alexander, 177
Lyotard, Jean-François, 14, 30

Madonna of the Rose Bower (Lochner), 10
Malaguzzi, Loris, 81
mancipium, 53, 55, 61, 115
Marcuse, Herbert: Great Refusal, 24, 35, 117, 176; new reality principle, 31–32, 38–39; new sensibility, 5–6, 21–24, 29, 65, 67–68, 79, 113, 116–18, 177, 180; utopia, xi, 1, 117, 175, 176
Marshall, Peter, 68
Marsico, Guiseppina, 78
Masschelein, Jan, 79, 119, 120
material. See shadow material
materialism, vital, 68
Matthews, Gareth, 46
McLaren, Peter, 173–74
Mead, George Herbert, 28
meaning: about, 19; dialogical schooling and, 47, 77–78, 83, 85, 137–38; field of, 125, 127, 129; philosophy of childhood and, 86, 87, 90, 94–95
Meares, Russell, 130, 134
Merleau-Ponty, Maurice, 16, 22, 30, 69, 76, 95–96, 130
metapositions, 70, 165–68, 169, 174, 177
modes, child-rearing. See child-rearing modes
monological pedagogy, 20, 80, 83, 127–28, 133, 138, 139
Montagu, Ashley, 25–26, 27–28, 34, 40
More, Henry, 48
My Name Is Myshkin (Kennedy): about, xii, 99–100; excerpt, 100–11

Nandy, Ashis, 14–15, 16–17
natality, 3, 4, 5, 31, 58, 76, 85, 122

nature: child as, 17; new relation to, 38–40; social democracy and, 71–72. *See also* first nature; human nature; second nature
necrophilia, 1
Negri, Antonio, 117
Neill, A. S., 123
neoteny, 5, 21, 25–26, 31, 39, 124, 178
Neumann, Erich, 11, 70
neuroscience. *See* brain
new ethic, 70
new reality principle, 21, 23, 31–32, 38–39, 65, 67, 69, 116–17. *See also* reality principle
new sensibility: about, xiii, 5–6, 30–31, 36, 121; anarchism, and, 116, 117–18; boundaries and, 181–82; dialogical self, and, 69–70; Marcuse on, 21–24, 38–39, 67–68, 113, 116, 176–77; school and, 177–80; social democracy, and, 63–64. *See also* second nature
Nietzsche, Friedrich, 84, 142
novels for children. *See* philosophical novels for children
Novum, 1, 28, 67, 80, 116

Ong, Walter, 22
ontology, 1, 55, 62–63, 78–79, 83, 146
organismic theory, 19
original plasticity, 25, 26, 27–28, 178
original unity, child as, 7, 9, 11, 30
other, becoming. *See* becoming other
other, time of the, 58–59

paedomorphism, 25–26, 26–27, 76, 84, 121–22
panpsychism, 68, 146
papier-mâché, 29
parenting, 15, 74, 76, 78
parrhesia, 4, 172

participatory democracy, 114, 115, 138, 180
Pearce, Joseph Chilton, 26, 67
Peirce, Charles Sanders, 28, 138, 140, 143
perception, revolution in, 24, 31–32, 116–17
philosophical inquiry. *See* community of philosophical inquiry (CPI)
philosophical novels for children: about, 30, 96, 97–99, 99–100, 145–48; excerpts, 100–11, 148–51
philosophical reasoning, 82, 135
philosophies of childhood (POC), 85, 86–87, 87–91, 91–93, 95
Philosophy for Children program, xii, 19–20, 30, 95, 97–99, 128, 131, 141
Piaget, Jean, 46, 77, 136
planetary crisis, 1, 39, 67–68, 118, 176. *See also* climate change
plasticity. *See* original plasticity
Plato: on childhood, 14–15, 140; model of subjectivity, 17–18, 19, 20; on philosophical play, 141; on the state, 16; tripartite self, xiii, 7, 8, 11–12, 66, 70, 166
play: about, 3, 10, 127; *aion* and *kairos*, 55, 130–33; -based curriculum, 92; CPI and, 129–30, 130–33, 139–40; deep, 3, 59, 81, 120; genealogy of, 128–29; language play, 46–47, 49; power, and, 138–39; risks in, 136–38; rules of, 133–36; space, 129–30; *spielraum* (play space), 60, 129–30; *spieltrieb* (play drive / impulse), 58, 59, 61, 63, 80, 129
play space, 60, 129–30
Plotinus, 9
POC. *See* philosophies of childhood (POC)

polymorph, child as, 14, 30, 31, 61, 76–77
positions. *See* I-positions; metapositions; promoter positions; we-positions
power struggles, 49–51
primal transgression, 56
primitive. *See* wild being
projective reaction, 73, 74–75, 78
project method, 33
promoter positions, 77, 78, 173, 179
prophet of futurity, child as, 9–10, 16, 22, 24–25, 53, 60, 63, 141
Proudhon, Pierre-Joseph, 117, 124
psychoclass: about, 63–64, 66, 70; anarchism as, 114, 117; democratic, 65, 71–72, 79; emergence of new, 120, 121–22

queer theory, 60

rational authority, 83
reactions. *See* empathic reaction; projective reaction
reality principle, 10, 14, 56, 67. *See also* new reality principle
reason: desire, and, 5; expanded, 16, 20, 22, 69; irrational, and the, 8, 16, 19, 22, 69; libidinal / sensual, 68, 176; new synthesis of, 67, 84. *See also* new sensibility
reasoning, 23–24, 34, 82, 98, 135, 156
reconstruction: authority, of, 36–37, 80–81, 113–14, 138–39, 158–59; education as, 6, 7–8, 17–18, 21, 25, 26, 27, 36, 180; second nature, of, 81, 122; systemic, of education, 31–32, 34–35, 36
regression, 74, 170
Reich, Wilhelm, 116, 177
relation. *See* adult-child relation
relational ontology, 78–79, 83, 146

reproduction, education as, 6, 26, 34, 71, 120–21, 157
The Republic (Plato), 16
revolution in perception, 24, 31–32, 116–17
Reynolds, Gretchen, 92
rhetorics of fate, 129
rhizome: conceptual structure, as, 154–55, 156; CPI and, 156–59, 159–61; curriculum as, 81–82, 159–61
Ricoeur, Paul, 76
Rimbaud, Arthur, 167
risks in play, 136–38
Ritter, Paul, 29
roles, taking on of, 47–48, 78, 80, 92, 128, 139, 173
Romanticism, 9, 10, 13, 15, 17, 26–27, 30–32, 77, 116
Rousseau, Jean-Jacques, 60, 75, 88, 121
Royce, Josiah, 80
rules of CPI, 133–36

Sartre, Jean-Paul, 132
Saturn. *See* Kronos
Schilder, Paul, 130
Schiller, Friedrich, 9, 10–11, 16, 30, 53, 58, 80, 129, 141
school as holding environment, 78–79, 83, 161, 180
schooling: about, 2; embryonic community / society, as, 4, 36, 37, 78, 79, 161, 179, 180; laboratory, school as, 4, 26, 39, 178; neoliberal, 71, 120; progressive, 2, 6, 17, 18–19, 27, 31, 72, 121; traditional, 2, 17, 71, 80, 119, 120–21, 140, 178; universal compulsory, 71, 72, 73. *See also* community of philosophical inquiry (CPI); education; *skholé*

schoolteachers. *See* teachers
Schutz, Alfred, 77, 131
scientific inquiry, 134, 138
second nature: continuum, and first nature, 65, 67–68, 72; human nature and, 116–17, 118, 119; Marcuse on, 6, 24; reconstruction of, 81, 122; social democracy and, 114. *See also* new sensibility
self: enlarged self, 76, 78, 180; subject-in-process, 7. *See also* Cartesian model; dialogical self theory; tripartite self
sensibility. *See* new sensibility
sensorium, 22, 116
sensual reason, 68, 176
shadow material, 70, 73, 82, 122, 164
Sharp, Ann, 95, 128, 145
Sheldrake, Rupert, 23
Simons, Maarten, 79, 119, 120
singularity, 54–55, 62, 70, 73–74, 81, 93, 122, 165, 172
skholé: about, xi, xii, xiv, 2–4; adult-child relation and, 35–38, 83, 94–95; *aion* and *kairos*, as, 81, 120; anarchism and, 119–21, 122–24; archetype, as, 122–24; Athenian democracy, and, 2, 79, 83, 114, 119; community of interpretation, as, 79–80; community of philosophical inquiry and, 82–83; embryonic community / society, as, 4, 36, 37, 78, 79, 161, 179, 180; neotenic shelter, as, 79; place apart, as a, 79, 119; weekly meetings, 83, 123. *See also* schooling
social character. *See* democratic social character
social democracy, xiii, 4, 63–64, 66, 113–14, 159, 174, 175–76, 177
Socializing (child-rearing mode), 72, 74, 122

Socrates: Argument, on following the, 125, 127–28, 132, 145; dialogue, philosophy as, xii, 2, 3, 95, 137; ignorance, on assuming position of, 135; on play, 135–36, 137, 141, 143
Sorin, Reesa, 141
spielraum (play space), 60, 129–30
spieltrieb (play drive / impulse), 58, 59, 61, 63, 80, 129
Spinoza, 63, 122
Spock, Benjamin, 74
state, the, 114–15, 117, 118–19, 120
state apparatus. *See* ideological state apparatus
strong democracy, 4, 36, 114
studium (study), 2, 79, 120, 123
subject-in-process, 7–8, 16, 17, 19, 69–70
subjectivity: *infans*, 59, 61; modal, as emergent, 5, 21–23, 39, 59, 67, 69, 142, 180; Platonic model of, 15, 17, 19, 20, 66; politics of, 15–16, 63–64, 177
Sulzer, J., 73
Summerhill school, 123
superego, 14, 67, 69, 164, 166, 167, 168, 172
Sutton-Smith, Brian, 129

Tateo, Luca, 78
Taylor, Charles, 67
teachers, 85, 86–87, 87–91, 91–93
technocapitalism, 23, 35
Thanatos, 13, 16
theories. *See* bioenergetic theory; constructivist learning theory; dialogical self theory (DST); dialogue theory; *infans* theory; organismic theory; vital materialist theory; Yerkes-Dodson theory
therapeutic regression, 74

thinking, 157–58
time: about, xii, 54–55; *aion* time, 30–31, 53, 63, 81, 120, 132, 170; other, of the, 58–59; play and, 130–33; transitional spacetime, 60–61; veritable time, 58–59. See also *aion*; *kairos*
timeless time. See *aion*
Tocqueville, Alexix de, 159
Traherne, Thomas, 77
transitional spacetime, 60–61
tripartite self, 7, 8, 11, 12, 66, 166

Uranus, 56
utopia: about, xi, 1; anarchism, and, 116–17; education, ideals of in, 31–32; philosophy and, 4, 5; we-positions and, 175

Vattimo, Gianni, 116
veritable time, 58–59

Virgin and Child with Saint Anne (Leonardo), 10
vital materialist theory, 68
Vygotsky, Lev, 125, 127, 129, 133, 134

Ward, Colin, 118, 119
weekly meetings, 83, 123
Weinstein, Mark, 82, 135
Wengrow, David, 176–77
we-positions, 174, 175
Werner, Heinz, 19, 170
Whitman, Walt, 169
wild being, 54, 55, 59–60
Winnicott, D. W., 10, 30, 78, 129
Wittgenstein, Ludwig, 135, 154, 157
Wollstonecraft, Mary, 60
Woodcock, George, 117
Wordsworth, William, 30

Yerkes-Dodson theory, 77
yetzer harov and *yetzer hatov*, 118

www.ingramcontent.com/pod-product-compliance
Lightning Source LLC
Chambersburg PA
CBHW030826230426
43667CB00008B/1393